D1246459

One White Man
in
Black Africa

From Kilimanjaro to the Kalahari
1951 - 1991

To Sylvia,
My mainspring,
And to Philippa, Julian and Justin,
Our offspring,
In love and gratitude

One White Man
in
Black Africa

From Kilimanjaro to the Kalahari
1951 - 1991

John Cooke

Tynron Press, Scotland

© *John Cooke, 1991*

First published in 1991 by
Tynron Press
Stenhouse
Thornhill
Dumfriesshire DG3 4LD
Scotland

ISBN 1-85646-011-8
All rights reserved

Cover by Solun A. Wan
Maps by Berneck Makwiti and Goitse Koorutwe
Typeset in Singapore by Linographic Services Pte Ltd
Printed in Singapore by Chong Moh Offset Printing Pte Ltd

CONTENTS

PREFACE

Something hidden. Go and find it. Go and look behind the Ranges —
Something lost behind the Ranges. Lost and waiting for you. Go!

Kipling, **The Explorer**

PREFACE

I first went to Africa, sub-Saharan Africa that is, in 1951 as a district officer in the Colonial Administrative Service. I went mainly in search of new experiences and challenges, and the opportunity to explore in the widest sense, not only faraway places, but also new peoples and ideas, all foreign to my European homeland, and therefore exciting. In the nearly forty years that have elapsed since then I have been doubly satisfied with what I have found and experienced. Travel and exploration there have been in plenty, on mountains, in caves, and through desert and the endless African bush, but also and just as exciting has been experience of people, individuals and societies with a fascinating variety of histories, cultures, attitudes, ambitions and drives.

I served for eleven years as a district officer in Tanganyika* as it was then called, and subsequently after the country became independent in 1961, as a teacher in school and university for a further thirty years both there and in Botswana. During this period Africa has gone through a series of traumatic changes, from the last years of the colonial era, through the euphoria of the early years of independence, to the time of troubles of today when catastrophe looms.

What I have written is not a heavy-weight commentary, but a simple, straightforward tale told by one who was there. Inevitably, I also comment on historical events, and the people involved in them, and in a concluding epilogue I try to summarise what I feel about developments in Africa since mid-century, and how I view the unsettled present and the unpromising future. The narrative is not structured in a time dimension, but rather in one of place, and I give roughly equal treatment to each of the places where I have lived and worked, irrespective of the length of time spent in each.

* Tanganyika became part of the Republic of Tanzania in April 1964 when it was united with Zanzibar.

PART 1
Imperial Administrator

Though she send you as she sent you long ago,
South to desert, east to ocean, west to snow.

*Flecker, **The Dying Patriot***

Chapter One

Background

Pull out, pull out, on the Long Trail — the trail that is always new.

Kipling, **The Long Trail**

I first applied for an appointment as a district officer in the Colonial Administrative Service in 1948. As an embryo imperialist I was an unlikely candidate, in terms of the popular concept of the colonial administrator. The district officer was the lynchpin of the colonial system of government. He was known as a district commissioner when in charge of a district, which was the basic administrative unit, or a provincial commissioner when in charge of a province comprising several districts. The present-day media image of such men is not very flattering, as the following quotations from recent authors will serve to demonstrate.

Paul Johnson, a British journalist turned historian, has this to say in his book *The Offshore Islanders*:

"The truth is, imperialism as a matter of practical necessity, corrupted the master-race. It forced ordinary white men to behave like gods — false gods. A tiny elite, governing multitudes, had to acquire, or assume, a Jupiter-like complex, simply to get through the business of decision-making. The thunderbolts had to be rained on the heads of the wicked, the good rewarded with miracles. To many of the elite, the illusion — the performance — became reality: they thought of themselves as gods. To others, the divine dispensation of rewards and punishments became a hollow and cynical routine. In either case, the imperialist made himself into a lesser man. The empire did not so much shape character, as deform it."

Professor A.H. Rweyemamu, an African, writes in similar vein in a paper presented at a meeting in Arusha, Tanzania in 1983, and reprinted in the *South African Journal of Contemporary African Studies Volume 3:*

"The British imparted to the colonies their system which included a generalist administrative class which constituted the top cadre of the administration. The entire system was geared to the maintenance of law and order, and the collection of personal taxes, using the colonial police forces, and the indigenous chiefs to facilitate the process. This led to the formation of a generalist class of elite officials who were socially and racially exclusive. These were men selected because of their university degrees in classics, history or philosophy. Many of them came from the English aristocracy and felt they had a mission to rule the rest of the world."

This sort of writing represents a travesty of the truth, but by frequent repetition it has become received dogma. I for one do not even remotely fit this image, as I hope to demonstrate. My background was rather unusual, but in my attitudes and in my work I was not an exception, at least amongst the men and women who were my colleagues and friends.

I had not been born into any ruling elite. Quite the contrary, in fact. My maternal grandfather was a coalminer. My paternal grandfather was a working hatter who had the tenacity and ability to build up his own hat-manufacturing business, only for his sons to see it disintegrate in the great depression of the 1930s. For four years up to the outbreak of war in 1939 my father worked as a labourer, doing daily double shifts from 6 a.m. to 10 p.m. for six days a week to earn the princely sum of £4.10.0 (£4.50) to keep his family going. In consequence of this

I did not go to a Public School and Oxbridge, but to the local grammar school and Manchester University on scholarships. I lived at home and cycled in and out of town daily. I had no driving desire to wield power over anybody. I knew enough and had experienced enough of exploitation to sympathise with the underdog anywhere. My ambition to go and work in the colonies, preferably in Africa, was based on far more harmless urgings, which are perhaps worth analysing briefly.

As a child I read all my father's old boys' books, written at the turn of the century. In these Africa and African exploration figured prominently. From these I graduated to anything I could find on exploration and wild places, and waded through the writings of Burton, Speke, Stanley, Livingstone and the rest. As a young teenager I took to the hills, moors and caves of my native Pennines, and later to more distant mountains, to satisfy the urge to wander and to explore. Eventually the Manchester University Mountaineering Club gave more organised opportunity to develop these all-absorbing interests. Mountaineering at this time was ceasing to be a middle-class preserve. We had little or no money, so that hitch-hiking or cycling had to take us everywhere, including to the Alps, and we bedded down wherever we could, in barns, bothies, caves or second-hand ex-army tents — the only criterion was that it should be free or dirt-cheap. Our equipment likewise was cheap and rudimentary, and by present-day standards totally inadequate.

I worked hard at university and got a good honours degree in Geography. I could not have done otherwise. The hard-work ethic permeated my background. To be poor was not a thing to be ashamed of — to be idle was. Honesty, loyalty, and freedom from debt were highly valued, and the importance of high standards in whatever one did was hammered into one, sometimes literally, at home and at school. If one wanted to get on in the world, one worked, and got on with it. The scholarship to grammar school and if possible to university was the passport to progress. I am eternally grateful to my parents for all the encouragement I got, and the almost total freedom "to do my own thing" — so long as it did not offend against their strict moral and ethical codes.

What my "thing", in other words my career, was going to be faced me when I graduated from Manchester University in 1948. My ambitions encompassed neither the acquisition of wealth nor the pursuit of power. I did want space, travel, challenge and excitement, however. Africa seemed to offer the promise of all these, but how to get there was a crucial question to which there seemed to be no easy answer. Then I saw an advertisement in the press for the Colonial Administrative Service. It spoke of challenge, hard work, early responsibility, and required a good honours degree, dedication, and powers of leadership. I put in an application, and then set off for the Alps. That was a hard and demanding trip, and to a degree traumatic in that we had a fatal accident. I did not give any more thought to the colonial service. On my return however, I found waiting for me an invitation to the Colonial Office for an interview. I had just got back in time to go down to London for it. As things transpired, I had two interviews, with two elderly gentlemen who had clearly had long experience in Africa. They were very good interviewers, putting me entirely at ease, and skilfully drawing me out. We talked about Africa and we waxed enthusiastic, they from memory, I from anticipation. I must have given a good impression, for shortly afterwards I received a letter from the Colonial Office. This said that they were certainly interested in me, but that as conscription was still in force I had better go off and do my military service, and inform them when I had completed it. I had been exempted up till then to enable me to go to university.

I soon heard from the services, to the effect that as I was a graduate I was to be posted to the RAF Education Branch. That sounded very dull and I managed to get my destination changed to the army. After a short spell of basic training I was posted to the Intelligence Corps, and thereafter my service career was very pleasant indeed. A year in Egypt at public expense was greatly appreciated, especially as for much of the time I lived with the other members of a small Intelligence Corps section in a nice flat in Port Said town and did not see a great deal of the army. I learned to sail and had a fascinating leave in Cyprus, and was in many ways sorry to have to return home to be demobilised in the very last release group No. 147.

The question of employment and a career loomed again. I wrote to the Colonial Office to inform them that I was available for their further consideration. I was a little concerned that my army career might appear to have been rather light-hearted, but I was gratified in due course to receive an invitation to attend a final selection board. This was clearly to be the crucial stage, and it turned out to be most interesting. I presented myself in a well-pressed suit, a new shirt and quiet tie, with shoes like polished glass — the army's basic training had done something for me. Eventually I was ushered into a large panelled room with thick carpeting. The atmosphere was hushed and heavy with *gravitas.* Facing me at the far side of the room, and under a big window, was a long table at which were seated the chairman of the board flanked by a number of very distinguished-looking elderly gentlemen. Off to the right three less important-looking mortals were seated at a separate table, clearly poised to record my ordeal. Boldness be my friend, was my dominating thought. The first question I was asked was so odd as to make me smile. "Who discovered Australia?" an obvious question no doubt for a Cooke, but when I replied that I thought James Cook had a good claim the chairman smiled craftily and wagged his head. "I thought you would say that," said he, "but you are wrong." The ice was broken, and thereafter a stream of questions, comments, and requests for my opinion on a multitude of subjects followed in rapid succession. One question impressed me above all the others. I had made it plain that I really wanted to go to Africa, and more especially to East Africa, and I was asked the question whether in due course I would be prepared to serve under an

African superior officer. My affirmative answer drew the inevitable interrogative "Why?" I threw caution to the winds, and said that I believed our stated policy was to prepare the colonies for self-government, and that if I found myself under an African superior we would be well on the way to achieving that goal, and so my career would have been justified. This answer was greeted with nods and smiles of approval. The year was 1950. Two weeks later I received a telegram which simply stated — "You have been provisionally selected for probationary appointment as a district officer (cadet) and will be posted to Tanganyika, after spending a year in training at Cambridge University."

The year at Cambridge was very pleasant indeed. We learned the elements of criminal law, the rules of evidence, with some introduction to civil procedure, to enable us to function as magistrates; the language of the country to which we were going, in my case Swahili; and a variety of useful subjects such as basic surveying and field engineering, the elements of tropical agriculture, some social anthropology, and rather less useful, an outline of Imperial History. Our tutor in law was a youngish barrister named Lane. I remember one of his more picturesque pieces of advice — "When you are sitting under your respective palm trees, gentlemen, handing out basic justice, try to remember what I have taught you". He is now Lord Lane, Chief Justice of England. Clearly our tuition was not lacking in quality. I enjoyed Cambridge immensely, and found Christ's College where I lived, a most comfortable and civilised place in which to spend a year.

Early August 1951 saw me aboard the *Llanstephan Castle* outward bound round the Cape for East Africa, with twenty other embryo stalwarts of Empire. We landed in Dar Es Salaam early in September. My African career had begun.

Chapter Two

Biharamulo

Yet all experience is an arch where through
Gleams that untravelled world whose margin fades
For ever and for ever as I move.

Tennyson, **Ulysses**

I

Dar Es Salaam harbour was a beautiful place, with all the conventional attributes of a tropical paradise: perfect lagoon with a narrow spectacular entrance, lovely beaches, waving palm trees, and a conglomeration of traditional African, old Arab-Swahili, and early European buildings. A very good friend who was at sea during the war, had called there, and used to enthuse about it, so that I was prepared for something special.

We spent a few days there and met the Governor, the Chief Secretary and various other V.I.Ps, and attended a series of functions: luncheon, dinner, drinks, and the like. I found all this rather stuffy and very conventional. We were each interviewed by the Chief Secretary who informed us to which province we were to be posted. I learned that I was destined for Lake Province. This was that part of Tanganyika which embraces the southern half of Lake Victoria, bordering on Kenya on the eastern side, round to Uganda, Ruanda and Burundi on the west. I had hoped for Northern Province where all the big mountains are, but at that time anywhere was going to be exciting, and in due course I was to find my way onto all those magnificent mountains.

To get to Mwanza, the administrative headquarters of Lake

Fig. 1   *East Africa showing places mentioned in the text*

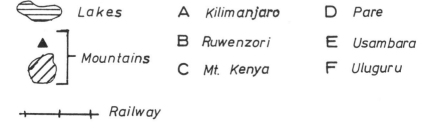

	Lakes	**A**	*Kilimanjaro*	**D**	*Pare*
▲	Mountains	**B**	*Ruwenzori*	**E**	*Usambara*
		C	*Mt. Kenya*	**F**	*Uluguru*

+—+—+   *Railway*

Province, involved a long train journey west to Tabora then north to the lake. Various of my colleagues dropped off at stations enroute, and I think it was three of us who eventually reached Mwanza. This is Tanganyika's main port on the lake, and the major town in a very productive region which is important for its cattle, cotton, and from the west side of the lake in Bukoba, robusta coffee. The central and original part of the town clings around the skirts of a series of rocky outcrops, and is very picturesque. In 1951 the port was a hive of activity, and the town bustling, clean and well-run.

I was not kept kicking my heels in Mwanza for very long. The provincial commissioner, a very fine man named "Jim" Rowe, called me in to his office and briefed me on my ultimate destination. This was to be Biharamulo, which he described as "a last lingering corner of ancient Africa". My evident delight at the prospect of going to such a place won his approval, and he complained of the burdens of high office, the paper work, committees, formality, and all that these entailed. He felt too far removed from the people he was responsible for and envied me my youthful prospects of grass-roots work.

Biharamulo district borders the south-west embayment of Lake Victoria which is known as Emin Pasha Gulf. To the north lies Bukoba district, and to the West Ngara district, Ruanda and Burundi. To reach my new station I had to take one of the lake steamers across to Bukoba. The boat I travelled in was the *Sybil*, a small ancient craft, one of the ships built in Britain at the turn of the century, then taken apart and shipped out to Mombasa, to be carried from there to the lake for ultimate re-building and launching. I learned quickly that the lake can be very rough indeed. It is relatively shallow, and strong winds quickly build up a short steep choppy swell. It was in this sort of sea that the little *Sybil* bucked and rolled her way forward. I was very sick even though on the long voyage out to East Africa I had never once felt sea-sick. When we arrived at Bukoba I felt less than enthusiastic for further travel.

My district commissioner, Ronald Smith was awaiting me on the quayside, and greeted me with an enthusiasm that I found slightly embarrassing. Sensing this he explained at once that I was the long-desired fruit of two years of persistent badgering of the provincial commissioner. Being a remote, sparsely populated and unproductive part of the territory, Biharamulo only rated one administrative officer, the district commissioner himself. Bigger and more important districts might have one, two, or more district officers in addition to the DC. Smith reckoned he needed an assistant to do the job properly, and now at last he was getting one. I was to find that, having been single-handed for so long, and being a bachelor to boot, Smith had developed routines, ways of doing things, and attitudes that had become rather fixed. Trying to adjust to these, without becoming a mere yes-man, gave early training in the tactful handling of my superiors that proved useful. However, that lay in the future, and my first impressions, later amply confirmed, were of a genial, generous and dedicated man.

We didn't hang around for very long. Breakfast was followed by a courtesy call on the DC of Bukoba. Bukoba was a large, prosperous and productive district and regarded as a senior administrative posting. Little did I guess in 1951 that in 1960, just nine years later, I would myself become DC there in the very delicate period of development leading up to Tanganyika's attainment of independence in 1961. The DC in 1951 was Tim Harris, a large bluff extrovert, who was having a very uphill task at that time in trying to introduce the concept and practice of local government democracy in the form of elected councils to the people. Up to that time they had been ruled more or less despotically by traditional chiefs or *bakama*; but more of this later when I come to relate my own experiences in Bukoba.

Smith had a landrover, a Series I specimen with an 11 horsepower engine. These had only been introduced in 1948, and I had driven one of the first to be delivered to the army in Egypt when I was there. In this we departed for Biharamulo on what was to be for me a memorable journey through quite magnificent scenery. Southwards through Bukoba the road often approaches the lake, but stays high up, offering splendid views. The banana and coffee *shambas* (the Swahili word for a cultivated plot) of the people gave an impression of tropical fecundity and the people looked prosperous and very dignified. Beyond Ihangiro, the last chiefdom before the district border, the scene changed and we eventually left the lake off to our left, and topped a rise. The panorama from there was superb. An immensely long bush-filled valley stretched into the far distance, and on its western side rose a prominent escarpment. The horizon was a purplish blue haze, and great cloud-shadows moved over the face of the land. The scene reminded me of some of the valleys of my native Pennines, the Alport or upper Derwent for example, but on a much vaster scale. The ribbon of road wound down the hill and disappeared into the enclosing forest. We descended quickly and motored on, bumping and crashing along the passable but rugged unpaved road. My reveries were quickly curbed by some sharp pricks on the back of my neck, and I was thus introduced to the notorious tse-tse fly, to many the steriliser of large tracts of otherwise potentially productive land, but to others the preserver and guardian of the ecological integrity and survival of large areas of African wilderness. I noticed that a line of telegraph poles followed the road, but saw also that this supported but a single line of wire. Commenting on this I was informed that this was our sole link with the world outside Biharamulo, and that at each end was a morse key and receiver. This fragile line of communication was made doubly tenuous by the elephants' habit of knocking down poles and line, presumably for the sheer fun of it.

After a four-hour drive to cover the 113 miles, we arrived at the district headquarters. A long straight avenue flanked by tall gum-trees led to the *boma,* the Swahili name for the district office. This was a squat, fortress-like building on a broad hill-top, built by the Germans some fifty years previously. Within six-feet thick stone rubble walls were enclosed the DC's house, the government offices, post-office, courtroom, stores and work-shops. Some distance half-way down the hill was the small hospital, and on the far side of the hill the houses of the agricultural officers and the settlement officer. That was the station. On enquiring where I was going to live, I was shown some newly dug foundations, and told that one of my first tasks would be to supervise the building of my house, and the sooner I got on with it, the sooner I would have my own place. So we got on with it, we being two Haya masons and a carpenter, a gang of labourers, and in due course a skilled thatcher, with myself as overseer. The only cement used was for an ant-proof concrete floor, the rest being built of rough local stone quarried on the spot, mud mortar and plaster, and a thatched grass roof. The ceiling inside was of hessian stiffened by a coating of limewash. Of plumbing there was none; water was carried up daily to a 44 gallon drum standing outside. Hot water for a bath was heated in a four gallon kerosene *debe* (Swahili for metal container) on the wood-burning stove in the kitchen, and carried in to a tin bath-tub. A rock-filled drain-pit took waste water, and a deep-drop dry pit latrine was located about twenty yards away. To the siting of the latter I gave special attention, locating it on the edge of a cliff, from which safe vantage point there was to be had a fine view over rolling bush-covered hills. A door was quite unnecessary. We finished the house in two months, and I had my first home in Africa.

The *boma* was an odd place that one tended to think of as an ancient monument, yet it was only fifty years old, and an old man in the village below told me he remembered the Germans building the place when he was a little boy. It seems he allowed his goats to tangle up the lines of string laid out for the foundations, for which he received a beating from the overseer. I was to live here for a while pending the completion of my own house, as the guest of Smith, and I greatly enjoyed his liberal hospitality. He was a very house-proud man, and one of his chief delights was a superb leopard skin mounted on green baize cloth. I had early acquired a bull-terrier pup who was given the name of Sambo, and I was utterly horrified one day to hear a loud commotion at the door of the house, and to see Sambo dragging out the leopard skin which he was vigorously shaking and worrying. Smith followed, roaring imprecations at the dog and its master. Fortunately we retrieved the precious object little the worse for its ordeal, but to this day I do not know why Sambo was not shot as a social outcast. In fact he lived on for several years to accompany me to the most unlikely places, learning amongst other things to climb like a mountain-goat.

The other personnel on the station were an interesting lot. Our police inspector in charge of about twenty NCOs and constables was Saidi Maswanya, an Mnyamwezi from Tabora. Little did we guess at the time, but he had quite a future in front of him. He became a stalwart of Nyerere's Tanganyika African National Union Party (TANU) and ultimately Minister of Home Affairs in the early years of independence. I met him again twenty years later in 1971 when I attended the Tenth Anniversary of Independence Celebrations in Dar Es Salaam to which I was invited as a guest. By that time he had become rather fat and pompous, and hardly deigned to recognise me. In 1951 however, he was young, pleasant, and a good policeman. One of his major duties was to prosecute criminal cases in our tiny magistrate's court. I practised as a magistrate of the third class, and Saidi and I got to know each other quite well. His posse of policemen was hardly an impressive arm of imperial might, keeping the "natives" in subjection. They were smart but very amiable, and would not have frightened anybody. Their arms were pre-1914 war vintage Lee-Enfield rifles of most unreliable appearance.

We had two agricultural officers. One, an elderly Scot named MacGregor was a specialist in the growing of tobacco. His wife Meg was with him, and they were a tough and durable pair. He had first come out to Nyasaland as it then was, as a very young man before the 1914-18 war. He worked in the tobacco growing industry, but during the war he had been a scout for the British forces chasing Von Lettow-Vorbeck in southern Tanganyika and Mozambique. His task was now to run the small tobacco nursery and curing factory, tobacco being the only cash crop in the district. He was assisted by Arthur Jenkins, a young field officer who came from Somerset. We also had a settlement officer, Tony Dodd, like Smith a wealthy bachelor. Biharamulo was a sleeping sickness area, and in the 1920s the people had been concentrated into tse-tse free settlements, about which more later. Dodd's task was to keep an eye on both the tse-tse and the disease they spread. He was an engaging character, slightly built and with a finely tuned cynical view of the world and his fellows. Some months after my arrival we were joined by Arthur Hammond as district assistant, responsible for building and road work, and vehicle maintenance. Our hospital was run by Gerald Kashozi, a Muhaya from Bukoba. He was not a qualified doctor, only a medical assistant, but he had long experience, and did a terrific job. Our chief clerk was another Muhaya named Edward Kayoza, and Hubert Feruzi was our inspector of schools. A treasury accountant and a postmaster completed our group, but their names now elude me.

Travellers sometimes came through the district, on their way north or south, and we often had to lend assistance to those whose vehicles had broken down, or who had thought they could travel faster and found themselves at Biharamulo at nightfall. Such people brought a touch of variety, fresh conversation, and news from elsewhere. A rather longer-staying bird of passage was an anthropologist whose purpose was to study the Bazinza, the major tribe of the district. He lived out at Runazi about 30 miles away, whilst pursuing his enquiries, but he often came into the station and was given a bed and food. He was good company, but caused some distress once when we asked him to help with a rather ticklish problem of succession in one of the subchiefdoms. He declined on the grounds that he did not wish to get involved with practical administrative problems that might have interfered with his academic studies. He was a classic case of the ivory-tower academic of those days. Fortunately not all anthropologists were like this. In Tanganyika Hans Cory did invaluable work in recording customary law which was of inestimable value to working administrators. In Botswana Isaac Schapera, in his monumental work on the Tswana, produced work which is still of great practical usefulness to government. Today the situation is wholly different, and social scientists fall over themselves in their haste to get involved in "development" work.

We had a number of missionaries in the district. Most important in terms of their length of stay were the Roman Catholic White Fathers. They had a large station with a fine red-brick church at Katoke about five miles from the *boma*. Doyen of their mission was Father Lavergne who had spent all his working life at Katoke since the early years of the century, returning but rarely to Europe. He was a grand old man with a flowing long white beard, and drove around in an immaculate Model A Ford car. His younger colleagues crashed and roared around their huge parish on motor bikes, displaying a profound faith in the Almighty. Roman Catholic missionaries were always most hospitable, and in all districts I worked in it was always a pleasure to visit them whilst out on tour, or safari as we called it. They liked visitors as it was an allowable excuse to open a bottle of wine.

Our other missionaries were of a very different stamp. A small Swedish Free Mission Station had been established relatively recently, staffed by both men and women. These were very pleasant and worthy people, but were very straight-laced and puritan in outlook. They up-staged the White Fathers in one way in that they had a Model T Ford car. This was extremely dilapidated however, unlike Father Lavergne's Model A, and how they kept the thing going was something of a mystery. There was of course no contact between the two missions. The attitude of missionaries in general towards fellow Christians of different persuasions was really most depressing, their common Christianity appearing to have little significance. The most underhand methods were in common use to secure advantage for a particular church, and government was fair game in this unholy struggle. I remember once in Biharamulo going out to measure and set out a plot of land which the White Fathers wanted for an outreach catechistic bush school. When I arrived at the site one of the fathers who was responsible for that area hastened to assure me that he had done the necessary measurements and so there was no need for me to trouble myself and waste valuable time. Greenhorn that I was at the time, I still caught a whiff of brimstone and quietly insisted on checking his measurements. I found he had taken fifty percent more land than had been agreed, but with a completely poker face the culprit remarked that of course anyone can make mistakes. I wondered if deceit was a pardonable sin when practised in the name of the church, but I said nothing.

II

The district we were responsible for was about 4,250 square miles (11,000 sq km) in area, with a population in 1951 of about 50,000 people, mainly of the Zinza tribe. The topography of the area was structured on a series of north-south trending ridges of outcropping sandstone dipping gently westwards, so that sharp escarpments faced east. The dip slopes of these ridges formed deep wide forest-filled valleys quite well-supplied with water. Speke and Grant came through this country in the 1860s, and Speke spoke glowingly of the pleasant aspect of the country at that time, with prosperous people owning large herds of the long-horned Ankole cattle. This prosperity was cruelly terminated in the 1890s by the great rinderpest pandemic which drastically reduced the cattle populations of the whole of East and Central Africa. A smallpox epidemic followed by famine completed the destruction of a flourishing society and culture.

The people were unable to keep the forest at bay and it slowly closed in on their shrinking settlements. With the forest came the tse-tse fly, making it impossible to rebuild the decimated cattle herds. From this series of catastrophes the Zinza people were unable to recover. The war of 1914-18 compounded the tragedy yet further, with the depredations of the warring armies. The Zinza became a demoralized and defeated people, and the outbreak of human sleeping sickness was a final blow. In the 1920s the government decided to move the people from their scattered settlements in the bush, into cleared enclaves where the bush could be kept back and the tse-tse fly under control. Regular blood-checks were made to give early warning of any new outbreak of sleeping sickness. The rest of the country outside these settlements became total wilderness rich in wildlife including large herds of elephant.

There were known to be old tracks across the grain of the country used by migrant labour from Ngara and the Belgian colonies to the west, who sought work on the farms of the rich African coffee farmers of Bukoba and Uganda further north. By the 1950s most of these migrants travelled by road, but the cross-country tracks still existed. I was anxious to see this country and badgered Smith to let me out on a long foot safari. He was by nature and inclination a desk man, insisting on meticulous accuracy in accounts, filing systems, answering of correspondence etc, and he wanted my nose kept firmly to the grindstone to inculcate similar attitudes in his protégé. Weekends were my own business however, so one Friday I took the weekly mail bus to Nyakahura, with the intention of walking the thirty-five miles back to the station cross-country. I took with me Daudi, one of our messengers. The *boma* messenger was a sort of district officer's general factotum, and called in Swahili a *tarishi*. We recruited a guide-cum-porter in Nyakahura and set off at dawn on Saturday. This was my first real experience of the African bush. The narrow foot-trail winding endlessly through the forest and over the hills astounded me, for this was the main pre-

European communication system of the continent. The elephant we met at close quarters scared me stiff, especially as we were quite unarmed; the tse-tse were murderous, and the heat was like a hammer. Though fit and long used to extended mountain expeditions, I arrived back in a tired state, to the amusement of my master, who assumed I would have learned my lesson. He was wrong and I continued to press for more field-work.

Smith relented somewhat and my next outing came when I was sent to the neighbouring district of Ngara to liaise with the DC there on a new road being built from Keza in Ngara district northwards into the western part of Biharamulo. I travelled up to Ngara on the mail-bus, a word about which may be of interest. It was a standard Bedford five-ton truck chassis on which was fitted a locally made timber body with open windows, and hard bench seats, and a huge roof-rack on top. This did a once weekly round trip Bukoba-Biharamulo-Ngara and return, carrying mail and all the other goods required at the two out-stations. It was run by one of the Indian merchants in Bukoba. Travelling on it was quite an experience, packed as it was with cheerful, noisy humanity, and great loads sharing the roof with goats and chickens, all well strapped down. This service seldom failed us, hammering through in all weathers, clouds of dust in the dry, and seas of mud in the wet.

The DC of Ngara was George Gordon, a man noted for his decidedly radical left-wing views on most things. With him I went to the road-head on the new road, which I found most stimulating and exciting. A cleared track was being hacked out through the virgin green forest, and entirely by hand, using axes, spades and pick-axes. Trees were cut down, the roots dug out, and the newly cleared trace levelled and trampled into a motorable track. This was tangible progress, and the new road would open up new lands to settlement, which in turn would help to drive back the tse-tse fly. It pleases me greatly to see at the present-day that this road we began is now marked on the maps as a main highway going northwards right into Uganda.

This question of extending settlement and pushing back the wilderness was, and indeed still is a serious one, and deserves some further consideration here. As I have noted above, by the 1920s nature had certainly got the upper hand in many parts of East Africa, and the Biharamulo area was a particularly badly affected place. A vicious circle had become established, and the population was shrinking. To protect the people and to make control of sleeping sickness easier the population was concentrated into sleeping sickness-free cleared settlements. Here it was also easier to provide schools, clinics and trading stores, and to organise communal labour turn-outs to keep the forest at bay. This policy has been variously condemned by critics of the colonial period as retrogressive, paternalistic, defeatist and ecologically disastrous, but even with my limited experience of the area in 1951/2 I cannot honestly see how any other policy could have helped the Bazinza people. It is ironic that many such critics of colonial policy were prepared to welcome Nyerere's policy of *ujamaa* (socialist) villagisation in the 1970s, pointing out the advantages of concentration in making easier the provision of social and extension services, and stimulating the community effort said to be traditionally African.

III

As a young district officer on my very first tour of duty I was closely involved at grass-roots level with problems of development. Let me examine just one of these which we faced in Biharamulo in the early 1950s. Development, both infrastructural, such as roads, water supplies, buildings; and social, such as systems of law and order, schools, hospitals and clinics, requires cash. The least degrading way of financing such things is for the people who benefit therefrom to provide at least part of this by their own efforts. In development theory at the present-day in fact, it is at long last being realised that self-help as opposed to external aid is in the long run an economically and psychologically healthier way of generating progress. Self-help can flow from selling what you produce or selling your labour. The former has the advantage of keeping the young male members of a community at home. Colonial policy encouraged both, and has been stigmatised for doing so, both cash crop production and migrant labour being anathema to radical opinion. Even amongst the radicals at the present-day however, there are signs that opinion is veering towards the realisation that foreign exchange has to be earned, and that you can only do that by selling things you produce, which in much of Africa means cash crops.

To return to Biharamulo. We were trying very hard to encourage the growing of tobacco, to which soils and climate were well suited. We had a nursery, experimental plots, a small factory for curing the leaf, and a tobacco specialist of great experience in the person of old MacGregor. Part of the proceeds of the sale of the people's tobacco crop would help to raise directly the spending power of the people, and part would be levied as tax to finance the local authority, to enable it to provide local services such as schools and clinics. In our endeavours we faced great difficulties. Firstly much of the tobacco produced found its way into the Congo where black market prices were very good. True, the people obtained cash, but this could not be tapped easily for tax. Independent Africa also faces this problem of smuggling and the black market, and handles things far more fiercely than we would ever have dared to do. A second major difficulty was that the young men preferred to go away to work, either long distance to the sisal plantations in the east, or to the coffee and cotton farms of the Bahaya and Baganda to the north. They preferred the former where they were better paid and treated. The absence of large numbers of young men meant that communal labour turn-outs to clear bush and keep the tse-tse fly at bay were less effective than they might have been. The only real solution to this problem of fighting the wilderness is where an expanding vigorous people simply clears and settles permanently new land.

An excellent example of this has occurred around the southern shores of Lake Victoria, extending now into Biharamulo. The Sukuma are just such a vigorous people and since the 1930s they have been pushing westwards, clearing the bush, planting maize and cotton, and bringing in their cattle. By the 1950s they had cleared and settled the whole of what became Geita district, assisted and encouraged in every way by the colonial government. This is an essentially folk movement and still continues, so that in time the whole of Biharamulo may be cleared and re-occupied by dense human settlement.

As a poor and thinly populated district in the 1950s, Biharamulo did not have a lot of cash to spend. Nevertheless roads were built and improved, schools and clinics were opened in even the remotest places, and progress though slow was taking place. A problem with the schools was filling them with pupils. The idea of modern education had not yet caught on, especially where girls were concerned. I frequently had to literally press-gang children into schools, and brow-beat their parents into keeping them there. When I say this today, few people are prepared to believe me, so pervasive has become the lie that education was neglected in the colonies.

The local government, or native authority as it was known, was still in a very early stage of evolution in Biharamulo. Such native authorities had been established throughout Tanganyika under the policy of Indirect Rule. Under this system, introduced by Sir Donald Cameron in the 1930s, traditional authorities were maintained in office, and under the guidance of district officers, carried out much of the routine administration of the country at the local level. Our policy was to progressively upgrade and increasingly democratise these authorities. The pace of change varied greatly from district to district. Wealthy districts such as Bukoba and Moshi were moving much more quickly than others, and I will describe developments there in which I was involved, later in my narrative. The traditional authority in Biharamulo was weak and very conservative and since there was no popular pressure from below to change things, progress was very slow. The problems of poverty and demoralization which I have described needed a much more dynamic approach than the chiefs were able or willing to give. We could not simply expel useless leaders, as to do so would have aroused the opposition of the local people and interested outsiders. Petitions to the Governor and UN would have followed. Such actions would have been portrayed as unwarranted interference in the traditional culture. Ironically, one of the first acts of Nyerere's government after independence was to sweep away all chiefs and traditional authorities like so much useless chaff before the wind, and to rigidly centralize all government operations.

The native authority controlled an annual budget, heavily subsidised by the central government. It employed an array of administrative and court clerks and a local police force; it built and maintained roads, schools and clinics; and collected its own revenues from a local head tax, market fees, beer licences and such like. The district commissioner was adviser to this body, but in the circumstances of Biharamulo he had a very big hand in actually directing its activities. One of my major tasks as a district officer was to keep a close eye on the accounts of the local treasury both at the headquarters and out in the sub-chiefdoms. Frequent checking was essential, but the process was really an educational one. The basic fundamentals of modern local government were being inculcated, but this was a long slow process. Another important task was to check local court records. Throughout Tanganyika, local courts presided over by chiefs and sub-chiefs administered tribal customary law, and all proceedings and records were kept in the Swahili language. The district commissioner was a court of appeal from the judgements of these courts, and since he also administered the central government system of courts based on English and Indian law and procedures, he was a link between the two systems. Of course there was usually a permanent resident magistrate in the larger districts, but he had no jurisdiction over the local courts.

IV

I was enjoying my work immensely, but continued to chaff at the bit at being kept too long in the office. Eventually I succeeded in persuading Smith to let me out on a long foot safari in one of the remoter parts of the district which was not often visited. To describe this safari I can do no better than quote verbatim a diary that I kept at the time. Here it is as I wrote it. Any explanations that seem necessary are shown in parentheses.

Friday   Arrived Nyakahura 3.30 p.m. Pointed out the new site for the police post to the provincial Police Commander who was touring the district. He seemed to like it. Found Tony Dodd in occupation of the rest-house. With his aid I roughly measured out a site for the new *gombolola* (sub-chiefdom) court and office on a small hill near the *mwami's* (sub-chief) house. Petro (the *mwami*) seems to be doing a good job. All the vegetation has been cleared away, and a large quantity of stone collected for the building.

Saturday   25 porters as requested turned up promptly at 6.30 am with Petro in attendance. I found 16 were enough to carry our loads. They left before me with *mwami* Ndahura of Nyabugombe (the next sub-chiefdom) who had very kindly come over to meet and accompany us into his area. The walk to Mutala was pleasant in spite of the heat. The hills are rocky and steep with their bones showing through. Cultivation is limited to the valley bottoms and small re-entrant valleys where to judge by the vegetation water is available at no great depth. A large concourse of people was gathered at the tobacco *banda* (shed) and as we approached they poured up the track to greet us. I must have shaken hands and said "*jambo*" (how do you do) at least two hundred times. They seemed very pleased that someone had come to take an interest in their affairs. I paid off my porters, had a bite to eat and a drink, and then went to the *banda* to hold a *baraza* (public meeting). I said how pleased I was to visit their country, and asked about the rains, and the crop prospects. I then launched into the subject of tobacco. There are only 100 growers this year as against 150 last year. A long discussion ensued on this theme. Many people got on their feet and said that they did not get enough money for their tobacco, and that many young men went to work in Uganda where they could earn more money. I argued that they were foolish to go to till the farms of strangers who made much money thereby. Surely it was better to stay in their own pleasant land and make it rich as the Baganda had done theirs. Did they wish their country to revert to total bush and their children become the servants of strangers for ever? There were loud murmurings of approval and I think the point went home. I am sure if more visits were made and the same theme repeated constantly, there would be more tobacco development. The next subject was school. They did not wish to send their daughters to school, so I had to deliver a lecture on the great benefits of education, especially for future mothers. We finished with some miscellaneous complaints, including one that the local Indian trader was not paying them enough for goat skins.

The *baraza* finished, I dealt with some applications for tax exemption and granted twelve to old men. I then went on a tour of the *shambas* with the two agricultural instructors, the local headman and the *mwami*. The tie-ridging (to check erosion) looks good. Much of the tobacco has flowered and cultivation has ceased. The instructors seemed pleased and I congratulated them on their work in helping the people. The bean crop was not so good. There were a few new banana plantings. Later in the evening I went out with the shot-gun to look for partridge but had no luck. This is a very pleasant place, the craggy hills giving me great pleasure. The people are most kind and helpful, and have cleared a very nice camp-site for us.

Sunday   Walked to Nyabugombe, sun very hot indeed. The Mutala valley is a cul-de-sac, and we had to climb a steep pass to get over into the next valley. From the top of the pass a fine view opened in all directions, with masses of tumbling rocky hills. Again the presence of luscious vegetation in the gullies spoke of the presence of water.

We arrived in Nyabugombe feeling a bit tired, but went straight into a *baraza*, with a large crowd in attendance. Used same arguments as at Mutala to discourage emigration. There are only six tobacco growers this year. The school is setting a good example with a flourishing acre of tobacco. The teachers told me of their problems, especially the high rate of drop-outs after only two years at school. I tried to point out to the people the futility of such a short period at school. The school was clean and efficient and I congratulated the teachers. The same could not be said of the clinic which was a disgrace, and I expressed my opinion to the dresser in no uncertain way. There was an old man there with a dreadful open sore on his leg. I told the *mwami* to have him carried to Nyakahura whence he could go by bus to the hospital at Biharamulo. Granted eight tax exemptions.

Monday

Walked to Kafua along the road. This is badly overgrown with vegetation but the bridges are intact, and there has been little erosion due to rain wash. On arrival I found a good camp-site cleared, and again a large crowd was waiting. I held a *baraza* and discussed the usual points as at Mutala and Nyabugombe. Very pleasing to note an increase in tobacco growers to 53 from 35 last year. There were pleas for a trading store, and I promised to approach Ismail Osman, an Arab trader at Nyakahura to see if he could help. Later went on a tour of the tobacco *shambas*, and was troubled to note some rust disease. I must speak to MacGregor about this when I get back.

Tuesday

Walked to Kasherazi. A very hot and sticky day, and we arrived in a weary state. Once more a great crowd streamed out to meet us, and they led us to a fine camp-site. I went first to look at the site of the new school which is being built. Foundations are going well. I also looked at the demonstration leopard trap built by the game ranger some weeks previously. Then I held a large *baraza*, and spoke on the following points:

1. The need to provide food and accommodation for John, the rural medical aid, on his regular visits. They are ready to do this, so I will ask the *mwami* to tell John to resume his visits.

2. The school. I told them that when the rains are

over, we would send masons to put in a proper
ant-proof course and finish the building.

3. Tobacco growing. I gave the usual exhortations
    to better efforts.

4. The leopard. This has already killed seven
    children. The game ranger had been and shown
    them how to build traps, and where to site
    them, but they had done nothing. I asked if
    they liked feeding their children to leopards.
    They strongly disagreed and said they would
    build the traps. Feeling that some strong
    persuasion was required I selected 50 men, and
    divided them into groups of 10 each. Each
    group is to build a trap. *Mwami* Ndahura is to
    return in two weeks' time, and if any trap is not
    built, one man from the group responsible is to
    be punished. This might work. Later I went on
    a tour of the *shambas*. There is deep, rich dark
    soil here in the valley bottom, but few tobacco
    growers. Vigorous people could make a good
    life here. Afterwards I held an inquest on the
    last child death attributed to leopard. The
    people are uneasy and talk of witchcraft, but I
    am sure an animal is responsible. (Note: The
    traps were built, and a very large old male
    hyena caught. There were no more deaths after
    this so he was obviously the culprit.)

Wednesday   Left early for the long walk to Rusumo. Clouds
            were gathering as we left, and a heavy shower
            soon broke which soaked us all to the skin. There
            was a great deal of very high grass, but the head-
            man had thoughtfully had this cut back from the

path to help us. This is rich-looking country but there are very few people because of its remoteness. Where there are pockets of people the crops look very healthy, and it is good to see proper tie-ridging even here. If the road can be pushed up here it should speed development.

We reached Rusumo in the late afternoon. It is a magnificent place. The gorge and falls are splendid. It is easy to dream of vast outputs of hydro-electric power from here in the future. The Belgians seem to have similar dreams, and they have built a road to their side of the river.

Thursday   We had to cross the river today. This we did in dug-out canoes at a point only about 500 yards above the falls. The canoeman's technique was to shoot downstream diagonally across the current, until he reached the counter-current near the far side, at which point he deftly turned the craft and we moved gently into the bank. This was rather frightening with the falls so close. Once on the far side we were in Ngara district, and faced a long walk of twenty miles and a climb of about two thousand feet to reach the district office. We arrived tired but satisfied. Smith had sent a truck up to collect us.

Shortly after this safari to the far west of the district I was given another interesting job out in the field. This was to supervise the initiation of a dam-building and bush-clearing project out in the Kalenge sub-chiefdom in the south of the district. This work was to be carried out by a communal labour turn-out. The object was to ensure water supplies through storage in a hand-built dam, and to clear encroached bush to keep the tse-tse at bay. The work went well, and I was very impressed with what a mass of human beings, armed with but simple tools, can achieve when properly led, motivated and well-organised.

Yet another interesting, if somewhat unusual task also cropped up later that year. We received a letter from the War Graves Commission requesting us to arrange inspection of some Belgian war graves out in the forest down towards the lake shore. Four Belgians and a number of their *askaris* (*askari* is Swahili for a soldier) had been killed in a German ambush in 1916, and they had been buried at the site of the skirmish. I volunteered to carry out the inspection. The place could only be reached on foot so I recruited some porters and a guide at Runazi sub-chiefdom headquarters, and set off with *tarishi* Musa and my personal servant Petro. We did the trip in fifteen-mile daily stages, two days out and two days back. Unfortunately the weather was rather wet, and down near the lake extensive areas were flooded, though only to a shallow depth. We waded for miles through water about a foot deep, viciously assaulted by tse-tse and mosquitoes. The site of the graves I found very depressing. There were headstones on the Belgian graves with name, rank, place of birth, and the phrase "*Mort au champ d'honneur*". The askaris were in a communal grave under a large pyramidal stone cairn. We cleaned up the whole area, and cut back the bush. It was hard to avoid moralising about the futility of such deaths, and such thoughts kept me awake most of the night, greatly aided by the chatter of my men round the campfire. There were lions prowling around, rumbling and grumbling, and my men, sensibly, chose not to sleep.

During this trip, it was interesting to talk to my porters about the 1914-18 war and what they had heard about it. One thing they were unanimous about was that the Belgians who took over this part of the territory from the Germans were hated and feared. I asked about the Germans and was told something I was to hear again later. This was that the Germans were strict and could be very fierce, but they were predictable and on the whole just. People knew precisely where they stood with them, and could act accordingly. I thought it would be tactless to ask what they thought of us British. I was to learn that slowly over a long period of contact.

V

Naturally, a large part of my time was spent in routine administration. The district officer was always known by the Swahili expression *"bwana shauri"*. A *shauri* can be roughly translated as a matter or affair which needs discussion and sometimes arbitration to be solved satisfactorily. So the *bwana shauri* is one who is concerned with disputes, arguments, complaints and such-like. Never a day would pass without a queue of people forming outside my office with matters they wanted to discuss. Though often busy with other things, account and audit queries, writing up court judgements, answering routine correspondence etc, I had to give time to these people. To refuse to do so, or to display impatience would have been resented, and would have quickly got me a bad name. It must also be remembered that rural people in Africa, or indeed anywhere else I suppose, have a rhythm of life which is foreign to the urban-based person. Time is not very important. Matters are not introduced at once or directly, and must be preceded by an exchange of greetings and enquiries regarding the other person's health, his family, his crops etc etc. I learned quickly the enormous range of meaning and implication involved in the apparently simple expressions "eeeeeh" or "eh-heeeee" which punctuated and lent tone and emphasis to a conversation. One of the commonest types of complaint was against an official such as a sub-chief or head-man, who had failed to deal satisfactorily with some grievance or other, or had in the complainant's eyes, been unjust. If the matter could not be dealt with there and then, I would write a note to the official concerned, or make a note to deal with the matter when next on safari in the area from which the complainant came. The DO was a safety net. The Roman riddle *"Quis custodiet ipsos custodes*" was answered at one level, but the question remains as to who controlled us, the top level of administration in the districts. The answer to that is not easy and is difficult to make convincing to the sceptics, but lies somewhere in the concept of *esprit de corps*, pride in a tradition of incorruptibility, pride in cultivating a good name amongst the people for whom one had responsibility. Arrogance and an arbitrary use of power got one nowhere. Tolerance, patience and an honest firmness, and perhaps above all a robust sense of humour did. To be a successful district officer was not easy. By successful I mean the achievement of rapport with the people one governed, so that a two-way relationship developed, involving mutual trust and respect. The majority of the people with whom one had to deal were rural or small-town dwellers, often illiterate, and such people have a sharp eye for character and behaviour, probably because close human contact and oral communication are the stuff of their lives. People are very real and important to them, and it is not easy to fool, mislead or "con" them. Quirks of character or mild eccentricities so long as real and not assumed, could be a great help. To acquire a nickname was often a sign of acceptance.

Court work was very interesting. I was initially a third-class magistrate with powers strictly defined by the Criminal Procedure Code. I had to study for my law examinations which we were required to pass successfully in order for probationary appointment to be confirmed. Papers were set in criminal procedure, the Penal Code, the law of evidence, and civil procedure. I managed to take and pass the examination whilst at Biharamulo, and could then graduate to be a second-class magistrate. Most of the cases I had to hear were concerned with petty larceny, minor assault, public nuisance etc, the daily diet of a magistrate's court anywhere. Where serious crimes such as murder or manslaughter were concerned, I had to carry out a preliminary inquiry, and then send the record off to the High Court for further action.

Quite often in court hearings I had to use an interpreter, as in this remote district, many people were not fluent in Swahili. The court proceedings were supposed to be carried out in English, and all records were kept in that language, but once I had acquired fluency in Swahili I allowed the proceedings to be conducted in that language, though I still had to record in English. This greatly speeded up the proceedings. Our little court house was a very cosy intimate sort of place, and I soon learned to appreciate the innate ability of illiterate people to act, which involves in a manner of speaking, a great capacity to lie convincingly. *Tarishi* Daudi used to act as my interpreter from Luzinza to Swahili and vice versa, and his technique was often amusing. I would direct a question at the witness, whereupon Daudi might launch into a long harangue with the addressee. Quite often the answer which eventually reached me was a simple *ndiyo* or *hapana* that is "yes" or "no". I generally trusted Daudi, but I wondered sometimes, when the court audience dissolved in laughter, just who or what was the subject of their mirth. The time at which some event in the witness's testimony occurred often caused problems, and a common means used to indicate this was to point at the sky, indicating the position of the sun at the time. Early morning time was usually judged by first, second, or third cock-crow.

The coroner's court took up quite a lot of time. The least pleasant part of this was viewing the body. This was obligatory on the court and had to be recorded in the proceedings. When someone had died in a remote part of the district in suspicious or unusual circumstances, and the sub-chief got to hear of it, he had to arrange for the body to be brought to Biharamulo. This could take time, and the consequences may be imagined, in a hot climate. Gerald, the medical assistant, had to carry out the post-mortems, and I used to view the body at the same time. On one occasion the body was brought in of an old man who had been burned to death in a hut fire. It had been wrapped in banana leaves and carried through the bush slung on a pole for three days. With that one Gerald and I just peeped through the mortuary door and left it at that.

After a longish spell in the office it was always good to get out again into the district. One regular task was paying the road gangs we had working more or less permanently on the district roads which were the central government's responsibility. A number of experienced road foremen were in charge of the gangs and they recruited their labour locally. The main work involved digging out the drainage ditches either side of the road and throwing the spoil onto the road crown to maintain a cambered surface to shed water. Pot-holes and ruts were systematically filled in, and bridges repaired. The latter were simple affairs built of logs with plank decking, or where appropriate stone drifts were put in. These roads were simple, cheap, and effective for the amount of traffic carried. Paying the labourers was a regular chore, and this involved carrying large heavy bags of coin. They refused to accept paper money, which to them was not nearly durable enough. It was not real money, and could be destroyed by fire or damp. Counting out all these coins was rather a tedious job. At appropriate times of the year I would be accompanied by a tax clerk who would relieve the men of part of their earnings. Perhaps rather unexpectedly, they did not seem to resent this, but welcomed the chance to be rid of their obligations. I never met any resentment at this sort of primitive pay-as-you-earn system.

Many of the sub-chiefdoms could be reached relatively easily and quickly by road or track. It became apparent that I needed a vehicle of my own to better carry out my duties. Walking was great but it took time, and Smith did not care over-much for what he chose to refer to as my "walking holidays". This irritated me as I regarded close contact with the people as much more important than routine correspondence with bureaucrats. I applied for a government loan and ordered a new Landrover from Dar Es Salaam. It came up by rail to Mwanza, thence across the lake by steamer to Bukoba where I went to collect it. I thus became the proud owner of my first capital asset. Thirty-five years later I still own a Landrover, my fourth with over 100,000 rugged miles on the clock. The toughest, most practical vehicle ever made.

VI

Work in Biharamulo was thus varied and of very great interest. I was enjoying my work immensely. There were however, other things to do of equal interest, and these occupied many of my weekends. The local sandstone forms sharp, steep escarpments, and the rock closely resembles the Pennine gritstone on which I had learned the basic skills of rock-climbing at home. Here were miles of virgin cliffs and crags, unexplored and unclimbed, a rock-climber's private paradise. None of my colleagues was in the least bit interested, so I either went alone or took the long-suffering Daudi, who was far too polite to say what he thought of my strange antics. The only explanation to him was that I was looking for something. So I was, I suppose, but not the tangible things he was thinking of, precious stones or some such thing. I very nearly came to grief one day, when, pulling myself up over the top of a crag I saw, at a level with my eyes, a snake. Fortunately instead of letting go and falling I froze, and realised that what I was looking at was not a live snake, but a recently sloughed-off skin. I climbed down, shaking and unnerved, and went home.

Hunting inevitably attracted my early interest. The whole area was rich in game. Quite near to the *boma*, birds such as partridge and guinea-fowl were plentiful, with duck and geese on nearby marshy areas. Smith was a keen bird-shot, and he had a beautiful Holland and Holland twelve bore made to his own measurements. I used one of the NA single barrel twelve bores of totally undistinguished origins. We often went out in the evenings, and had some good sport. But I was eager for bigger things, not surprising in view of my youthful reading about Africa and exploration. Smith was not so keen, and he sold me his rifle, a

Husquarna 9.3 mm. Thus armed I prepared to sally forth. Many of the locals hunted, using ancient muzzle loading pieces referred to in Swahili as *gobori*. With these powder was poured down the barrel followed by the shot which could be old metal rubbish or ball ammunition. This was then well rammed down. Firing was by means of a percussion cap ignited by a trigger-operated hammer. Daudi recruited a local hunter of note to accompany us, and very early one Sunday morning we set off for some swampy country to the north where buffalo were said to be plentiful. My ambitions clearly outdistanced my capabilities, since my experience was nil, and looking back I realise how incredibly foolish I was. Buffalo can be very dangerous beasts especially if wounded, and have to be followed up. We found buffalo alright, in large numbers, but they caught our wind and disappeared into a papyrus swamp. We followed, and found ourselves moving along tunnel-like passageways made by the great beasts. The mud and water were quite deep, and my early enthusiasm had cooled off markedly. My companions however, had total faith in me and the beautiful lethal weapon I carried, and were eagerly looking forward to a bonanza of fresh meat. I had perforce to go on with the venture. By the grace of God we never got near enough for me to take a shot, though I had to restrain my hunter from peppering them from a distance with his *gobori*. I was at least aware of the danger of wounding one of these formidable animals, and having now seen them at close quarters, I had no stomach for a long hunt after a wounded one in that environment. When I got back and told Smith of the day's exploits he was half amused and half angry that I should be, as he put it, "such a bloody young idiot".

Wildlife in the district was abundant, and nowhere more so than down near the lake where a large tract of uninhabited land had been designated as the Nyamirembe Game Reserve. This was largely the creation of Bryan Cooper, the game ranger who lived down there. Nearby was the tiny port of Nyamirembe, which had a small pier and a godown, from where the arabica coffee from Ngara district was exported, and through which we imported bulk goods such as cement. The population of this place was about fifty people, with whom Cooper waged a sort of cold war. He suspected them, with some justification, of poaching in his reserve, but he could seldom catch them. It wasn't really serious, but Cooper, like so many wildlife enthusiasts, was a total fanatic, and had no time at all for human beings. He was distinctly eccentric, and living alone, he got few opportunities for discourse with his own kind. When he did get amongst Europeans, he never stopped talking, and so earned the nickname "walkie-talkie" Cooper. I got to know him well and liked him. He taught me a great deal about African wildlife and bushcraft. I often went down to Nyamirembe at weekends, and we would spend whole days wandering about on foot, observing the teeming game. I was also allowed to go out alone or with a game scout. We once came across a party of honey-hunters, and spent some time with them. I heard and saw for the first time the African honey-bird (*Indicator indicator*) which guides human beings to bee nests, flitting from tree to tree with its funny chattering call. Sure enough one of these led us to a hive, and the men proceeded to smoke out the bees with smouldering grass and twigs. I was astonished and delighted when these people made fire by the ancient method of twirling a stick in a slab of different wood, and thus igniting a small clump of dried grass. I tried my hand at this, but could not master the knack of maintaining a continuous high twirling speed. We sucked the honey straight from the comb, and it was delicious. By tradition we left some comb for our little guide.

On these expeditions I used to wonder at the remarkable ability of the "bush" African to navigate and not get lost in very confusing country, and their deep knowledge of their environment. This early realisation of the innate ability of so-called primitive people has often led me to ponder on the nature of intelligence. In those early years in the African wilderness I often felt foolish and incompetent in comparison to my companions.

Over time I have myself acquired such skills, but one should remember that modern man, of whatever race or colour who goes back to the wilderness for recreation or whatever and learns how to travel and live there, is simply reverting to atavistic skills long buried in the sub-conscious. *Homo sapiens* after all, has been a hunter-gatherer for the greater part of his existence as a separate species. For an unsophisticated African however, or any other person from surviving Iron Age or earlier cultures, to move into a modern industrial-urban way of life and thought, involves a big jump forward, not a reversion to inherited but dormant skills. The European for example has evolved the modern technical environment and has developed with it over centuries. The African by and large has not, and he is being asked to adapt with dramatic suddenness. As a teacher in Africa one must ponder these things. Most of the students I have taught over the past twenty-five years are only two or sometimes only one generation removed from a cultural and technical environment similar to that of my forbears of a dozen and more centuries ago. The astonishing thing to me is that they adapt so fast, a tribute to their innate ability. Western people, and there are many who tend to brand the rural African as slow, unadaptable, unintelligent, or idle, would do well to think rather more deeply and critically on these matters.

But to revert to my friend Cooper. He had a rough sense of humour, and once gave me a bad scare, to his enormous amusement. We were out walking one day, and came upon a sleeping black rhino, not the best-tempered of animals. A gleam came into my mentor's eye and he ordered a retreat to a nearby ant-hill from which point of vantage he proceeded to throw stones at the slumbering giant. It snorted and leapt to its feet with amazing agility, and rushed around angrily sniffing the air. To my great relief it took off in a direction away from us, clearly intent on venting its irritation on something. Tension gone, I testily asked Cooper what he was trying to do. He stopped laughing and airily informed me that he knew all about rhinos, and if this one had charged us he would have put a bullet in front of its nose to distract and divert it. He would never have shot it of course, and I am quite sure would have sacrificed me rather than one of his beloved animals. However, for some reason he loathed and hated baboons, and shot them on sight. An American big-game enthusiast was once staying with Smith as his guest, and it was arranged that Cooper should take him out to find and bag a large tusker. Apparently they found a big bull and stalked it for several hours to try to get in position for the American to kill the beast with a perfect *coup de grace* single shot — he had been reading Hemingway. Just as the dénouement approached however, Cooper spied some baboon on a nearby hillock and immediately blasted them. The elephant of course vanished rapidly and the hunt was off, to the immense chagrin and fury of the American.

I was very happy in Biharamulo, but young district officers were not usually left in peace in one place for very long. Sure enough early in 1953 the order came to move across the lake to Musoma. There were still many things I had not had time to do in Biharamulo. I wanted to make a foot safari to Lake Burigi in the far north of the district, which Speke had described in glowing terms, likening it to Lake Windermere. I had also intended to carry out a study of the traditional iron-making industry which had flourished near Runazi, and which had been temporarily revived during the war to make hoes for the Sukuma cultivators. However, I had no time to lament these failures. Musoma was a large district and was to prove to be as exciting and challenging as Biharamulo had been.

Chapter Three

Musoma

The views were immensely wide, everything you saw made for greatness and freedom.

Blixen, *Out of Africa*

I

Musoma is a much larger district than Biharamulo, being about 6,560 square miles (17,000 sq km) in area, and with far more people, about 150,000 in the 1950s when I was there. The small town of Musoma itself had about 6,000 people. It is situated on the south side of Mara Bay where the river of that name enters the lake. From a lake frontage of about fifty miles, the district stretches eastwards for about one hundred and fifty miles right up onto the high Serengeti plains, where it marches with Masailand to the east and Sukumaland to the south. The climate on this eastern side of the lake is far less favourable than that on the western side, being much drier. The landscape as a result looks very different. Musoma is a land of lightly wooded grassy plains, though in the western parts, a series of rocky hill ranges, which may be wooded, give variety to the landscape. The whole way of life and economy of the people is very different on the opposing sides of the lake. Their history and culture too are dissimilar.

The west lake peoples of Bukoba and Biharamulo were politically organised in a series of small states in which the mass of the ordinary people were dominated by a ruling caste derived from an immigrant cattle-owning aristocracy. Bananas (*ebitoke*) grow well there and are the staple foodstuff. Few cattle are kept, and the main source of wealth is robusta coffee in Bukoba, and tobacco in Biharamulo. One language, Luhaya, is dominant, and to this Luzinza is closely related. Musoma shows no such relative simplicity, but rather it is a confusing mosaic of peoples, languages and cultures. The major groups or tribes are the Jita, Kwaya, Shashi and Luo near the coast, the Zanaki in the western hill ranges with the Ikizu close by, and the Kuria, Ngurimi, Nata, Issenye and Ikoma further inland, and some Masai in the far east. The coastal peoples have some cultural and linguistic affinities with the west lake peoples, though the Shashi are Sukuma speaking, and the Luo are a totally different group speaking a Nilotic language. The economy of the coastal people is based on cultivation, though they also keep cattle which are culturally very significant. They grow maize and sorghum, with banana, and sweet potatoes along the lake edges. Cotton is a very important cash crop. The inland peoples are culturally distinct, being mainly pastoralists, with many habits and customs derived from the Masai, by whom they were for long molested. They do cultivate, but depend on drought resistant sorghums and millets, with cassava as a famine reserve crop. In very general terms the importance of cultivating declines progressively eastwards. A rather strange and distinctive small group are the Tatoga or Tatiru who live mainly in the grasslands of the Ikizu chiefdom. Their language is Nilotic, though very different from the related Masai and Luo. They probably represent a very early intrusion of Nilotic speaking peoples southwards long before the Masai came.

The traditional customs of all these peoples vary greatly, and this applies particularly to their laws regarding such things as the ownership of cattle, marriage, inheritance and the holding of land. This made the sorting out of disputes a major headache, whether at the official level in the hearing of appeals from Local Court judgements, or at the unofficial level. None of these laws had been written down when I was working there, and I had to learn fast as I went along. This was altogether a confusing and difficult area in which to work, and a far cry from the relative simplicities of Biharamulo from where I had just come. It was also totally absorbing.

The bulk of the population was concentrated in the better-watered and thus more agriculturally productive lands close to the lake coast, and thinned out progressively eastwards. In the early 1950s pressure on land was not yet acute, and though large numbers of cattle were kept, overgrazing and land degradation were not really serious issues. There were still large expanses of unspoiled savana grasslands dotted with acacia thorn trees, with denser woodland along the river courses, often teeming with wildlife.

II

Musoma township lay well back from the lakeshore. Its centre was a simple gridiron pattern of unpaved streets, along which were built the shops or *maduka* of the mainly Indian traders. The only other group of non-locals engaged in trade were the Somalis, who controlled the trade in cattle. As one moved out from the centre the quality of the buildings declined, and the houses on the outskirts were typical mud-brick and thatched roof structures. The polyglot population was made up of people from all over the district, and as usual in East African towns there was a strong Muslim element.

When I arrived in Musoma there was no public water supply, and all water had to be carried up from the lake. It was not until 1954 that a reservoir was built on a hill in the town and water pumped up to it from the lake, to be reticulated from this storage throughout the town. Neither was there an electricity supply, and the paraffin lamp and refrigerator reigned supreme. However, Musoma's links with the outside world were good, and one did not feel cut off in a remote back-water as in Biharamulo. Musoma was a lake port, with the quay and installations about a mile out of town on a small peninsula jutting out into Mara bay. The two main lake steamers, the *Usoga* and *Rusinga* called weekly on their round-the-lake schedule, going clockwise and anti-clockwise respectively. We also had an air-strip, used by a twice-weekly service run by Caspair Air Services of Nairobi. This was also a round-the-lake service and operated by two ancient De Haviland Rapides, which were twin-engined biplanes. We had a hospital with a European medical officer, two nursing sisters, and an assistant MO. A dental assistant came on tour periodically, bringing his dental drill with him. It was operated by a foot-treadle, so that filling a tooth was a slow and painful operation.

Musoma had long had two and sometimes three administrative officers, the DC and one or two DOs, so that my arrival was a purely routine matter. The DC was Brian Hodgson, who had all the right antecedents and fitted perfectly the received image of a colonial administrator. He was an old Etonian and had been at Oxford where he had earned his rowing blue, stroking Oxford to victory in the 1937 boat race. But he was a worker, and totally dedicated, so that working under him was both instructive and pleasant. He was married with three delightful children, and as the station complement was much larger, with several married couples, the atmosphere was very different from that at Biharamulo, where we were all bachelors except for old Mrs MacGregor. Our origins were mixed, and in addition to locals included British, Irish, Canadian, New Zealanders and South Africans. Out in the district were a number of mission stations, Roman Catholic, Mennonite, Africa Inland Mission and Seventh Day Adventist, all of which were largely staffed by Americans. There was also a small productive gold-mine thirty miles out at Buhemba, which had a very mixed population of Australians, South Africans, Canadians, Greeks and British, with a local labour force. They were a collection of rugged individualists, and not at all easy to deal with, though very hospitable. I once had the misfortune to have to deal with a very tricky *shauri* out here.

One of the South Africans, an Afrikaner named Van Maltitz, kept pigs, and these had got out one day to do a lot of damage to a maize *shamba* belonging to one of the local people. The inevitable complaint came to me, and I had to arbitrate on the question of compensation. I knew what would happen. The Afrikaner would be convinced that I, a British administrator, would inevitably favour the black man, while the latter might suspect that I would favour a fellow white man who moreover was very large and threatening. There was however no element of doubt in the matter, for clearly the pigs had got out and done a lot of damage to the growing maize. I ordered Van Maltitz to pay compensation, but told the local to fence his land properly. Van Maltitz was not pleased.

On arrival in Musoma I was able to move into a comfortable house, and as my cook, Michaeli had accompanied me from Biharamulo, the domestic side of life was quickly organised. I also employed a local Mukwaya named Namko, of whom more later. My new home was right on the lake shore, and so I was able to swim daily, keeping a weather eye open for the odd crocodile. It was this habit of swimming in the lake which undoubtedly first gave me bilharzia or schistosomiasis, though I also swam regularly in the lake from Bukoba and waded through countless rivers in later years.

III

Musoma was a very busy district, and there was probably more work than the DC and I could cope with. We received periodic visits from a peripatetic resident magistrate, and in due course we were to get a permanent appointee, but until that happened we had to do all the criminal court work. The visiting RM only had time to cope with the backlog of civil work. My main tasks were to do the bulk of the court work and to supervise the work of the native authority treasury. The treasury was a busy one, but fortunately the treasurer was capable, experienced, and efficient, having been trained by the Germans when a young man. He was a very dignified elderly person named Maato, but invariably known as Mzee Maato, *mzee* being the Swahili word for an elder, and very much a term of respect. He was grey haired and had a trim little goatee beard, so that apart from the colour of his skin, he bore a striking resemblance to General Smuts. Reference to this always greatly amused him.

My role in the treasury was really that of auditor and training officer for the staff, and I used to sit for hours at the month's end checking and balancing the books. One incident that occurred one day while I was so engaged is worth recalling. A young African of about my own age poked his head through the office window and chatted to Mzee Maato. The latter, always a model of courtesy, called me over and introduced me to his visitor. His name was Julius Nyerere, and he had recently returned from studies in Edinburgh, and was enjoying a short holiday at his home in Uzanaki, where he had been born the son of a minor chief. I met him once or twice more during that visit. He struck me at the time as careful and guarded, not surprising as he must have felt very unsure of himself. I was to meet him again on a number of occasions in later years, and once spoke at one of his meetings, getting into some trouble thereby as I will later relate.

One overriding impression that I think anyone who has known Nyerere must have, is one of genuine simplicity and sincerity, which makes him stand out, with Seretse Khama of Botswana, amongst the modern leaders of emergent Africa.

The court work I had to carry out was a real burden. Hodgson did not like it, and so I had to do it all. I was a second class magistrate with limited powers, but there was a provision in the Criminal Procedure Code allowing a lower class magistrate to take first class cases when the DC was unavoidably away from the station. This clause was fully exploited, and I never understood why the High Court never enquired what it was that kept the DC away so much. I did all the criminal work, for the resident magistrate who visited us from time to time was only able to clear up the backlog of civil work on each visit. Fortunately we had a very efficient clerk of the court who kept everything in order.

The court-house was a big open-sided building with a corrugated iron roof, and with the bench raised up on a platform at one end, with access to the chambers behind. The magistrate had to record all the proceedings in his own hand, and it must have been at this time that my handwriting deteriorated into an almost unintelligible scribble. In most cases the prosecutor was an African inspector of police, and to speed up the proceedings I again, as in Biharamulo, allowed Swahili to be used directly, though I had to record in English. This simultaneous translating helped to polish my Swahili very considerably. We had an official court interpreter for defendants and witnesses who could not cope in Swahili, and with the multiplicity of languages in the district, his linguistic abilities impressed me greatly. He never faltered. His English too was excellent, and I often sought his assistance on points of Swahili grammar. With this practice I managed to pass my Higher Swahili Examination after eighteen months in the territory.

In my practice as a magistrate I tried to apply the precepts and knowledge that Mr. Lane had tried to instil into us at Cambridge, and though I found this work absorbing and fascinating, it was also exhausting both physically and mentally. It is a heavy responsibility for a young man to have the power to deprive another person of his or her freedom for periods of up to three years, and I often agonised for hours over whether to find someone guilty or not of the offence with which he or she was charged. I am sure I was often far too lenient, but rather that than its opposite, I think.

The peoples of Musoma were a far more violent lot than the Bazinza of Biharamulo, and I had many cases to deal with of assault, and wounding with spear, arrow or knife, with murder and manslaughter quite common. Illicit distilling of *moshi,* a potent and dangerous alcoholic spirit, and smoking of locally grown *bhangi* (*Cannabis sativa*) were also very common. There were of course lighter moments, and the humour on such occasions was often of the earth, earthy. On one occasion a policeman was describing his search of a suspected thief, and of how he told him to drop his trousers and bend down, whereupon several twenty shilling notes fluttered to the ground. With a dead straight face and sound logic he went on to inform the bench that he thought that a very strange place for a man to keep his money, and he therefore arrested him. One could write a book of such anecdotes as no doubt could any magistrate.

One unwelcome result of all this work at headquarters was that I found it difficult to get out into the district, and I could only do this when the RM was visiting. I got so fed up at one stage that I asked John Blower who was Game Ranger out at Banagi on the Serengeti, to enquire if I could transfer to the Game Department. I knew what the answer would be for the powers-that-be would not dream of releasing me, but the attempt relieved some tension.

I did get out for short safaris down the lake coast to Mugango and Majitha, and carried out the normal touring duties of attending local council meetings, checking sub-treasury accounts, inspecting the crops, examining the local court records, and hearing a multitude of complaints and personal problems. The task of sitting in as adviser at local council meetings was an important one. These were always held in the local sub-chief's court-house, normally an open-sided building of concrete blocks with a corrugated iron roof. Such meetings were always packed, and in the hot sun, the temperature got very high, and the smell of sweaty, smoky humanity very pervasive. Debate was invariably long and often heated, and the flow of rhetoric elaborate, and it went on all day from morning to dusk. There was nothing inhibited about the speakers or the subjects they raised, and government came in for a lot of criticism, which the attendant district officer had to cope with as well as he was able.

Once I had passed my Higher Swahili I could begin to hear

appeals against local court judgements, and this was work I greatly enjoyed. In hearing these appeals I had the record of the lower court, in Swahili, and I could call and question both parties to the case and their witnesses. Almost all cases were of a civil nature and usually involved disputes over land or cattle, or were concerned with marriage or divorce settlements. I always made a point of trying to visit the village of the parties, and always when land was the subject of the dispute. This took me right into the homesteads and *shambas*, and thus into very close contact with the people. Where difficult points of customary law were involved I had the assistance of two assessors, invariably respected old men. There were no specific rules of procedure in hearing these appeals, and so I could patiently dig for the truth. It was time-consuming but absorbing work, and quite fascinating. Particularly amongst the pastoral peoples, a case could be immensely complex, and could take hours to unravel. Amongst such people bride-price or dowry is paid in cattle by the suitor to the father of the woman he wishes to marry. If a divorce is sought, maybe years afterwards, because the wife has been unfaithful, or maybe barren, repayment of the cattle paid in dowry may be reclaimed in whole or in part. Some of the cattle may have died in the meantime, others may have produced off-spring, and some may have been given in dowry elsewhere, and may in their turn have reproduced. Given these people's total attachment to cattle, it is not I think difficult to imagine the complex arguments and subtle lying that could bedevil attempts to track down the cattle in question and arrive at a satisfactory settlement. A special problem attached to cattle cases concerned language. Pastoral peoples have an immense vocabulary to describe cattle in all their shapes, colours, sizes, horn shapes and other aspects, and such words are not translatable into Swahili which has no such vocabulary. The necessary circumlocution to try to describe a given animal gave me a lot of trouble.

Quite often the hearing of an appeal would be attended by a crowd of interested onlookers, and the longer a case was drawn out, the more interesting it was to the assembled throng. I often had to draw deeply on reserves of patience and good humour to survive. To have shown anger, or impatience, or to have been too direct and lacking in subtlety would have quickly lost their respect, and to give a valued and acceptable judgement I had to have that respect. I remember hearing a case that involved cattle amongst a group of Tatiru, pure pastoralists to a man, in Ikizu chiefdom. The location of the dispute was out in the middle of a great grassy plain, and we sat under a big camelthorn tree to try to resolve the dispute, with a large throng of interested people as observers. It was hot, and the flies, inevitable in cattle country, were pestilential. The argument went on for a whole day, from early morning to dusk. Finally, weary and dispirited, I gave my verdict, whereupon to my surprise, the appellant who had lost the case, a venerable old man, stood up and accepted my decision, and thanked me for my conduct of the case. I felt that in some vital but intangible way I had arrived.

To return to my short coastal safaris. The people planted extensive areas of the lake-edge sands with sweet potatoes, which flourished in the damp environment. These were a prey to hippo which could consume a large mass of vegetable matter in the space of a single night. At meetings the people complained bitterly about this and about the apparent reluctance of the Game Department to do anything to help them by shooting a few hippo. Once they got to know that I possessed a rifle at home, I just had to take it with me and shoot the odd hippo as a deterrent to the rest. This hippo hunting could be quite exciting. We went out in canoes, not the hollowed-out trunk variety, but a type common on Lake Victoria which is made of long planks fixed together, with a high prow and stern. African hunting methods are seldom subtle, and the long slow stalk followed by a swift *coup de grace* are largely unknown. We would paddle up to a school of hippo, and I was then expected to blast away in the hope of fatally hitting one. I tried to be cool and scientific, and take careful aim at a selected beast. All that are usually visible of a floating hippo are its ears, eyes, and nose, and taking aim at this small target from a canoe full of excited people was not easy. At the sound of the shot, the beasts made off, sometimes leaving a dead companion behind. I was always afraid of an angry hippo deciding to attack our canoe and overturn us into the water, but none ever did. If the dead beast could not be immediately retrieved, the people would wait until the expanding stomach gases floated it up, and then tow it ashore. The subsequent butchering operation was not pleasant to behold, and the stench of escaping stomach gases was appalling, but one hippo yields a large quantity of meat and fat, both of which are very palatable. Excellent soap could also be made from hippo fat boiled up with caustic soda.

The lake coastline was in places very attractive, with sandy beaches and rocky headlands. I loved it when there was a strong wind blowing, driving low wet clouds and piling big waves onto the shore. We northern peoples may crave the sun, but there is something in the blood that also yearns for rough cold weather, especially when one lives in tropical climes — at least that is the case with me. I often insisted on going out in such weather to inspect *shambas* along the coast, greatly to the puzzlement of my local companions. They must have thought me quite mad when I would stand for several minutes at a time just leaning into the wind and driven spray blowing off the lake. I was obviously homesick, but that would have been very difficult to explain.

1953, my first year in Musoma, was the year of Queen Elizabeth's coronation, and appropriate festivities had to be organised. One thing that particularly impressed me was the enormous and genuine enthusiasm that everyone put into this occasion. The oft-peddled view of colonialism is of sullen oppressed people smouldering with resentment, but nothing could be further from the truth in my experience.

The day was marked by a big march past of the police, and contingents of the various other public services, and hundreds of school children from all over the district. This was followed by a huge display of tribal dancing, with troupes of dancers coming from every tribe of the district. A good deal of careful staff work was required to organise the transportation, housing, feeding, and eventual return to their homes of the large numbers of people coming in from many distant places. My special responsibility was organising the dancers. With its complex mosaic of peoples Musoma can produce more exciting, colourful and varied dancing than probably any other part of Tanganyika, and the spectacle we enjoyed on Coronation Day 1953 was magnificent. The coastal peoples' rhythmic drumming and colourful costumes were splendid. The Luo wore high ostrich plume headdresses, and necklaces of hippo teeth, and on their feet were clogs full of pebbles, with small bells around their legs, and thus attired they leapt and gyrated, making a superb rhythmic sound and spectacle. The Kuria and Ngurimi were dressed for battle in feathers and skins, and armed with spears and shields they mimed combat in short angry rushes which had the crowds screaming with excitement. The Ikoma from up on the edge of the Serengeti wore magnificent lion's mane headdresses that waved wildly as they leapt high in the air, backing and advancing for hours on end. The energy expended was prodigious, the dust and noise and colour and excitement overwhelming. Unfortunately I only had a Brownie box camera so that my photographic record is miserable, but I have only to look at these old black and white prints for all that excitement to come rushing back to my mind. On a purely practical note, our estimate of the amount of local beer or *pombe* likely to be consumed had appeared ridiculously excessive, but it all went, and we had no complaints of niggardliness. That was truly a day to remember.

There was no shortage of interesting things to do in Musoma town, and though I was always anxious to get up-country, life was never boring. We had a Middle School just along the road which was run in an exemplary manner by a very fine man named Emmanuel Kibira, a Muhaya from Bukoba. He came from a very gifted family, his elder brother having been a key figure in the development of local government in Buhaya, while his younger brother became Bishop of the West Lake diocese of the Tanganyika Lutheran Church. Emmanuel was a striking man in both appearance and character. His face was long with a strong jaw, and a powerful slightly hooked nose, and he exuded energy and enthusiasm. His school was a model institution and it was always a pleasure to visit there. I tried teaching the boys to play rugby, and in fact they got on well with it, playing with vigour and enthusiasm, but alas there were no teams from elsewhere against whom they could test their prowess. I also tried running English classes for locals, though my skill in that field was minimal. One of my students was one Selemani Kitundu who was a trader and fisherman. He later got deeply involved in politics and became a leading light in Nyerere's Tanganyika African National Union (TANU). When I became district commissioner of Morogoro after independence he appeared on the scene as my regional commissioner. Later he became Chief Political Commissar of the Tanzanian Defence Force and I met him again in that role at the Tenth Anniversary of Independence celebrations to which I was invited, in Dar Es Salaam in 1971.

IV

Eventually the time came when I could apply for some local leave, of which one could take three weeks annually. I had for long decided how I was going to spend that leave. I planned to drive across the Serengeti plains to Arusha and on to Moshi, and from there climb Kilimanjaro, the highest mountain in Africa at 19,340 feet (5950 m). This great mountain is an almost extinct volcano, and has three major peaks: Kibo, the highest, Mawenzi at 17,000 feet, and Shira at 13,000 feet. Kibo is in fact a huge caldera or crater, and the highest point of the mountain lies on the outer rim of this. This point is now known as Uhuru peak, but had the earlier title of Kaiser Wilhem Spitze, given to it by the first German explorers of the mountain. A major problem in achieving my aim lay in finding a companion of like interests and intent, and able to get away at the same time as myself. This was not easy, but by great good fortune I learned that the Sheffield University Department of Geology were organising an expedition to study the geology of the mountain in co-operation with the government department of geological surveys. David Sampson was prominent in the organisation of this. He was an ex-Sheffield geologist then working for the government. I had known and climbed with him when we were members of the Sheffield and Manchester University mountaineering clubs. I wrote to him and asked if I could join the expedition for a couple of weeks, and this was agreed upon. I had brought all my mountaineering gear to Africa with me, such things as boots, ice-axe, crampons, windproofs and sleeping bag, so all I had to do was to jump into my landrover, load up the gear and plenty of spare water and petrol, and set off for the mountain. I took Namko, my house servant with me. He was overjoyed but didn't quite understand where we were going. He expected me to be aiming at the fleshpots of Nairobi or Dar Es Salaam, and appeared on the morning of departure in his best clothes. Eventually he did enjoy himself for he had some new and novel experiences to savour.

Our first task was to cross the Serengeti plains, not quite as simple and straight-forward as it is at the present day when a good gravel road cuts across from Seronera to Ngorongoro. In 1953 there was only a rutted two-wheel track through the dust, sometimes braiding into a broad series of tracks where people had attempted to avoid progressively deeper ruts. We stayed overnight at Banagi, the game ranger station on the western edge of the plains, and pushed on the next day. Unfortunately a flying stone had broken my windscreen so that our crossing was perishingly cold and appallingly dusty. We camped on the slopes of Ngorongoro and Namko was alarmed by the lions roaring in the vicinity at night.

Eventually we joined the Sheffield people at Marangu on the slopes of the mountain, where they were using the comfortable hotel as a base. From there I set off on my first ascent of the mountain. Namko stayed below. He drew the line at some of his employer's crazy ideas and flatly refused to go any further. He was quite happy down below, with the beer and bananas and nice Chagga girls. The geologist I accompanied had already been up the mountain and was accordingly well-acclimatised to altitude. He moved quickly. Pride forbade my requesting a slower pace, and pride got its just deserts in a fearsome hammering headache, a common manifestation of altitude sickness. First we went to a camp below the sheer slopes of Mawenzi. The geologists were busy here with their tasks, but I wanted to seize the opportunity to climb this rocky peak which rises to over 17,000 feet. I intended to go alone, but there was another spare man in the camp, a hydrologist from Kenya who had been sent to join the expedition to see if he could pick up anything of interest to the Kenya water people. He had absolutely no mountaineering experience, but was keen to have a go. There was a lot of cloud about and visibility was poor as we set off from the tents, and it remained thus all day. However, I had made a visual inspection of the mountain the previous evening when it had been clear, and I knew roughly where I wanted to go. The best route lay up one of the northern ridges, and then along a narrow ledge into a big gully which went straight up to the summit ridge. We got up the ridge safely but somehow missed the ledge, and found ourselves in a gully alright, but a narrow and difficult one which eventually petered out in a formidable face. I began to feel perplexed and a little nervous. Nothing was visible either up or down, and before me was a wall of what appeared to be consolidated volcanic ash with large lumps of harder rock sticking out from this in a random pattern, rather like the artificial climbing walls on which the present generation of climbers practise their skills in gymnasia. I firmly belayed my companion in the gully and instructed him how to handle the rope to me. I then ventured on

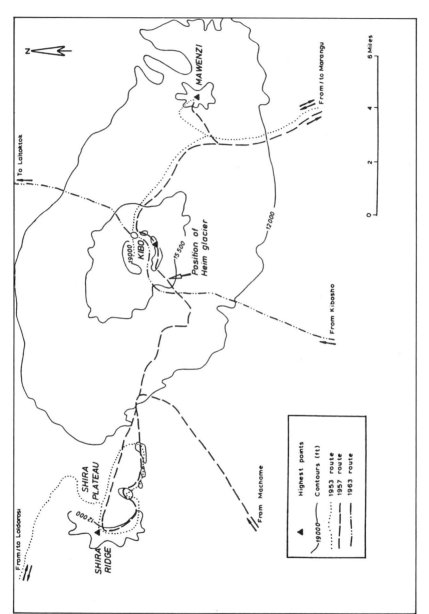

Fig. 2   The upper zone of Kilimanjaro showing routes used

a tentative exploration of the wall. Each nervous foray upwards was quickly followed by retreat. My head was throbbing, and if I was nervous, my companion was positively jittery. He eventually pointed out that he had a wife and child to think about, and insisted we go down. I agreed with alacrity to this perfect excuse to retreat, and down we went. As we got back onto the ridge the mist cleared briefly, and we were able to see where we had been, on a sheer one thousand foot wall that plunged to unknown depths below and soared up to the unseen summit above. My companion paled visibly, and I muttered a prayer of thanks for deliverance from folly. Two days later a party of four of us had a very enjoyable climb on a clear day by a new route straight up and into the main gully and to the summit. I was by then acclimatised to the altitude and revelled in the whole experience.

From the Mawenzi camp I went across the high saddle that links Mawenzi to Kibo and climbed the latter by the abominable tourist route which goes up a dreadful utterly boring scree slope. We had a camp in the crater of Kibo and from there explored much of the summit area with its remnant ice sheets, and the inner or Reusch crater. Geologists collect rocks of course, and rocks have to be carried down. The system we used was to carry two rucksacks, fore and aft, each loaded with about a hundred pounds of rocks, and run down the screes so loaded. Running down immensely long scree slopes with such loads taxed the leg joints which were not designed for such work. This sort of behaviour, a sort of mis-spent youth, probably accounts for the arthritic knees and ankles of my later years. Everything has its price, as my medical friends take pleasure in reminding me.

A day in the fleshpots of Marangu was followed quickly by a move to the western side of the mountain. One of the geologists wanted to visit the Shira plateau and if possible examine the glacier snouts on the western side of Kibo. We went up through some European farms to a high glade in the forest called Loldorosi, where one of the farmers was experimenting with pyrethrum as a crop. We made a base camp and from there spent two very frustrating days trying to find a way upwards through the dense mountain rainforest, which was full of elephant, buffalo, rhino and other less alarming beasts. There were four of us, David Humphreys the geologist, two African survey assistants and myself. Eventually we found a way through to emerge above the forest in the zone of giant heathers and other remarkable plants such as helychrysum and lobelia of enormous size, which form a dense barrier to easy progress. We were on the right bank of the Ngare Nairobi river, and just at the head of the forest we found a strange thing. This was a long, smooth, helter-skelter-like groove plunging from the lip of the gorge straight down to the river at the bottom. It was an elephant slide — what a sight it would be to see the giant pachyderms using it.

We were caught out at dusk on the third day literally nowhere in the giant heather belt, and were without water. In the distance far below us we could hear the river, a sweet sound to thirsty men. Throwing caution to the winds we plunged down the steep valley wall, with only a pencil torch to light our way. Hanging from trees, slipping and sliding, we got down. The water tasted sweet indeed and we bivouacked that night amongst the boulders in the river bed. Next morning we saw our route of descent and marvelled that we had got down safely. To ascend in daylight we had to use a safety rope and climb with care and deliberation.

Eventually we reached the edge of the Shira plateau and established ourselves in a very handy cave in the wall of the now shallow upper valley of the Ngare Nairobi. From there we spent two days exploring the plateau, and climbing all the Shira peaks. This plateau has a lost-world-like atmosphere. It is at an altitude of 13,000 feet (4,000 m) and to the east rise the formidable and impressive south and west faces of Kibo, seamed by long glaciers and dominated by the Eiger-like Breach Wall Peak or Brechswundspitze as the Germans called it. On the other sides the ground falls away out of sight, usually into a sea of cloud which in the afternoon wells up onto the plateau itself. Amazingly there was life up there and we saw both klipspringer and eland. This place really fired my imagination, and I was to return twice more in later years, once en route to make the first complete traverse of the mountain and the first ascent of the Heim glacier, of which more later.

When we got back down to Loldorosi Namko was very displeased. He had been worried about me, but more for his own skin, for their flimsy tents had been surrounded on most nights by roistering elephants. My leave was nearly up, and we had a long journey still to face back to Musoma, so we departed at once. The journey was not without incident. Crossing the Serengeti, and being rather careless, I took a wrong track, and realised after some time that we were travelling north towards Loliondo. Not wanting to retrace our tracks, I cut off across the open plains, and was relieved when eventually the familiar shape of Banagi hill appeared hull down on the far horizon. We reached the Seronera river, near where there is now a luxury game lodge for tourists, and tried to find a suitable crossing place. Leaving Namko in the landrover, I walked to the bank and along it until I found a practicable spot. When I reached the vehicle again, Namko's eyes were almost popping out and he was pointing at a small kopje I had walked past. Two superb black-maned lions were sitting there looking at us with mild interest. I had twice walked past them without seeing them, and thus without showing any fear. If I had seen them when they were between me and the landrover, I am not sure what I would have done. Namko had very sensibly kept quiet for fear of alarming both them and me. Actually, Banagi lions were so well fed that I doubt if they would have even bothered to get up. Nonetheless my legs suddenly went weak and I jumped into the landrover with alacrity and slammed the door shut. The rest of our journey home was uneventful.

V

Back in Musoma it did not take long to settle back into the routine of work. Once we had a permanent resident magistrate on the station I was relieved of all the court work, and was thus able to get out on safari more often. Once more I will quote from an old diary I kept at the time, to illustrate a typical working safari up-country. Points of explanation are in parentheses.

Saturday   Left home at 11 am. Called at Zanaki chiefdom headquarters to arrange for a *baraza* on the way back next Friday. Called on Chief Makongoro at Ikizu, and delivered the council minute book. He seemed well.

Between Ikizu and Issenye saw plenty of game. Chief of Issenye was not at home, so carried on to Nata. The road is awful. Called on Chief Rutiginga and had a chat over a jar of very nice buttermilk he offered me. He knew nothing of the recent Kuria raid on the Masai. Between Nata and Ikoma saw very large herds of game including about five hundred zebra. Spent about an hour at Ikoma talking to Chief Nyihocha before carrying on to Banagi. Stayed with Blower there. In the late afternoon we went out onto the Serengeti. Game was abounding everywhere. We saw a leopard up a tree with a Thomson's gazelle it had killed, and some very somnolent lion.

Sunday   Got off to early start. Settled in at the Ikoma rest-house, and then collected the Chief and went on a long tour of several *magunguli* (headmen's areas). We passed through Masaka, Manyatta, Bukumi, Nyangari and Maherera. At Masaka some bush clearing is going on, while at Nyangari a start has been made on a new cattle-watering dam. I poked into a number of food stores and estimated that most homesteads have at least two full of grain. In the evening went for a walk to the old German fort at the Grumetti drift — a rather gloomy place.

Monday   Attended meeting of the Ikoma *chama kikuu* (chiefdom council). Spoke to the council about hunting, the cattle census and cattle raiding. They had few comments on these points, but were very voluble on the subject of Waikoma irredentist claims on the far side of the Grumetti river in Nata. Went through the registers of *ushuru wa wilaya* (local government tax) and found that many people had not yet paid. I spoke to the councillors about this, impressing upon them the importance of prompt tax payments to their treasury.

After the meeting went to inspect the site of the new chiefdom headquarters, and then went on to Negoti where a local man named Alphonse has a small gold mine. He has sunk two shafts, and seems very pleased with progress.

Tuesday   Used a track which is in good shape to reach Sibora. Picked up Chief Rutiginga on the way and went on a tour of the area. There is plenty of good land here and ample room for more people to settle. Held a meeting with the local councillors who were ready with a number of points for me. They want the medical officer to come and have a look at Sibora, and I promised to talk to him about this. They want a school and are willing to start building it themselves. I promised to help get this organised as they would need some skilled help.

After the meeting I dealt with a number of individual *shauris*, and then went on to Nata village. The road is quite good, but I was puzzled by the number of abandoned homesteads. I was told that Masai cattle-raiding was the main cause of this. I camped at Nata, and in the evening went hunting and shot a topi, which made everyone happy at the feast of fresh meat.

Wednesday   Proceeded to Issenye. Camped in the mission school house. In the afternoon went on tour of the area with the Chief. Poked into a lot of food stores and estimated people have enough food for about three months. This is good-looking country and there is a line of permanent springs along a hill-ridge. More people could settle here.

Thursday   Held meeting with Wanangwa and Wanachama (headmen and councillors). They raised a number of points. Like the people of Nata they want a school and are prepared to start the work themselves. Again I promised to help. They need a new headquarters building. I said I would advise that it be considered for next year's NA expenditure estimates. They need cassava cuttings for planting out, and I said I would pass the message to the agriculture officer.

In the afternoon I went on to Ikizu, and took a couple of hours off to climb Chamliho, a prominent local mountain, en route. I went on to Busegwe where I camped.

Friday   Dealt with a *shauri* concerning plot 6 in Busegwe trading centre, then attended the meeting of the Zanaki chiefdom council. This was a well-run affair, Chief Edward being very efficient, with plenty of sensible things to say (he was Julius Nyerere's half-brother). The only point needing action concerns the border trouble at Tegeruka on the Mugango-Zanaki border. In the afternoon I went with Edward to Kiabakari and held a meeting with the local people to explain the nature of a prospecting licence and a mining claim. I think they understood, but in any case there are very few people on the area of the claim (at that time intensive work was in progress to prove a gold ore body, which was later successfully exploited).

Got back to Musoma well after sundown.

One or two of the subjects mentioned in this extract are worth some further comment. Chief Rutiginga of Nata was a splendid old man, solidly built and tough, with a wrinkled crafty face framed by long pierced ear lobes from which dangled large copper rings. He was a man of few words. I remember once at a native authority or district council meeting when the perennial problem of Masai cattle raiding was under discussion, Rutiginga roused himself suddenly from a doze, and strongly supported a motion from one of the councillors. The suggestion was that cattle should be branded, to help identify stolen beasts, but the old man had misunderstood — he thought the suggestion was that the thieves should be branded when caught. The Masai were persistent thieves and caused a lot of trouble. They firmly believe that Ngai, or God entrusted all cattle to the Masai so that removing them from the custody of other lesser peoples was simply the assertion of God-given rights. I was always amazed at the speed with which these people could move cattle over very long distances after a raid. The police had special officers whose sole concern was with stock theft and its prevention. These men were invariably Afrikaners from the community at Oldeani where they had settled in the early years of the century. They were very tough and hardy individuals capable of taking off at very short notice, often to spend weeks chasing cattle thieves.

Ikoma fort was a gloomy and forbidding ruin in those days, but I am told that it has now been rebuilt into some sort of tourist lodge. It was built like a Norman keep, with tall corner towers and connecting walls, and securely in command of the old Grummeti river crossing before the bridge was built upstream. During the 1914-18 war a British force had attacked it unsuccessfully and suffered a lot of casualties. One could still find the odd bone or skull lying around, though a medical officer some years previously had cleared away most of the grisly relics still unburied. It had eventually been taken by the British and partly demolished. It was this history no doubt which made it such a sombre sort of place.

Banagi was always a good place to visit. It was the residence of the game ranger responsible for the east lake region including the Serengeti, probably one of the finest wildlife regions in the whole of East Africa. The Banagi lion had been made famous by Monty Moore, a pre-war ranger who had half-tamed a number of lions by feeding them on carcasses towed behind a truck. A number of wealthy, mainly American big-game aficionados had thus been attracted to the area.

A major task of the game ranger was to try to control the poaching of game which was rife, especially in the corridor extension of the Serengeti National Park which gives access to the lake shore in Ushashi. The Shashi and Sukuma were ardent poachers, and I often had to deal with culprits caught by the game scouts. Whilst being a conservationist at heart, nevertheless I felt a certain amount of sympathy for these people. As some wise man once put it, "it is difficult to ignore the equivalent of Smithfield meat market freely available on one's doorstep", and this resource of plentiful meat had long been exploited by these people well before the inscrutable European said it should stop. The people naturally regarded the game ranger or *bwana nyama* with a good deal of suspicion and displeasure. Once at a council meeting in Ushashi I was asked by a councillor why they could not prosecute the *bwana nyama* when *his* animals raided their *shambas* and did a lot of damage. That was an embarrassing question and very difficult to answer. I prevaricated. Poaching however was illegal and the law had to be upheld. Once by accident I caught a gang of poachers red-handed. It was in the Ngurimi chiefdom just south of the Mara river. I was with Chief Simeon, and one of his *tarishis* named Masudi. We were travelling cross-country in my landrover after a visit to Ikorongo, when we stumbled on this gang. They were carrying a very large quantity of dried meat in big wide slabs, the product of two or three weeks' effort by about a dozen men. They were all armed with their big longbows and spears. In such circumstances one cannot turn a blind eye. They all knew Simeon and myself and they knew the law. Masudi, a big strong robust fellow, was quite definitive in his attitude. "*Tutawakamata, bwana*," ("we will arrest them") said he aggressively, chin thrust forward. That was easier said than done. How do you arrest a dozen or more well armed men out in the bush, miles from anywhere? I had no intention of spending hours shepherding them all the way back to Maji Moto, the chiefdom headquarters, assuming they had been willing to be so taken. I suggested to Simeon that he should exert his authority over these men, who were his people, and tell them to load all the meat into the landrover, and clear off as quickly as possible. This was done and we drove off. The meat was given to the clinic and the school at Maiji Moto. I wondered afterwards what we would have done if these far from docile people had refused to comply with Simeon's order. As it happened boldness and lack of hesitation on our part had taken them by surprise and had paid off. Masudi was chortling, but Simeon looked nervous as we drove off.

Poaching of wild animals was in fact quite a serious problem, although in those days it was not organised on a commercial scale as it often is nowadays in many parts of Africa. As I have said, I felt a certain amount of sympathy for local people who were what one might call subsistence poachers, though obviously some sale of game meat did take place in the villages. For others I had no sympathy at all. Particularly bad were the South African miners at Buhemba. They tended to hunt and kill for the "fun" of it, and I have seen the trail of death and mindless destruction they could leave behind them. Sometimes more apparently worthy people could be involved. I once caught a Mennonite missionary with a truckful of topi carcasses. On being questioned he replied, "Aw, c'mon Mr. Cooke. Ah have to feed God's children, y'know." "Of course," I replied, "but Caesar has ruled that you need a licence to feed them on God's animals; may I see your licence, please." Of course he had none, and was duly prosecuted. On another occasion I heard yet another missionary describing how he and several others had shot an elephant — for the ivory to provide funds for the mission, naturally. "We saw this big tusker," he said, "and we got real close, and then let it have a volley. It dropped to its knees, and we let it have another couple of volleys, and I guess that just about finished it off." Hardly an example of clean precision hunting, and I often wondered if these men of God ever thought of a wild animal as part of God's creation and susceptible to suffering just like humans.

John Blower was ranger at Banagi during my first year in Musoma, but when he left, his place was not filled at once, and the station was left in charge of a few game scouts. At that time the Mau Mau was active in Kenya and anxiety was expressed about the rifles and ammunition left at Banagi. They would prove a fine haul for a gang of dissidents who might have heard of this place. It could be reached from Kenya through totally uninhabited country. I was sent to retrieve the arms. It happened to be the rainy season, and when I got to the Grummeti drift, the river was in full flow, so that I could not drive across. Leaving my landrover with my cook and *tarishi,* I waded and swam across the river, and walked to the Ikoma police post. From there I took two constables to accompany me to Banagi, another twenty miles farther on. We commandeered three bicycles in the village and set off. As we approached Banagi the eerie silence gave me a little concern, but we needn't have worried. The game scouts were pleased to see us and fed us. We cleared the armoury of weapons and I told the scouts to hide the ammunition. We three set off back to Ikoma with the weaponry slung around ourselves and the bikes, so that we looked like old-time bandits. This gave us great amusement as we set off, but this changed to a dull resignation as thus accoutred we struggled over the sandy and often stony track on our ancient machines. When I eventually got back to Musoma with the haul of arms, I felt very pleased with myself, but the whole affair was treated as quite routine. My sense of a mildly heroic venture was totally deflated.

VI

During one safari to the Ikoma chiefdom I travelled north-wards in my landrover along the edge of the Serengeti where the grass savanna tends to give place to rather thicker woodland. I followed an old track which went from the derelict old gold workings at Kilimafedha to Nairobi via Narok. I went as far as a place called Klein's camp. There was nothing there but a good camping place which had been used by an old Kenyan hunter named Klein. The amount of wildlife in this area was amazing, and the number of lions especially notable. A prospector whom I knew well named Arnold Kuenzler, who was looking for traces of kimberlite for Williamson's Diamonds of Mwadui, found these lions a nuisance and a hindrance in his work. He argued, understandably, that he should be given licence to shoot them when they threatened him, but needless to say this was refused. Arnold survived, so I am sure several lions bit the dust.

Beyond Klein's camp the track goes on through magnificent country, and crosses the Mara river into what is now the popular Masai Mara National Park in Kenya. Edwin Ratzburg, an old-timer who lived in Musoma, had run a transport service using Model T Fords, from Kilimafedha to Nairobi in the 1920s, and he had some fascinating yarns to relate of his adventures in those far-off days. I decided I would like to walk through this country, and asked Hodgson if I could undertake a two-week safari, with the ostensible object of looking for illegal settlers, poachers or even fugitive Mau Mau remnants. I received the half-expected response that there was plenty of office-work to do, and I should get on with it. Not to be deterred I solved the dilemma by using two weeks of local leave to do the trip in 1954. This was regarded with official favour, and I was even given an official allowance to pay for my porters.

My plan was to start from Maji Moto in Ngurimi, and to go via Ringwani and Ikorongo into the Mara valley which I would follow as far as the Kenya frontier before turning south towards Negoti and Ikoma. From there I would march back northwestwards to Ringwani and Maji Moto. This country was unmapped in those days so I would have to rely on my porters' knowledge of the country they were familiar with, and on my own bush-sense, and what one might call geographic logic or feel for the lie of the land. Chief Simeon found me some porters, and my old friend Masudi was to keep them in order. I also took along a game scout named Saakumi, his porter, and my cook Michaeli. We kept food and equipment to a minimum. For the men, we took a large fly-sheet and for myself, a small bivouac tent, and for food maize-meal, rice, curry-powder, tea, sugar and biscuits. This was less spartan than it sounds, for the area we were to explore was teeming with game, and we feasted like kings on fresh meat daily. Saakumi and I carried rifles, and the men their longbows and arrows. These bows were formidable weapons, about five feet long like an old English longbow, and needing a powerful arm to draw. We felt safe against all possible threats. I have travelled widely in East, Central and Southern Africa but I have seen nowhere else the wealth of wild life that we met with on that safari. There were large herds of elephant, buffalo in their thousands, black rhino, giraffe, all the major and minor antelopes, predators such as lion, leopard, cheetah, hyena, wild dogs, and all the scavengers, jackal, fox, vulture etc. At each evening's camp it was but the work of a few minutes to go out and shoot something for the pot. Here I learned to wonder at the prodigious capacity of my companions to consume red meat. Every twenty-four hours they managed to polish off a largish antelope. My own consumption was puny in comparison, though I am fond of meat. I was allotted the liver and part of the fillet, the choice bits that is, but I could never eat all I was given. The men skewered large hunks of meat on sticks which they leaned to the fire so that the outer parts turned brown. The fact that they ate the meat in this semi-raw state probably accounts for their ability to digest such large amounts. I was glad I marched at the head of our column, for their eructations of wind were as prodigious as their appetites, and the air in our wake must have been blue. Sitting round the camp-fire with them in the evenings was entertaining and instructive. Saakumi, Michaeli and I did not speak Kingurimi, so we all had to discourse in Swahili. The level of conversation reminded me of a British army barrack room, with the same sort of banter and low humour, most of it well below the navel. My willingness to hunt and kill our food each day pleased them greatly, but at other times they thought me distinctly odd and told me so. I only had my old Brownie box camera, and so had to get very close to animals to get reasonable photographs. Fortunately, since this was true empty wilderness penetrated by very few people, the game was undisturbed and not much concerned at our presence. I found I could walk right up to herds of buffalo without frightening them, though eventually they would wheel around and thunder off, a truly stirring sight. The men refused absolutely to let me try the same technique with lions. Consternation was caused one day as we were emerging from some dense riverine bush. A large rhino, with a calf at heel, burst from cover, snorting with annoyance. I have never seen people scatter so fast. One moment the men were around me, the next they were up trees. Saakumi and I retreated with rather more decorum, and subsequently we poured mock scorn and derision on the others. The large beast trotted around for a while, sniffing the air, but then she made off with her baby in close attendance. We all assembled together again in a great hubbub of chatter and laughter, and the event was retold and discussed in great detail over the next few days. Their own discomfiture at the sudden appearance of the rhino was great cause for mirth. I found their robust, self-deprecating sense of humour very endearing.

We made our most easterly camp short of the Kenya border, and I gave the men a day's rest while Saakumi and I went on to where the Mara crosses the border. From a high rock bluff above the valley we had a stupendous view. The broad valley at our feet stretched on into Kenya Masailand, while beyond the river, to the north, lay the long blue line of the Issuria escarpment disappearing into the milky blue haze of the far horizon. A great silence enveloped us, with only the sound of the wind in the thorns, and the subdued buzz of insects to disturb it.

The only human beings we came across on our journey were a group of illegal Luo settlers right up the Mara. They were cultivating a small area, and obviously doing some hunting, for there were skins stretched out to dry in their camp. They were so nice, and so pleased to see someone that I hadn't the heart to be severe with them. I simply reminded them that they should not really be there, and that they ought to go back whence they had come when they had harvested their crops.

An interesting sequel to this journey occurred only last year, some thirty odd years later. A good friend and colleague, Godwin Adika, a Ghanaian who worked in my department at the University of Botswana for several years, but who is now working in Kenya, called to visit us again. He showed me a map he had designed and made using LANDSAT satellite imagery. On looking at this map I realised that this was the very country I had walked through in 1954. When I told Godwin and described the country he was quite surprised. In the south of the area there is now much settlement, and a new town at Mugumu. I am told there is much land degradation due to overgrazing and woodland clearance.

Other more normal safari work continued as and when I could get out of the office. Sometimes this work was of a very specific nature. The native authority council had a programme to build a number of small cattle-watering dams during each dry season, using communal labour turn-outs. Our modern critics would call this forced labour, but in modern Tanzania it is called "self-help" and is applauded by the self-same pundits. These dams were simple affairs. The site, usually in a declivity in the plain, was chosen and roughly surveyed. Then a large open pit was dug out, and the spoil carefully formed into a curving dam wall on the down-slope side of the excavation. These proved very effective in storing water in the dry season. I had supervised this sort of work in Biharamulo for village water supply, but my first experience of it in Musoma was in the Kiagata chiefdom, the home of the Kuria people. These are a pastoral people, amongst whom manual work for men is just not acceptable. In consequence it was the women who turned out to do the dam-building work, and most of them were young and lissom. It was a not unpleasant experience to watch these young women, stripped to the waist, and balancing *karais* or shallow earth pans on their heads, swaying gracefully up in long lines to dump their loads on the growing dam wall. They used to giggle and shout remarks to each other as they passed me, the import of which I could only guess at, not understanding Kikuria. But my *tarishi* understood and was often convulsed with laughter.

The Kuria, or Watende as the army called them were favoured recruits for military service, and large numbers of them volunteered for the King's African Rifles in the last war. There was a tale told in Musoma of an occasion during the war when the recruiting officer was on a visit to sign on new recruits. He announced that the need was at that time not for riflemen or fighting soldiers, but for service personnel such as drivers, pioneers and the like. On hearing this, the crowd melted away in disgust. They were admirable people, but less realistic in this regard than the Masai, who were totally uninterested in military service in spite of their prowess. They argued there was no point in going to fight people they did not know, who probably had no cattle anyway. One other notable feature of the Kuria was their extreme litigiousness, in which their only rivals were the banana-eating Haya, Chagga and Nyakyusa.

Shortly before the end of my first three-year tour of service, Brian Hodgson called me into his office, and said with a grin that he had a job for me that he thought I would enjoy. How right he was. Apparently the provincial commissioner of Lake Province, one "Fanny" Walden at that time, was disturbed by reports of large numbers of Masai grazing their cattle on the Lake Province sector of the Serengeti and related reports of an increase in cattle raiding on the Sukuma. He wanted a rough census of the Masai cattle carried out, and Hodgson had suggested that I be told to do the job. I thanked him for this and prepared to depart. I was to be assisted by Peter Bramwell, who was game ranger at Banagi, and Peter Venter, a stock theft preventive officer from Arusha. The task took us two weeks to complete.

My companions were an interesting pair. Bramwell was a Kenyan and had been at Banagi for about a year, during which time he had completed the first phase in the construction of what was to become the Seronera game lodge for tourists. This first stage consisted of only a few concrete rondavels with thatched roofs, and a water collecting system from a nearby rocky kopje. He was a trifle eccentric, and his method of travel across the Serengeti plains for example, was highly original. The dust was atrocious, and Peter used to travel in a completely open landrover, clad only in an old army greatcoat. On arrival at his destination he simply removed this, shook it violently to detach much of the accumulated dust, and then got dressed in clean clothes, all of which was really very practical. Just as Cooper at

Nyamirembe had an obsession about baboon, so did Bramwell about wild dog, and tended to shoot them on sight. Venter was a typical tough, confident young Afrikaner born and bred in Oldeani. As well as speaking fluent Swahili, he had enough Kimasai and Kisukuma to enable him to do his job effectively, which was dealing with the problem of cattle raiding between these two peoples.

We based ourselves at Seronera and went out each day, criss-crossing the plains on a more or less grid-iron pattern, counting each herd of Masai cattle we encountered, and questioning the herdsmen as to their place of origin, and how long they had been grazing where we found them. By enormous good fortune we had a game scout with us of Masai origin, a most unusual man, since Masai do not hunt, and do not normally seek paid employment. This invaluable man knew cattle as only a pastoral nomad can. Often we would come on a herd and start counting it, whereupon he would tell us as though we were fools, that we had already counted that herd a day or so previously. On being asked how he knew this he would shrug and say with laboured patience the equivalent of "for heaven's sake, it's obvious, can't you recognise them?" All we ignoramuses could see was a collection of undistinguished and miscellaneously coloured and shaped bovines. This absolute familiarity of pastoral people with cattle is truly amazing to someone from a totally different culture. With this splendid fellow as our guide and mentor, we were able to avoid double counting and come up with a reasonably accurate result.

Three incidents on this trip have remained especially clear in my mind. One day we were counting a herd, and the young herdsman spoke to me in very good Swahili. I was rather taken aback, and asked him where he had learned to speak it so well. When he said that he had been at school in Arusha for several years, I ventured to ask him further why he had come back to this life, standing on one leg, leaning on a spear, and dressed in nothing but a blanket, and gazing at cattle all day and every day.

He looked at me, then let his gaze roam over the great sweep of grassland, and come to rest on his cattle, and said quietly, "This is my life, I want nothing else." I felt quite humbled. That summed up the Masai as I knew them in Musoma and later in Lushoto. They were and no doubt still are an anachronism, but a proud one. Perhaps alone of all shall we say unsophisticated peoples (I abjure the use of the word primitive which has acquired pejorative overtones), they have remained unimpressed by western culture and the material things it offers. African nationalist movements have all tried to argue that colonialism attempted to denigrate their traditional cultures which the European was said to despise. Yet ironically, the new leaders have to a man swallowed whole all the material trappings which the imported culture offers, such as ostentatious life styles, expensive clothes, big cars etc, all summed up in the name given by the common people in East Africa to the new elites — the *wabenzi* (from the Mercedes-Benz cars so beloved of the newly rich). At the same time the Masai have been branded as shameful, primitive, and a disgrace to the new dispensation. In Arusha in Tanzania, the local politicans tried to insist on the proud young Masai wearing trousers and T-shirts instead of the traditional toga or blanket when coming into town. Yet it is surely these people who still value and uphold their own culture and life-style, and spurn the cheap trappings of an alien life-style. I have often voiced my views on this paradox to African friends. Some have agreed with me, but others have brought out the old argument that Europeans have a sentimental attachment to the "noble savage" and would like to keep rural Africans in a state of suspended animation as museum exhibits or as examples of how primitive the African was before the European came, with his civilising mission.

The second and third incidents I recall from this cattle census task concern Venter, the stock theft preventive officer who assisted in the work. He always carried a small Beretta .22 calibre pistol in his pocket, no doubt a sensible safety precaution in his rather hazardous job. One day towards evening he suddenly became very agitated and told us that his pistol was missing, and he could not find it. We could only presume it had fallen from his pocket somewhere on the wide open plains. Two days later a tall Masai came striding into the camp, and stalking straight up to Venter, handed him his pistol. Then without a word he turned on his heel and departed as soundlessly as he had come. He had found the pistol, and had sensibly put two and two together. Venter wore uniform and was thus easily recognisable. It seemed a fine example of simple and uncluttered honesty.

The third incident was rather alarming. In the Moru kopjes area we came one day upon a group of young Moran, the warrior grade. They were camped in a cave and were fully armed with their long spears and *simis* or short swords. Clearly they were up to no good, and most likely bent on a raid southwards for Sukuma cattle. Venter's reaction was interesting, but rather frightening in the circumstances. Without hesitation he walked straight up to the biggest of the young Moran, and slapped him across the face. Speaking in Kimasai he apparently told them that he knew they were going to steal cattle, and that they must drop their weapons at once and clear out of sight — quickly. What seemed a long silence followed, and the men looked murderous. The moment of doubt was broken by another peremptory bark from Venter, after which they slowly dropped their weapons and slunk off looking extremely sullen and angry. Tension relieved, I angrily asked Venter what the hell he thought he was trying to do, get us all killed or what? He laughed, and said when I had as much experience as he had of dealing with these young bloods, he might listen to what I had to say. One thing was clear — resolute boldness is a sound policy in some situations, of which this was undoubtedly one. We collected the weapons and left. I still have two of those beautiful spears.

VIII

Eventually my three years were up, and a long leave in UK became due. I was entitled to six months, but this seemed an awful long time when there were so many interesting things to do in East Africa. I wanted to climb some more mountains, and decided on the Ruwenzori in Uganda. Fortunately I had a keen and willing partner to accompany me. This was Barry Weightman, an agricultural officer. We had done some walking and scrambling together on the rocky hill ranges of western Musoma, and had to some extent distinguished ourselves by climbing the unclimbable kopje behind the district office, and planting thereon a large flag for the Queen's coronation. This was apparently visible from well out on the lake, according to the steamer officers.

We read all we could get hold of on the Ruwenzori, which wasn't much. Barry bought the necessary personal mountaineering equipment in Nairobi, and we set off on the long drive to the mountains in my landrover. These mountains, usually identified as Ptolemy's Mountains of the Moon, lie on the edge of the western arm of the Great Rift Valley, or politically on the Uganda-Zaire boundary. They are not of volcanic origin like the other great East African mountains such as Mount Kenya and Kilimanjaro, but represent an upthrust block of the earth's crust, rising to over 16,000 feet (or about 5000 m) in several great peaks, the most important being named after Stanley, Speke and Baker, the nineteenth century explorers in these regions. They are snow-covered and have some sizeable glaciers, and are notorious for bad, cloudy, wet weather. The upper alpine zone is guarded by a belt of dense mountain forest which gives way to bamboo thicket, and finally to the unique East African mountain flora of giant heathers, lobelia, helychrysum and others. A number of roaring torrents plunge through the forest, fed all year by snow-melt and heavy precipitation. Some very simple Nissen-type huts had been erected by the heroic efforts of members of the Uganda Mountain Club at key locations in the mountains, and we planned to use these. To do this we obtained permission from the Mountain Club who instructed us to obtain the keys from the district commissioner at Fort Portal in whose district the mountains lie.

Our journey to Fort Portal took us through the Kenya Highlands, where we stayed with friends near Kericho, and on into Uganda. The atmosphere of prosperity, the strong sense of order and good government, the excellent roads, the impressive Owen Falls dam and hydro-electric scheme, and the beautiful city of Kampala all impressed us greatly in that country. It is horrible and almost unbelievable to contemplate the dire straits to which that rich and beautiful country has been reduced since independence. One must fervently hope that the people will be able to rebuild their country and their lives to that old level of prosperity and peace. It will be a long haul but they will succeed for they are a gifted people. They will need all the disinterested help that the outside world can give them.

We eventually arrived at Fort Portal in a somewhat travel-stained and dishevelled state, and went to the district office to collect our keys. We were ushered into the presence of one of the several district officers which this wealthy and large district boasted. He was immaculate in suit and tie, sitting in a well-furnished office. We introduced ourselves, and he looked vaguely shocked that we should appear in the state we were in. His style and dress were typical of the Uganda and Kenya services. In Tanganyika, thank goodness, we were far more relaxed, easy-going and informal. This DO however, was very friendly and helpful. He gave us the keys, and also a letter to the headman at Bugoye asking him to help us recruit a few porters. Thus armed we departed. We were in the country of the Bakonjo people, and our porters were of this tribe. We provided them with blankets, food and tobacco, with a cash payment on completion of the trip, and they gave us sterling service, as I will relate.

We started into the forest early one morning, and it was not long before we were ascending steeply. We followed what appeared to be an ancient glacial moraine ridge on the right bank of the Mobuku river, and eventually reached our first camping place at Nyinabitaba where there was a corrugated iron bivouac shelter. The porters used a nearby cave which was in fact roomier and more comfortable than the shelter. Late that afternoon a severe storm blew up, and the air was crackling all round us with static electricity. Suddenly we were knocked off our feet by a tremendous flash and a simultaneous deafening report that sounded like the crack of doom. Lightning had struck our camp. Barry and I were alright though a bit shaken, but the porters were in a state of disarray. One of them had a nasty burn through falling on their fire, and was badly shocked. They quickly calmed down but it was obvious that the injured man would have to go down, with a companion to assist him. Our carrying capacity was thus greatly reduced, and we all had to add to our burdens, even Kule, the headman agreeing to carry a load.

The next morning we set off again, heavily burdened. For some reason which we could not divine, since the porters' Swahili was very rudimentary, they did not wish to use the usual route which crosses the Mobuku by a rough log bridge. They insisted that we continue further up the right bank and then cross higher up. This crossing proved to be rather hazardous. The river was a foaming torrent, from which a series of wet and slippery-looking boulders projected. Leaping from one rock to the next with a heavy rucksack swinging about on one's back was a tricky business. For the porters with their head loads we rigged up a safety line, and we all got across without mishap. Later we had to cross the Bujuku river, but that was spanned providentially by a large fallen tree. We were now getting high and the aspect of the forest was changing. It was very wet, and everything was festooned with streamers of grey-green moss, while underfoot was a morass of mud and dead, rotting vegetation. There were large masses of exotic fungi everywhere, and the environment was distinctly gloomy. Bamboo thicket slowly became dominant, and forcing through this was quite tiring. Eventually we reached Nyamleju and one of the Mountain Club huts. It had been raining all day and we were soaked, so we spent the rest of the day trying to dry out at least part of our clothes over the primus stove. Above Nyamleju are a series of bogs. These seem to have caught the imagination of most travellers in the Ruwenzori, and all accounts include graphic descriptions of trying to leap from one giant grass tussock to the next without falling, or alternatively ploughing through the cold black mud beneath. Once more it rained all day, though now the rain was mixed with icy sleet. Though we were well into the mountains we still had not seen them. This in fact was to be the keynote of our expedition: continuous rain, sleet and snow, ten-tenths cloud, with only a few brief and tantalising, but magnificent glimpses of the great mountains we were trying to climb.

Finally we reached Bujuku, which lies in a great amphitheatre set in a rim of mighty mountain walls, the outer bastions of Mounts Stanley, Speke and Baker. We ensconced ourselves in the hut there, while our porters again retreated to a nearby cave, and we prepared for some serious mountaineering. Barry had zero experience of high mountains, or of snow and ice climbing, so we could not be too ambitious. The porters would have a few days' rest, holed up in their cave where they kept a smoky fire going, creating an atmosphere in which surely only they could survive.

Our first venture was towards Mount Stanley, whose twin peaks of Margherita and Allesandra are the highest in the range. Driving snow, total lack of visibility and discretion forced us back from about 15,000 feet. Nothing daunted, the next day we decided to attempt the 16,080 foot high Mount Speke. We set off very early in the direction that compass and intuition suggested, and climbed slowly upward, up wall after wall of messy loose rocks which led us eventually to snow. We just kept on ascending until we found ourselves on a heavily corniced snow ridge which became progressively more narrow and exciting. We were in a totally white environment and could see nothing, but we sensed profound space all around us. Finally we reached the summit, or so it appeared, for the ground fell away steeply on all sides. We had been going for about five hours, and we presumed we had reached the summit of Speke. It was snowing gently but persistently, and there seemed no point in hanging around waiting for an improbable clearing and a view to prove our success. We retreated and got back safely to the hut without incident. Barry was having a very rough introduction to the glories of high mountaineering, but he didn't complain.

Having apparently succeeded on Speke, our confidence was rising, and we decided to make an attempt on Mount Baker, just under 16,000 feet high. The flanks of this mountain overlooking Bujuku are said to be sheer and impregnable, so we had to go over the Scott-Elliot pass to Kitandara, and make an attempt from there. At Kitandara we found another tiny hut, and once more tried to dry out our soaking clothes and gear.

The next morning the weather was still awful but we set out for Baker. We forced our way upward through the ubiquitous tangle of giant plants until we reached a rock ridge. Route finding was hardly a rational exercise. We simply climbed upward on the first ridge which presented itself. We were roped up, but initially we could climb together and thus move fairly quickly. Soon however the rock steepened and we came up against a massive buttress which appeared to block the ridge completely. It was snowing and there was a cover of treacherous verglas on the faces, with loose snow on the ledges. We had no clear idea where the ridge we were on would lead us, and so discretion once more forced a retreat. We got down off the rocks safely, but then lost our route of ascent through the vegetated slopes below. We were not lost, but certainly perplexed. We knew the general direction we needed to follow, but we also knew that these slopes were liberally broken by a series of precipices, and cut by deep, gorge-like valleys, and we had no desire to get tangled with either of these hazards. We were soaked to the skin, cold, and angry with ourselves, the weather and the mountain — a dangerous state of mind to be in. But fortune smiled on us. I noticed an old knife cut on some heather, then another and another. Someone had been this way before, hacking through the tangle. We had a trail, albeit a very vague one, and following it we managed to get down to the valley, and so back to the hut, exhausted but greatly relieved.

Our time was now up, and food supplies running low. We had to get out of the mountains, which we did without further incident. Once down, the pleasure of drying out in warm sunshine was indescribable. We enjoyed the long journey back to Musoma, going this time round the southern end of Lake Victoria, with a brief call at Biharamulo to see old friends.

IX

Shortly after getting back to Musoma I departed for the UK on a long leave, my first tour of duty in Africa completed. To say that I had found my work both challenging and satisfying would be an understatement. All my expectations had been fulfilled. As a geographer by inclination and training I had now seen at first hand the nature of tropical environments, and the diversity of human responses to them. I had come into contact with cultures very different from my own, and acquiring fluency in an African language, had learned to appreciate the subtler aspects of totally different ways of life. From all this I hoped I had become more tolerant, and had learned that we Europeans do not have all the answers to human problems. I had been given to understand the perfectly understandable desire of many Africans for a greater say in the running of their own affairs, but had also seen that if they really wanted many of the more material things of our culture, then they had a long way to go in acquiring the philosophies and attitudes that make those things attainable for the masses of the people and not just for small élites. On a different plane I had experienced and travelled through what were to me wholly new landscapes, and had been able to climb some wonderful mountains. As I left I wondered where my next posting would take me to, and what new experiences lay in store.

It was winter when I arrived back in England, and I rejoined my school's old boys rugby club. I wallowed in some cold, wet, muddy games, a far cry from African sunshine (but perhaps not from the Ruwenzori). I managed to get in four weeks skiing in Norway, but I was not sorry when my leave approached its end. I was informed that I would be returning to Tanga province, and more specifically to Lushoto district which lay in the Usambara mountains. That sounded very interesting, and so it was to prove.

Chapter Four

Lushoto

So and no otherwise — so and no otherwise — hillmen desire their Hills.

*Kipling, **The Sea and the Hills***

I

Lushoto district occupies most of the western Usambara mountains in north-east Tanganyika, together with parts of the surrounding plains country. It occupies an area of 1,350 square miles (or 5,497 square kilometres), and in 1957 had a population of 152,687 people. It is thus much smaller than either Biharamulo or Musoma, though it has a much higher density of population. It is also very different in a number of other significant ways. The mountains are like the Ruwenzori, an upthrust block of the earth's crust defined by major faults. There is still periodic movement along these faults, and twice during my stay in the district we experienced minor earthquakes. One of these was most impressive. It occurred at night, and took the form of a distinct tremor accompanied by a loud sound like that made by a train emerging from a tunnel. This reached a crescendo, and then died away to be replaced by an uncanny silence.

These mountains rise dramatically from the plains, from which they are a splendid sight, to a height of over 7,000 feet (2,100 m). Most of the population lives above about 4,500 feet (1,300 m), in broad valleys and upland basins above the steep bounding escarpments. Large areas of the upper regions are covered by natural mountain rainforest, to which has been added by man a large area of planted soft-wood forest. Rainfall is generally very good, Lushoto town for example having a mean annual rainfall of about 40 inches (1,000 mm), though there is considerable variation from place to place both in the amount of rainfall and in its seasonality. Temperatures are greatly reduced by the altitude, and at our house we used to have log fires in the lounge every evening throughout the year. The climate is therefore almost temperate in many ways, and the overall impression is of cool, green, healthy uplands, with many streams of clear water. An added blessing is the absence of the malaria-carrying mosquito. One imagines that such a region must be fertile and productive, and indeed the German colonists thought this was so at the turn of the century. The reality is rather different however, as I will relate.

The Shambaa are the dominant people of the mountains, and they have close affinities with the Zigua and Bondei of the surrounding plains. They were ruled by a distinct group or clan known as the Wakilindi, who claimed descent from a semi-mythical ancestor named Mbegha, a great hunter who came up to the hills from the plains, and taught the Shambaa how to protect themselves from marauding predators and vermin. The Shambaa made him their king and called him Simbamwene. A small relict group of people also live up in the higher reaches of the hills. They are known as the Mbugu, and are a pastoral people who speak a language which is something of a puzzle to linguists. It has a Bantu-type grammar but its vocabulary is mainly related to Cushitic, the language group of most peoples of north-eastern Africa. Their origins are a mystery.

In the nineteenth century a great leader arose in Usambara, known as Kimweri ya Nyumbai. He consolidated the Shambaa state and extended its power over the mountains of the western and eastern Usambaras and the surrounding plains. This well-ordered and agriculturally productive state was commented on favourably by contemporary European travellers in the region. Kimweri died in 1862 and the state disintegrated thereafter, subject peoples breaking away, and dynastic struggles within the ruling Kilindi clan further weakening and dividing the polity. These feuds and quarrels continued unabated into the later years of this century, and assumed a complexity and ultimately a paralysing futility of Byzantine proportions. Nobody who worked in the Usambaras could ignore or fail to observe this debilitating disease which militated against many attempts to develop the district. I will return later to some important aspects of this.

The Germans regarded these cool uplands as an ideal place for European settlement. They established an important agricultural research station at Amani in the eastern Usambaras, and alienated large blocks of land to European settlers. Their railway line from the port of Tanga to the fertile land on the slopes of Mount Kilimanjaro and Mount Meru to the north, passed along the foot of the Usambara escarpment, and from this line roads were driven up into the hills. The settlement at Wilhelmstal was established where now is the small town and district head-quarters of Lushoto. Attempts were made to develop arabica coffee and temperate vegetables and fruit as important cash crops. The promise was never realised, however. Though forest grows well, the soils are acid and poor, and lacking in important nutrients, so that crop yields are seldom good unless the land is heavily fertilised and carefully managed.

The British in their turn made very great efforts to improve and develop peasant agriculture, and at the same time to conserve and improve the soil on the often steep cultivated slopes, but by and large we failed. The government of independent Tanzania has had even less success, and at the present day with a vastly increased population, problems of soil erosion, declining fertility, and consequent social and economic poverty are much worse. Try as one may, it is difficult to explain fully why the fruitful development of such an apparently attractive environment, populated by an intelligent people, should have proved so elusive.

II

For three full years from 1955 to 1958 I was closely and intimately involved in the struggle to make this environment more productive, through rational organisation and management of its physical and human resources. The struggle was not only with nature, but also with human waywardness and short-sightedness, a situation containing all the ingredients of a tragedy which is still relentlessly unfolding at the present day.

I had little or no knowledge of these things when I arrived in Lushoto in April 1955, very happy to be back in Tanganyika and entranced with the prospect of working in these beautiful mountains. I moved into a comfortable house, built of red brick with a cedar shingle roof, and a big open fireplace in the lounge. It had mains electricity, a piped water supply, and full plumbing. Outside was a pleasant garden with an abundance of coniferous and broad-leaved trees. All this seemed a far cry from the relatively primitive conditions of Biharamulo and Musoma. Namko had decided to join me from Musoma, and with a local cook and a gardener, my domestic arrangements were soon complete.

My district commissioner was Ian Glennie, whom I had met before when he was DC of Kahama, the next district south from Biharamulo. My bull terrier Sambo let me down with Glennie as he had with Smith in Biharamulo. The DC's residence was a large flat above the district office, to which an open stairway gave access. Sambo accompanied me everywhere, including to my office. One day I was alarmed to hear Glennie shout, "You bloody thieving hound!" and I rushed out to see Sambo on the stairs with a large parcel of meat held perfectly symmetrically in his mouth. Facing him stood my irate boss in a sort of *High Noon* situation. Fortunately a good sense of humour prevailed, and my erring hound was forgiven, though he was barred on pain of death from ever entering the district office again.

The administration comprised the DC and two DOs, a locally employed European chief clerk, and several administrative and treasury clerks. The other major departments of government were well represented in the district. Agriculture and Forestry were very strong, since Lushoto was the provincial headquarters for these departments. We also had the main sylvicultural research station for the whole territory. The Police had at various times European, Indian, or local officers. We had a small hospital with a European medical officer, an Indian surgeon and several nursing sisters. There were two quite good hotels, one in Lushoto town, the other up in the hills at Magaamba, and these were well patronised by people escaping the heat of the plains and the coast.

The attractive climate made Lushoto a favourite place for retirement by Europeans who did not wish to return to Europe. Most of these were elderly of course, and this had its more macabre aspects. Going down into the cellar of the district office shortly after my arrival, I was alarmed to find a stack of long wooden boxes which looked suspiciously like coffins. Indeed they were just that. Funerals had to be arranged quickly in those days, and so the wherewithal had to be ready to hand. Sometimes a priest of the correct persuasion could not be summoned in time, and on two occasions when I was acting DC I had to conduct the burial service. The DC really was in many ways a general factotum, and in religious matters was obviously regarded as neutral.

Some of the old people were very interesting characters, and well worth the trouble of getting to know. Dr Williams or "Battling Bill" as he was popularly called, was a case in point. He had been a medical officer with the British Army in the 1914-18 East African campaign. He had stayed on after the war as a civilian medical officer, and then retired to Lushoto. We had several ex-service characters, including an air vice-marshal, and some of these required careful handling. One day Captain Philip Brindley, MC, came storming into my office, clearly extremely annoyed. He slapped on my desk a letter addressed to him by one of our clerks as "Mr P. Brindley". "I don't mind them forgetting the gong (his Military Cross medal)" he roared, "but I am not plain bloody mister!" Another medical man was Dr Suffrin, who must have been about ninety. He had spent all his working life in Nigeria as a medical officer, from where he had retired to Tanganyika. He was something of a recluse and lived up in the hills. One day his house was broken into, and a shot-gun stolen, whereupon the Police charged him with failing to keep it securely locked up. His case came up before me, sitting as magistrate. I read the charge to him, and asked him to plead, at which point he left the dock, stalked up to the bench, and wagging an admonitory finger at me, exclaimed in his old cracked voice, which still, however, carried a ring of authority, "Young man, I was handling guns long before you were born. How dare you accuse me of not being able to keep my shot-gun safely. This is absolute nonsense!" The African inspector of police who was prosecuting didn't know whether to be frightened or amused. I had to find the old man guilty, but bound him over to be more careful in future. This seemed to irritate him more than a fine would have done, and he hobbled out of court muttering imprecations against upstart young bureaucrats and all their works.

There was a strong missionary presence in the district. The Lutherans had arrived first during German times, and were dominant, with their main station at Mlalo in the centre of the hills. The Roman Catholics were fairly low key, and were represented by the Rosminian Order. They had a large mission station at Gare, and also ran a preparatory school down at Soni. The Universities Mission to Central Africa (UMCA) which was the major Anglican mission, was strong in Tanga Province, but not so much in the western Usambaras. We had however, the inevitable St. George's church, a pleasant little stone structure. There was the usual uncharitable competition between the various persuasions. The Lutherans, however, were so strong that they must have felt the others were not worth bothering about, so instead they quarrelled amongst themselves to produce some bitter in-fighting. Islam was very strongly represented, as was to be expected so near to the coast, whence came the Arabs with their faith. The majority of the Shambaa were in fact Muslims. Religious controversy inevitably had linkages to the political schisms within the Shambaa body politic, making confusion even worse confounded.

Administratively the district was divided into a number of sub-chiefdoms each of which was presided over by a sub-chief or *Zumbe Mkuu*. These were Vuga, the traditional capital of the Shambaa state, Lushoto, Bumbuli, and Mgwashi in the south, and Mlalo, Mlola, and Mtae in the north. Other Shambaa sub-chiefdoms lay within the Korogwe sub-district, but I had no responsibilities there. The paramount chief or *simbamwene* was Kimweri Mputa Magogo. He was a grandson of the Semboja who had played a major role in fomenting the strife which followed the death of Kimweri ya Nyumbai in the last century. His position as chief was disputed by a number of Shambaa and Kilindi factions, so that his position was by no means secure. He was undoubtedly sustained in office by our support. Without this support the whole Shambaa polity would have been in a far worse state of continuing and vicious internecine strife. It is futile to argue, as some historians do, that our support for Kimweri was wrong. Any other alternative would have met equally strong opposition from those not in power. The whole traditional structure has been swept away since independence, but I am sure that the old rivalries and feuds must still control the wayward currents of the political base-flow in the Usambaras today.

III

In the 1950s the native authority was being developed slowly, as in the rest of the territory, towards greater responsibility and independence. The native authority council was known as the *bawanjama*, and it contained an elected element, as did the subordinate sub-chiefdom councils. Our policy as elsewhere, was to increase the powers of the councils and decrease the controlling influence of the district commissioner as the representative of central government. The wealthier and more developed a district, the more rapid was its progress, and in districts like Bukoba or Moshi, the councils became very powerful organs of local government as I will describe. A continuous education effort was required from district officers in instructing, guiding and checking the work of the officers of these councils at all levels. This formed an important element of our work especially when out on tour in the district.

All our work in the 1950s in Lushoto was undoubtedly dominated by the Usambara Development Scheme. Essentially this was a soil conservation and agricultural development scheme. It has lessons to offer at the present day when the rapid improvement of African agriculture is of key importance in the context of an exploding population, and the demand for ever-increasing production from the land, for foodstuffs and for cash crops to earn the foreign exchange necessary for the financing of development.

The Shambaa are traditionally cultivators, using the hoe as their main working tool. They grow permanent crops such as the banana, coffee and wattle; and annual crops such as maize, cassava, beans, sweet potatoes, sugar-cane (for beer-making) and green vegetables. They had developed quite elaborate irrigation systems, taking water from hill-streams, and conducting it by furrows along the hill-sides, to be fed eventually by gravity to terraced fields in the lower valley bottoms where fertile soils could be found. In these terraces they grew beans, sugar-cane and vegetables. The latter became in due course an important cash crop in favoured localities within reach of a market. With the break-up of the Shambaa state, and the decline in the authority of the traditional rulers, these irrigation systems had tended to decay in many areas. Where there was a vigorous headman or sub-chief, they were still to be found in good shape.

The Shambaa prefer to live in villages, and each family holds plots of land scattered through the surrounding area. A family might hold three or four such plots making up a total area of perhaps three to five acres in the 1950s, but undoubtedly much less at the present day with the increase in population pressure on land. They also have access to areas of communal grazing for their few cattle, sheep and goats, which are also grazed on the stubbles after harvest. The complex relief of the mountains has a marked effect on the quality of the land, and also on the seasonal incidence of rainfall which is greatly affected by the aspect of a slope i.e. the direction in which it faces. In general terms the northern hills get better precipitation in November-December. These rains are known as the *vuli* and come from the north-east. The southern hills benefit more from the long or *mwaka* rains in March to May, which come from the south-east. So the main cultivation season in the two areas varies, though also within each zone there are considerable local variations superimposed on the general pattern. As might be expected, the people are very aware of the effects of soil quality and rain season on the varying potential of their plots, and their cropping patterns and seasonal work programmes are closely adapted to these. With a relatively static population in the nineteenth century, the Shambaa system of agriculture was well-adapted to their environment, and yielded the wherewithal of a good life.

With the rapid growth of population made possible by the colonial imposition of peace and order, the area under cultivation rapidly increased. Once the flatter land and the lower slopes had been occupied, it became necessary to extend cultivation up the steeper slopes, clearing forest to make this possible. Without an adaptation of techniques to control soil creep and rapid run-off of rainwater, and to conserve fertility, this expansion led to incipient soil erosion, and more rapid leaching out of already scarce nutrients. Land degradation began to be noticeable. Mountainous regions with a high incidence of steep slopes are especially prone to accelerated soil erosion, and the standard response of peoples the world over, for example, in Japan, Switzerland or Peru, has been to counter this by cultivating along the contour rather than up and down slopes, by more elaborate terracing, or by planting permanent crops on steeper slopes to hold the soil in place. Similarly, declining fertility can be countered by the use of wastes and compost, or animal manure if available. Soil conservation practices are not the invention of modern western agriculture.

In the late 1940s administrative and agricultural officers in Usambara and in other similar environments in Tanganyika began to draw attention to these problems and efforts to counter soil loss and land degradation were made. In Lushoto district one of the worst affected areas was in the Mlalo sub-chiefdom, a densely populated upland basin hemmed in by steep hills in the central part of the western Usambaras. The Mlalo Basin Rehabilitation Scheme was devised and put into operation in 1949 as a pilot scheme to test some simple and easily applied soil conservation measures. From this beginning the scheme was later extended to cover the whole district, and was applied with vigour and success until cancelled by a vacillating government in 1958 shortly before independence, in response to ignorant and hypocritical political pressure.

The scheme has been referred to frequently since that time by a variety of mainly academic critics who have brushed it aside as irrelevant, as ecologically misguided, or as an example of colonial mismanagement and a heartless trampling on the traditional practices of the common people. One eminent historian has referred to it as "imposed drudgery and regimentation" and said that such schemes attacked the "symptoms' and not the "causes" of deprivation. One is forced to ask: "Is then soil loss and land degradation not a *cause* of a people's progressive impoverishment"?

One must not confuse the Usambara Scheme with the similar one mounted in the Uluguru mountains in Morogoro district. There some of the technical solutions to land deterioration were in fact wrong, and the scheme was withdrawn when this became obvious. The mistakes made in Uluguru, and the undeniable failure of that scheme have been seized on enthusiastically by biassed commentators in later years. They have tended to extrapolate from that scheme and to brand all agricultural and land conservation schemes as similar failures, and equally wrongly conceived.

I was very intimately involved with the Usambara Scheme at grass-roots level, and so can describe it as it was, and not as it may be made to appear from the depths of an ivory-tower armchair at a distance of years.

The requirements of the scheme were simple and were as follows. Steep slopes (over 25°) were not to be used for annual crops, but were to be planted with permanent crops such as bananas, coffee and wattle. This was to prevent excessive soil disturbance, to maintain a protective cover from heavy rain, a permanent root system to bind the soil and absorb moisture, and a physical barrier to rapid downslope movement of high energy run-off water. Secondly, all annually cropped land was to be cultivated in ridges (in Swahili *matuta*) along the contour of the slope. All waste plant material from the clearing of the land was to be buried in the ridges rather than burned. There it would rot down and improve fertility and soil structure. These ridges would act as a barrier to run-off and be a means of maintaining soil quality. As a concomitant to this, livestock were not to be grazed on stubbles and harvest residues, but were to be kept in byres (in Swahili *mazizi*) and hand-fed on green material specially grown or collected from the forest. This would leave the wastes available for burying in the ridges, and livestock so kept would be of better quality, and would yield easily available manure for the fields, and milk for consumption and sale.

Simple rules promulgated by the native authority council encapsulated these requirements. Clearly such new practices could not be introduced and applied at one fell swoop, so a period of five years was allowed for, to enable each farmer to slowly apply them to his fields. Provision was made for failure to apply the rules to be punished by small fines in the local courts. No other force was used, and only a very small number of miscreants found themselves in prison for non-compliance. Of course the work required was hard, drudgery if you like, but is any progress possible without this?

Most of the ground work of overseeing the application of the rules was done by agricultural department field staff. Sub-chiefs and headmen were expected to co-operate fully, and offenders were dealt with in their courts. District officers were expected to do all in their power to foster and encourage progress whilst on tour in the district. As a geographer with a professional knowledge and understanding of the physical environment, land, soil, climate and plants, I could easily appreciate the necessity of trying to reverse the progressive deterioration of the land which was the basis of the Shambaa people's livelihood, and of their children's future. I also understood the human dimension: that change could only come through steady, firm pressure, accompanied by persistent persuasion and explanation. I put my convictions into action, and spent a great deal of my time touring the hills on foot, exhorting, arguing and explaining what we were trying to do. I must have visited every village and cultivated area in the hills on this work. I learned to speak Shambala, but oddly enough got on better with Swahili. I spoke the latter as well as the people themselves, but Shambala only haltingly, so that whilst using it I was at a psychological disadvantage which intelligent folk were not slow in exploiting in any argument or debate, pleased though they might be that I was learning their vernacular.

I used to argue at district team meetings and on any other appropriate occasion, that the agricultural field staff paid too much attention to inspection and the prosecution of offenders, and not enough to education and persuasion. I tried to practise what I preached and was always loth to apply the pressure of the law in my own work. My views had some effect, but not quite as I had imagined. A star of the Social Development department of government was one Horace Mason, and he was called in to advise on extension methods. He had made a name for himself in work amongst the Wameru in Arusha district who had become disaffected (with good reason) by the alienation of part of their land to European farmers by the government, a major *faux pas* of the Twining era. Mason took a lot of the credit for calming the Wameru and re-establishing normal conditions. He advised us in Lushoto to start using modern visual aids to put across the basic elements of the scheme's agricultural improvements. He arranged through the government for a visual aids expert to be sent out by the colonial office, in an advisory capacity. This expert duly arrived, armed with flip charts, and board displays and diagrams. He was an artist and produced the most superb materials. We were however rather dubious regarding the effect of some of these on our very unsophisticated audiences. Our people were mainly illiterate, but very practised in public harangue, eloquent masters of the spoken word and verbal argument, which was a principal occupation and entertainment in their lives. Most of them however, had never seen a display screen, and were unfamiliar with structured visual imagery. But our expert was confident of the universal applicability of his magic, and played down some of our reservations. I remember an early demonstration when it was being explained that terraces and contour ridges had to be parallel and along the contour of the land. Diagrams were produced to explain this. Now our expert was a trained artist to whom perspective is a normal fact of life, and shown in drawings by well-accepted and understood techniques in a two-dimensional image. The audience looked at these from all angles and I could see that they were clearly puzzled. Eventually they asked me what on earth this visitor was trying to do — explaining that ridges must be level and parallel, but then drawing them on his board sloping towards each other. Such are the pitfalls awaiting the western expert in a pre-literate society.

The scheme was naturally unpopular with many people, as must any scheme be when introduced to a conservative peasantry anywhere in the world. It involved a change in ingrained habits and customs, and it involved a lot of hard work. This natural resistance to change could have been in time overcome by gentle sustained pressure, and by a slow realisation of benefits as they became apparent over a period of years. No agricultural betterment scheme can achieve immediate miraculous results. In Usambara local politics inevitably intervened. Chief Kimweri and the council supported the scheme, promulgated the necessary rules, and did their best to enforce them. This created a golden opportunity for those elements traditionally opposed to Kimweri, and they seized it eagerly, using every trick in the agitators' manual to encourage and whip up ancient passions and animosities. The cry *hatutaki matuta* (roughly "down with ridging") became the rallying cry of the opposition. In the early years of the scheme the disgruntled elements organised a near riot at Vuga, which was firmly dealt with. Thereafter subtler tactics were employed, though sometimes a mob could be organised for a specific occasion or purpose.

I was once the object of one of these. I was visiting Vuga for a normal sub-chiefdom council meeting, and on my arrival I found a large crowd of women waiting for me. As I arrived they began to chant *hatutaki matuta*. Obviously this was an organised demonstration to either impress or frighten me. My support for the scheme was well known. We started the meeting, but Hemedi, the sub-chief was clearly worried, and when the screaming and abuse reached what he thought was a threatening level, he advised that we leave. Fortunately my landrover was standing by the council building back door, so that we could easily reach it. We jumped in and managed to drive away, though as we did so the canvas canopy of the landrover was ripped open. Discretion is often the better part of valour, and definitely so in this case. Mobs are less than human, and I tremble to think what a mob of excited women might have done to us. Hassani, my *tarishi*, looked very thoughtful as we drove away.

By the middle and late 1950s the scheme was progressing well. It was a wonderful and encouraging sight to see whole hillsides beautifully contour ridged, and long deep groves of banana plantations developing along the steeper slopes. In the valley bottoms we strongly encouraged the cultivation of fresh vegetables on low irrigated terraces, and this again made an impression of organised productivity. Agricultural production was increasing steadily over this period.

Sadly all this progress came to an end. As TANU intensified its opposition to the government, it was prepared to use any existing local organisation which was against established authority. In the Usambaras such an opposition was present in a readily exploitable form. Much of the opposition to Kimweri was itself divided, but a sizeable group of dissidents had gathered round a man named Shem Shemsanga, who had himself almost been made chief in 1947. TANU swallowed this group whole, and campaigned against *matuta*. The party was proscribed for a while in Lushoto, but then allowed to re-enter the lists. As the drive for national independence intensified under TANU, the Usambara scheme became a victim of larger issues, and as I have said, it was brought to an abrupt, untimely and tragic end. Whilst living in Tanga years later I used to visit Lushoto quite often, and the spectacle of degrading land and a general sense of hopelessness was awful and very depressing. Today I am told, it is infinitely worse.

IV

While a good deal of my energy and enthusiasm was channelled into the furthering of the aims of the Usambara scheme, I had much else to do. Ian Glennie was not averse to his district officers getting out on tour, and he was in fact a great walking enthusiast himself. The district had a good network of roads so that one could get quickly to the various administrative centres, and tour from these on foot. The roads were of beaten earth or gravel, but as might be expected in this hilly district there were many twists and turns, and some sharp gradients. Heavy rainfall made maintenance an important and continuous occupation, which we were involved with. Negotiating these mountain roads in wet weather was a hazardous business, for the earth surfaces became very slippery when wet, and protecting walls on the outer edges were unknown. It was often a comforting assurance to have the landrover's four-wheel drive, though some colleagues managed happily with two-wheel drive Chevrolet or Ford pick-up trucks.

New roads and tracks were often opened up with communal labour turn-outs, and I got involved with one such in the Mgwashi sub-chiefdom. We planned, surveyed and built a new stretch of road from the Mgwashi headquarters to a place called Baga, a distance of about six miles. We contoured the route as far as possible, but some steep gradients and hair-raising bends were unavoidable. There were also some deep-cut stream beds to cross. In doing this sort of work, a district officer had the inestimable assistance of a small volume entitled *Field Engineering* which had been written in the 1930s by a government engineer named Longland. It was a *vade mecum* of everything one needed to know when carrying out simple engineering tasks in rural areas. It contained detailed advice and procedures on the design, layout and construction of buildings, roads, bridges, culverts and drifts, the sinking and lining of wells, the organisation of sanitation and refuse disposal, and many other very useful practical things.

In such work one also had to use whatever local talent was available, and often this was of great value. In building the Mgwashi to Baga road we were greatly assisted by an old man who many years ago had been trained by the Germans to build culverted revetting walls to hold a road on a steep slope, or to carry it across stream beds. He had in turn trained his son in these skills, and the two of them did some splendid work for us. They were quite illiterate, and innocent of mathematics, the laws of physics or principles of engineering design, but they were real specialists, and built the most superb dry walls at accurate angles, of raw local rock without aid of cement or concrete. A second expert was one of the district office *tarishis*, a foxy little man named Abdallah who at some stage in his past had been taught the techniques of blasting with dynamite. He removed the rock obstacles in our path. The first time I observed him at work I was very nervous. He had already organised the drilling of his shot-holes which had been bored out with hand-drill and sledgehammer. In my presence he placed his charges, calculated his fuse-lengths, then fitted and lit them. We retired to a safe point of vantage and waited expectantly. He had laid six charges, but only four went off. I was wondering what would happen next when Abdallah nonchalantly beckoned to me saying *"twende"* which means "let's go", and trotted off to the site. Willy-nilly I had to follow him, and I stood in a state of great apprehension while he prodded for the unexploded charges in the drill holes, pouring in water at the same time. I hope he was impressed by my apparent faith in his expertise, which was in the event justified, otherwise I would not be here to tell the tale. When this road was finally completed I took my wife Sylvia along it in the landrover. She does not have a very good head for heights and exposure, and was reduced to tears. My hopes for a degree of adulation were thus dashed.

With the increase in population, good land in the district was becoming more scarce. At the same time the excessive fragmentation of holdings by inheritance was reducing the average size of plots. As a result of these factors, litigation over land rights was on the increase. Many cases heard in the local courts were coming up on appeal to the district commissioner. Since I was known to like this work, most of these cases were given to me to deal with.

Amongst almost all African peoples, land is regarded as the property of the whole community, and individual rights in land in a European sense are not generally known. A man could only have user rights in land, though in practice these rights were inheritable. In densely populated districts, particularly where permanent crops like bananas and coffee were important, these rights in land were approaching the status of what we would call freehold occupancy. In Bukoba and Moshi districts for example, the Haya *kibanja* and the Chagga *kihamba* holdings had just about reached this status, of which more later. The Shambaa had not yet reached this stage, but nonetheless disputes about land were keenly and hotly contested. In handling cases in Lushoto therefore, I was able to acquire experience which was to serve me in good stead later in Bukoba and Moshi.

Disputes arose from a variety of causes. Boundaries of land were usually ill-defined, not a matter of any great consequence when land was plentiful, but this had changed. The agreeing of boundaries led to much dispute. Quarrels about the inheritance of holdings were also common, especially where valuable permanent crops had been planted. In hearing these cases it was always advisable to visit the land at issue, and also to recall and question witnesses whose testimony had been recorded by the lower courts. Other types of cases also had to be dealt with, such as arguments about a will, or a debt, or marriage and divorce problems. This work, as in Musoma, took me to all parts of the district, however remote, and into very close personal contact with the people. Usually the only persons I took with me on such work were my *tarishi* Hassani, and a local court clerk who knew the area in question. Hassani was a tall, thin, rather gaunt-looking man, but he was a tireless walker, always willing and very loyal. He would keep me well-informed of all the comments being made in Shambala which I often failed to pick up adequately, but which often gave subtle clues on the matter at issue.

My other legal work as a district court magistrate was all carried out in the small court-house adjoining the district office. Glennie, like Hodgson in Musoma did not like this work, and so I found myself doing the bulk of it. This was not the arduous burden it had been in Musoma, as the Shambaa were far less explicitly violent and quarrelsome than the people of Musoma district. I usually found that one day a week in court was sufficient to keep pace, and I was greatly assisted by an efficient court clerk named Evariste Mzirai.

Whilst out on tour in the district, or on safari as we called it, we stayed in the small and simple rest-houses at each main centre. These were usually built of mud or cement bricks with a thatched or corrugated iron roof, and had one or two rooms. Outside was a small kitchen, a servant's quarter, and further off, a deep-pit latrine. Many of these rest-houses had been built to command pleasant views over the hills, so that it was very relaxing to sit outside as the sun went down, and the day's work was done, and often chat to the odd person who came by, just to talk, or maybe discuss some problem. The Mtae rest-house in the northern hills had a particularly fine situation, on the very edge of the escarpment, commanding magnificent views northwards. Once when I was there, very early on a crystal clear morning, I was enthralled to see on the very far horizon, a tiny but perfectly clear silhouette of the whole Kilimanjaro massif with its three peaks of Shira, Kibo, and Mawenzi. At that moment I conceived the idea of following that whole outline in one single continuous mountaineering expedition. I was to realise that dream in 1957 as I will later describe.

Other rest-houses had their peculiarities or special attractions. Vuga was infested with scorpions, and the first task on arrival was always to spray the many cracks in the wall with insecticide. I have nothing against scorpions except that their sting can be very painful. It was always a pleasure to arrive at the rest-house at Gare, where the sub-chief was young and very enthusiastic. I would always find waiting for me a choice selection of fresh vegetables from Hamisi's own fields, laid out on a big banana leaf. Also at Gare was the main mission station of the Rosminian order. The fathers were all Irish, and very hospitable. I recall several pleasant evenings spent there, after which I would find it slightly difficult to wend my way back to the rest-house, and would wake up the next morning feeling less than one hundred percent eager for work.

There were several Europeans living out in remote places, and such folk naturally welcomed a visit if one was in their vicinity. One of the most interesting was an old German lady, Frau Von Den Bussche. Actually she had been born British, but had married Count Von Den Bussche and had come out to Tanganyika long before the 1914-18 war. She was very old, and lived an isolated life, surrounded by her equally ancient retainers. Her house was perched on the edge of the escarpment overlooking the Luengera valley and towards the eastern Usambaras beyond. It could only be reached on foot, either across the hills from Bumbuli or by a steep climb up from the valley below. She lived in a dignified old-style manner and was definitely a relic from a bygone age. She liked to relate her experiences in the Tanganyika of her youth, but she wandered a lot, and sometimes seemed lost in some remote recess of her memory, when one had to wait patiently for her to take up the threads of her story again.

Another couple of relics from the past were the Brands who had a small farm near Vuga. They looked as old as Methuselah, leathery, bent and rheumy, but the old man always wore shorts and an open-necked shirt. He had come out to Kenya in the early years of the century to experiment with the growing of cotton on the coast near Mombasa. In 1957 we had an escaped convict loose and at large in the district. He was dangerous. As a precaution we collected all the arms from outlying farms to forestall any attempt to form an armed gang of criminals. I went to the Brands to collect any arms they had. Old Brand was most reluctant to part with his which he must have had for many years. He said he was quite capable of handling any marauder. I had to insist however, but as I was leaving old Mrs. Brand called me aside conspiratorially and whispered that *he* had hidden a rifle under his bed because he was very stubborn. I didn't have the heart to demand it. Old people have their touchy pride which it is cruel to trample on.

Walking in the hills was very pleasant. The Shambaa themselves were real hillmen, and could move uphill at a testing pace, though they never seemed to be out of breath. Paths were steep, winding and narrow, and in wet weather slippery and treacherous. Older men usually sported a long stick with an iron ferrule on the end. My wife Sylvia used to accompany me on safari when we were first married, before parenthood put a stop to that, and the people were most solicitous and impressed. We had problems once on a steep slope near Bumbuli which caused concern. On our next visit to the same area, we were delighted to be presented with a specially made walking stick "*kumsaidia mama mlimani*" — "to help pull mama up the hills". We still have it, a treasured possession which has been in constant use to this day on many a remote mountain range far from the green hills of Usambara.

Not all our work was in the mountains, for Lushoto district extended down over the surrounding plains. The Shambaa did not like the plains which were hot and malarious. Some however had gone to settle, partly because ample land was available, which they could irrigate from the streams coming down from the hills. We had tried to encourage such movement, and a hair-raising road with fifteen hairpin bends had been built from Mlalo to Kitivo. We had rest-houses down there at Mnazi, Lunguza, and Mashewa. They were not used all that often, and the toilet facilities, deep pits with a box on top in a grass-roofed mud hut provided excellent haunts for all manner of wildlife such as snakes, scorpions, spiders and above all, bats. I was once at Mnazi with a new colleague of rather delicate sensibilities. Shortly after arriving one afternoon, I was sitting outside, dozing in a chair when I was aroused by a shout of alarm from my colleague, who came running from the latrine, buttoning up his shorts as he came. "There's something in there," he exclaimed, "that came up and tickled my arse." "Bats," said I, "and quite harmless." "I'll fix them," he muttered, and disappeared. A few minutes later I was roused again, this time by a flash and a roar from the same place. My affronted friend had poured half a gallon of petrol down the hole, followed by a lighted match. The consequences may be imagined.

V

One major task which involved a lengthy stay down on the plains involved me once again with the Masai. For some time it was known that they had been infiltrating across the Ruvu or Pangani river into both Pare and Lushoto districts, and moving through the Mkomazi gap between the Usambara and Pare mountains to fan out on the Umba steppe in search of grazing. They had absolutely no right to be there, traditional or otherwise, and the Shambaa greatly resented their presence. The district commissioner summoned a meeting with them, which was also attended by the Masailand DC, and informed them of all this, adding a polite request that they go back whence they had come. The Masai acquiesced, but of course did nothing. Further steps became necessary. A removal operation was planned and the order went out that they were to move. They were instructed to assemble all their livestock on a certain date at Mnazi, from which they were to be driven westwards to the Ruvu at a ford known as Langata Ndorobo, where they would cross back into

Masailand district. The task of ensuring that they did move was assigned to me, with the assistance of two veterinary field officers and as many assistants from the veterinary and agricultural departments as could be mustered.

We went to work and rounded up a vast mob of cattle which we estimated at about six thousand head. From Mnazi it was a three-day trek to get them to the river at Langata Ndorobo, with stops each night at a good watering place. We split them into three herds, and moved them in sequence to avoid too much pressure on the water points at one time. The Masai co-operated as they knew they had no right to be where they were, and they recognised that we meant business.

Inevitable problems cropped up. Some foolish Wapare carried out a hit-and-run attack on one of the herds out of sheer spite, and killed some beasts with arrows. It was difficult to prevent a Masai follow-up which could have proved nasty. But the greatest problem was with the numerous calves. They couldn't stand the trek, and the Masai elders asked me to hire a large truck which they said they would pay for. I managed to find a truck at Mkomazi owned by an Mshambaa, and in this the calves were ferried to Langata in a series of trips as requested. At the end of the trek the truck-owner came to me for payment, and I summoned the senior Masai elder to settle. This dignified man, attired in his cloak worn like a toga, duly arrived, but would have nothing to do with the Mshambaa whom he clearly regarded as of very inferior status. From the depths of his toga he drew a fat wallet which he handed to me with the peremptory order "*lipa yeye*", bad Swahili for "pay him". He then turned away. The wallet was stuffed with twenty shilling notes, a great deal of money in those days. I selected enough to pay the truck-owner, and handed the wallet back to its owner. He took it without a word and stalked off. There was no haggling, no bargaining, no checking of what had been taken. Cash was clearly of no significance to him, and the recipient of payment was utterly beneath contempt.

I was amazed at the degree of control these people exercised over their cattle. They were not mounted on horses, but controlled the beasts on foot, remaining close to them and seeming to communicate by whistling and singing to them. The best example of this control I observed one evening at the watering place at the Mkomazi river. Two thousand odd dusty and thirsty cattle wanted to drink, but they were allowed to do so only under perfect control in small groups in ordered sequence. There were no galloping horses, no shouts and screams, no crises; a remarkable example of a sort of empathy between man and beast. Incidentally the scene was one of great visual and aural beauty. A red-gold sunset, seen through clouds of dust which filtered and diffused the light, the lowing of the herds, the sounds of the herdsmen whistling and singing to their cattle; all made a perfect ensemble against the backdrop of the Usambara escarpment which glowed deep red in the last light of the dying sun.

Once we had driven the herds to the river at Langata, we faced the task of getting them across and into Masailand on the other side. We had alerted the Masai administration, and a district officer, Gerry Finch, was there, and a large number of young Moran to help get the cattle over the river and drive them away. We camped on one side and they on the other. I shall never forget the sight at night of the Moran, on the other side, gathered around their huge fire. They were roasting meat on long sticks angled to the heat, and every now and then a lithe naked form would step into the firelight and take meat. The light of the fire flickered over the crouching and reclining forms, reflecting from shining bronze skins, and glinting on tall spears driven into the ground amongst them. The spectacle was deeply moving, and undoubtedly stirred some vague memory of a far ancestral past, buried deep in the sub-conscious.

To move from the sublime to the ridiculous. One night Finch invited the two field officers, Geoff Kenyon and Frank Miller, and me over to his camp for a drink. We accepted and had to wade across the waist-deep water carrying our clothes. The evening developed inevitably into something of a party, and very much later we faced the prospect of re-crossing the river, in which there were both hippo and crocodile. In our rather inebriated state we thought this a huge joke, but we did take one precaution. Finch had a rifle with him, and he emptied a magazine of shots into the water as a prelude to our crossing to deter any ambitious beast that might be lurking nearby. We then launched ourselves, arms linked, into the water, and eventually after a rather staggering passage, we reached the other side and our own camp. Another volley of shots rang out as a sort of *feu de joie*.

On another night at our camp by the river, I awoke with a sixth sense of danger. We were sleeping out in the open without tents, it being the dry season. As I had no torch, I could not see anything and so went back to sleep. Next morning we saw with interest the footprints of a large hippo that had walked through our camp, moving between our camp-beds. It must have stepped very delicately, for nothing had been disturbed but my sleep.

Getting the cattle across the river was a major operation in itself. A good deal of pressure had to be applied to get them moving, for this was a medium they were not used to. They were extremely reluctant to launch themselves into the wide stretch of flowing water, underneath which was an unsure footing. Once the first few had been persuaded across however, the rest followed, but the movement had to be continuous, and again I was impressed by the discipline these people were able to impose on their cattle. It was a stirring sight to watch the crossing, which made a fitting conclusion to two weeks of hard unremitting effort by all concerned.

VI

It was not long after this work with the Masai that I got involved in an event which could have ended my career. Early in 1956

TANU was allowed to operate in Lushoto district, and Nyerere himself came on a tour to hold a series of meetings which were really part of a recruiting drive to secure more members for the party. One of these meetings was being held at Bumbuli, an important and populous sub-chiefdom, whilst I was there on a routine visit. I decided to go along to the meeting to observe what went on. I re-introduced myself to Nyerere who remembered our first meeting in Musoma. Courtesies were exchanged and I asked if I might sit in on the meeting — a request which was granted. My presence may have toned down the content and tenor of the speeches made, but in all honesty I could find no great fault in them. Nyerere's speech was typical of his style, neither patronising nor aggressive, simple in content but quite penetrating, with a clever use of half-truth and generalization to get his point across. I have always thought that he would have made a brilliant academic historian. The basic thrust of his speech was however straightforward; independence was coming, but it would not introduce an immediate Utopia; that could only be achieved by long, hard, unremitting toil in an atmosphere of unity. I was impressed. Perhaps rather foolishly I decided to make a speech too. The gist of what I said was that if this man Nyerere was calling for work and effort to build the nation, then I agreed with him, and he had my support. I larded my offering with a few sentences in Shambala which the crowd liked, but Nyerere did not. When the meeting was finished there was a rush to join the party, and I suspect that my presence and support gave a big boost to party funds that day. Some weeks later Nemesis struck. The DC called me into his office, saying, "What the hell have you been doing? H.E. (His Excellency the Governor) wants to see you sharpish." The Special Branch of the police had been at the Bumbuli meeting, and a report had gone in that the district officer of Lushoto had not only attended a TANU meeting at which Nyerere himself was present, but had also made a favourable speech. This report eventually reached the Governor himself, Sir Edward Twining, who was apprised of my errant behaviour. It so happened that he was in residence at the governor's lodge up in the hills above Lushoto town, where he spent the hot season away from the heat of the coast. This was probably my salavation for otherwise the affair might have been handled by some lesser, and almost certainly less magnanimous official. As it was, however, I was summoned to appear one morning before the great man himself. I put on my suit, composed myself for the ordeal, and duly presented myself at the lodge. As I entered the governor's office he greeted me with "Ah, Cooke, how are your friends in TANU, and your good friend Nyerere?" At my rather perplexed response, he told me to sit down, in a not unkindly voice. He came straight to the point, telling me what had been reported to him concerning my conduct, and he requested an explanation. I sensed that quite a lot was at stake and therefore went into some detail. I stated what I thought our policy was, namely to bring African countries to self-government as quickly as possible. I added that for this to be achieved, unity, hard work and a sense of realism were critical factors, and that Nyerere in his speech at Bumbuli, had emphasised these. He had not delivered a harangue or anything which I could construe as subversive or inflammatory. I had therefore, decided to lend him my support *at that meeting*. Twining listened to me very attentively, asked one or two questions, and then sat staring at me for what seemed an age. He then abruptly stood up, came and put his arm around my shoulders, and said, "Never mind, my boy, I can see you didn't really make a balls-up after all. Come and have a drink." He gave me a stiff scotch which I felt I needed badly. I was bowled over by the sheer, broad-minded magnanimity and humanity of the man. The matter was never mentioned again, and I know from later events that nothing regarding it was put on my confidential record.

There was a particularly compelling reason why I was more than ordinarily concerned at the possible consequences of this peccadillo. I was contemplating matrimony, and couldn't very well approach this as an unemployed ex-district officer. The young lady of my desire was Sylvia Kaufmann, whose parents lived on a sisal estate near Tanga, where her father was manager. We met briefly twice in Lushoto without the apparent kindling of any serious mutual attraction, but then Sylvia came up to Lushoto to sing at a concert being given at the Lushoto school. She had a fine soprano voice and had trained at the Nairobi Conservatoire of Music, the Royal College and Guildhall School of Music in London. We became more closely acquainted that weekend, and not being one to waste time or opportunity, I announced my rapidly developing affection. I was greatly gratified to learn that this was reciprocated. From that point we never looked back and were married within six months. Sylvia had planned to go to Germany to continue her musical studies, but that now went by the board. We had a private medical practitioner in Lushoto, a Hungarian named Padar, and he met me in the street shortly after we had announced our engagement. Shaking his fist at me, he exclaimed, only half jokingly, "How dare you ruin such a promising career, and rob us of that lovely voice."

For the six months before we were married, my weekends were all fully occupied. I used to drive down to Potwe where the Kaufmanns lived, and we would often go on down to the coast between Tanga and Pangani. Here there were miles of glorious empty beaches, warm blue sea, fine coral reefs and waving palms — a perfect tropical paradise. There was also the Mkoma Inn, a broken down old place run by an elderly monocled German. This had all the character and atmosphere of a beachcomber's retreat, and smelt of drying fish, coral, curry and dry-rot, with the sound of the surf always in the background. What more could we have wanted?

We were married in Tanga in June 1956, and spent our honeymoon in a shack on the beach at sleepy Bagamoyo, in a tent in the wilds of Handeni, and finally in the fleshpots of the Norfolk Hotel in Nairobi, with long stretches of motoring in my landrover in between. Once married, my life-style had to change somewhat. A bachelor household is one thing, a married one quite another. Namko was an early casualty. He was more than a bit of a male chauvinist snob, and thought of himself as very much a "gentleman's gentleman". Being driven to polishing floors and dusting furniture to a housewife's standards, was not at all to his taste. So reluctantly we parted company, and he returned to Musoma. He was replaced by a more amenable Mshambaa. Fortunately I had already found an excellent cook, Saidi, who co-operated very well with Sylvia, from whom he was to learn a great deal. The garden quickly took on a cared-for look, and masses of flowers began to appear.

My spare time activities had to change, and they took on a more domesticated slant. I exploited the resources of my environment and took up carpentry. There could not have been a better place to do this. The Usambaras still had very extensive areas of mature rain forest which contained many excellent timber species. Much of the forest was designated as reserve land, to preserve it from clearing for cultivation. This was vital, since in mountainous terrain with a high and concentrated rainfall, the forest acts like a gigantic sponge, holding water and slowly releasing it into the streams and rivers. Once such forest is cleared, erosion soon denudes the upper slopes, and rivers become raging torrents of water and debris after rain, and dry useless boulder beds at other times. The timber of these forests had for long been exploited by the Shambaa who knew the quality and usefulness of many timber species. Perhaps naturally there were many skilled carpenters working in the hill villages. Traditionally they had obtained their timber by hand-logging and pit-sawing, but by the 1950s there were saw-mills operating in many places. Commercial exploitation had begun with the Germans who had at one stage built an aerial ropeway to get timber down the escarpment to the railway line below. British policy was to clearfell some areas, especially those over-exploited in the past, and re-plant with fast-growing tropical pine species, and very large plantations had been created around Shume in the very highest reaches of the hills. Other areas of forest were exploited on a sustained yield basis, concession areas being granted to private logging companies, whose offtake was carefully controlled. Obtaining good seasoned timber for my hobby was therefore no problem, and with it I made such things as coffee tables, book cases and curtain pelmets. I also made chests and boxes for the storage and transport of our growing body of possessions for the inevitable time when we would have to pack up and move elsewhere.

VII

In fact a move came rather sooner than we had expected, but fortunately it was only of a temporary nature. The large and important Moshi district was having problems due to sickness among its district officers, and I was sent up there to help out for a few months. The order to move came shortly after the birth of our first child Philippa, so it was not entirely opportune, but we managed. In fact this move to Moshi was not at all unpleasant in many ways. The district commissioner was Brian Hodgson, under whom I had worked in Musoma, so that I didn't have to adapt myself quickly to a stranger's ways of doing things. Sylvia's Uncle Hans lived just outside Moshi on his farm, as did his daughter whose husband Fritz Veit had a large coffee farm high up on the lower slopes of Kilimanjaro. We were able to stay in both homes where we were very hospitably received. From the Veit's house Kibo seemed to loom very close, and there were wonderful views of the snow-capped summit from the garden.

I was very excited at the prospect of working amongst the Chagga, an enterprising and vigorous people. The lower slopes of the mountain were solid with their banana and coffee groves, amongst which their houses were dispersed. The Germans had shown that arabica coffee grows well in the fertile volcanic soils,

Ikoma dancers and spectator - the old and new Africa.

Masai belles with game scout, Serengeti 1954.

Head porters on foot safari up the Mara valley.

The acme of natural elegance - Masai Moran, Ruvu crossing.

*Safari companions - tarishi Stephen and my cook Issa,
Lushoto 1955.*

and an early British district commissioner, Major Dundas, had encouraged the Chagga to grow this crop. They had done this with enthusiasm, and the growers had eventually, though not without many vicissitudes, organised themselves into co-operatives which became the Kilimanjaro Native Co-operative Union (KNCU). The Chagga were fortunate in their environment: deep rich soils developed from the geologically recent lavas of the volcano; adequate and reliable rainfall; and permanent streams fed through the forest zone from the melting snows and precipitation of the upper slopes. They had made full use of this and evolved a flourishing agriculture based on the banana as the staple food crop, supplemented by maize grown on the lower lands below the mountain. Interplanted coffee provided a good cash income. They also kept cattle which they housed in byres (*mazizi*), and hand-fed on banana wastes and grass cut and carted from wherever it was available. These cattle yielded manure for their crops, and milk for consumption and sale.

On observing this pattern of intelligent mixed farming, I was forced to ponder why it was that the Shambaa were so reluctant to adopt similar practices, which we were trying so hard to inculcate. Was it the relative poverty of their soil? Or was it that in economic terms, the marginal return from the extra labour the Shambaa were being asked to put into their land, was just not worth that effort, and so they did not want to bother? Problems like this still bedevil efforts to improve African peasant agriculture, and they will have to be solved soon to cope with the massive and rapidly growing demand for food from the continent's burgeoning population.

The close settlement on their lands, and the overall importance of permanent and semi-permanent tree crops had greatly increased the intrinsic and cash value of land amongst the Chagga. The *kihamba* or permanently planted holding, had assumed the nature of freehold, and land which had acquired a cash value was openly being bought and sold. Another major consequence of their fertile land, and their intelligent use of it was that the Chagga had become a relatively wealthy people. Many of them were rapidly becoming entrepreneurs in the modern economic sense, acquiring larger holdings of land by purchase, entering trade, particularly the transport business, and seeking to organise themselves to better advantage. The problems associated with the emergence of this new class or element in society had created another complication in a political scene already complex enough.

In the nineteenth century the Chagga had become organised under chiefs, or as the Chagga call them, *wamangi*. This came about partly from a need to defend themselves against the rampant Masai at the height of that people's power. The *wamangi* also quarrelled amongst themselves and there was little peace on the mountain. In spite of their divisions however, they did offer a spirited resistance to the Germans when they appeared on the scene towards the end of the century. The latter however, defeated them by the well-proven European technique of combining utter and calculated ruthlessness with an inspired ability to play off one local ruler against another. Even though the Chagga had guns, and greatly out-numbered the newcomers, they succumbed as most indigenous peoples have always done since Cortes and Pizzaro perfected the technique of conquest by small determined groups in the sixteenth century. As in Usambara however, the undercurrents of internecine conflict and intrigue continued under German and later British rule, and as I have said were acquiring an additional dimension with the growth of trade and commerce.

By the time I reached Moshi in mid-1957, an apparent calm had descended on the Chagga lands, and they were enjoying a period of unprecedented prosperity and peace. A popularly elected paramount chief or *mangi mkuu* was in power at the head of a strong and influential Chagga council. The price of coffee was soaring, and the KNCU was a much-lauded model of African economic advancement. Every *mangi* had a Mercedes-Benz car paid for by voluntary subscription from their loyal peoples. It was a heady sort of atmosphere in which to work. Usambara seemed very backward in comparison, Musoma even more so, while Biharamulo seemed light years behind.

A major task which faced me when I arrived in Moshi was to organise the national census in the half of the district allotted to me. I had just finished setting up the organisation for this in Lushoto before I left, and so did not find much difficulty in adapting to the task in Moshi, though I did have to learn very quickly the geography and patterns of population distribution in my area. It gave me the opportunity to get to know the people, for I held explanatory and training sessions for the enumerators in every section of the area, which I was thus able to get to know quite rapidly. This was to stand me in good stead when I started on the task which was to take up a good deal of my time, namely hearing a large backlog of local court appeal cases. Almost all of these were inevitably land cases, disputes regarding the exact boundaries of land holdings, or arising from the sale of land which was frequently disputed by relatives, or problems with disputed allocations arising out of the settlement of wills. Land carrying mature coffee trees was very valuable, and people were prepared to go to law over remarkably small parcels of land, and to bear the considerable costs involved in paying court fees and witnesses expenses. Rules of inheritance were complicated and very different from those in Musoma and Lushoto where my experience lay up till then. Amongst the Chagga for example, the youngest son got the lion's share of the inheritance on his father's death.

I didn't have much walking to do in this country, for roads and motorable tracks penetrated to every part of the settled area. There was an amusing tale told of some enthusiastic young district officer who had come to Moshi some good few years earlier. He thought he would operate in the old style, and walk everywhere. Arriving at a chiefdom headquarters one day, he told the Mangi that he intended to tour the area on foot, and requested that a dozen porters be ready for him the next morning.

Early the next day, sure enough twelve sturdy young men were lying and sitting around outside apparently waiting for him. They made no move however when he asked them to take up his various boxes and bundles. As he spoke to them he noticed a truck standing in the roadway outside, and on enquiring whose this was, he received the polite reply, "Just carry on walking, sir. The truck is on us, but just pay us the standard porterage rates." The good old days were definitely long past in Uchagga.

It was in Moshi that I had some brief dealings with Somalis. There was a colony of these people settled on the Sanya plains between Moshi and Arusha. Most of them were involved in the cattle trade. They were of varying origins, belonging to different clans, and in consequence harboured mutual hatreds and antagonisms of an intensity I found quite alarming. They had complex feuds and quarrels in which on one or two occasions they asked me to arbitrate. I would have been wiser to avoid such entanglements. Individuals would come to my office, but would only enter after carefully looking round outside. They would then close the door, and coming close to me, speak in urgent and sibilant whispers. They would revile and slander their opponents in the most outrageous way imaginable. I made valiant attempts to get to grips with their disputes but was quite defeated. They were far too devious, complex and totally alien for my simple mind to grasp what they were fighting about, at such short notice. Perhaps in fact there was nothing tangible to grasp; perhaps they acted out their feuds as other people play chess or bridge, and almost certainly their subtleties were not really comprehensible in a foreign tongue like Swahili, which in any case they were far from fluent in. I formed a healthy respect, but no envy whatsoever, for district officers who had to work in Somaliland.

I had to work very hard in Moshi. It was not easy to cope with the many tasks I had to get on with quickly, at the same time as I was trying to acquire the necessary local knowledge to enable me to do the work adequately and efficiently. I became rather run down, and like Job suffered from a plague of boils. I lost a lot of weight, and when we got back to Lushoto many people commented on my reduced appearance. *"Umekonda kweli, bwana"* was a frequent comment, or in Shambala more picturesquely" *Uzagogozoka, zumbe"*, both of which mean "your face is really sunken in". In retrospect, I suspect that bilharzia was getting a grip on me, but I wasn't to know that then. My good friend Dr Padar diagnosed chronic bacillary dysentery and pumped me full of antibiotics and vitamins, which certainly seemed to put new life into me.

VIII

My health and stamina were of major concern to me at that time, as I was planning a major expedition on Kilimanjaro. Already since arriving in Lushoto, I had made one short trip up to the northern mountains which were only a long day's drive distant. That was over the Christmas holiday of 1955, when Ian McNaught-Davis came up from the coast where he was working in oil exploration. Together we climbed Mount Meru, a very splendid mountain and like Kilimanjaro, of volcanic origin. It rises to over 16,000 feet (nearly 5,000 m) above the town of Arusha. We motored up on Christmas Day, and made a camp at the edge of the forest belt, from where we climbed to the summit on Boxing Day. The following day we drove back to Lushoto.

My plans for Kilimanjaro had been maturing for some time. All parts of the whole massif had been reached by mountaineers, geologists and surveyors, and the main summit of Kibo had been reached by thousands of people by the normal trade route of ascent from Marangu, which poses no technical problems. However, I could find no record of a complete, continuous traverse of the whole mountain, taking in all the main peaks of Shira, Kibo and Mawenzi. This I planned to do. A second aim was to attempt a first ascent of one of the unclimbed glaciers on the south face of Kibo. The west and south faces of Kibo are separated by a massive breach in the crater rim and wall, which is very spectacular. The glaciers to the north-west of the breach, namely the Penck and the Credner, offer no great problems, and had been climbed. Those to the east, the Kersten and the Heim are formidable ice-walls and had not been climbed. I proposed to tackle the Heim as a route to the summit area of Kibo as part of the traverse of the whole mountain. From photographs it looked very challenging, and so it was to prove.

The first problem to be overcome was finding companions for the venture. They would have to be experienced and competent mountaineers, for the Heim would be no place for tyros. By enormous good fortune two excellent men turned up. They were Ax Nelson and David Goodall. In background, character and temperament they were totally different. Ax was an American who was at that time working as an adviser with the Meru Co-operative Union based in Arusha. He was a man of deep religious convictions with a driving urge in life to champion the cause of those he considered to be downtrodden and exploited. He had got involved with the Meru land case when he met Kirilo Japhet, the Meru spokesman in New York at the United Nations. The Wameru were petitioning against the Tanganyika govern-ment's alienation of a part of their land to European farmers. Ax espoused the Meru cause and came out to Tanganyika to work with them, ending up as an adviser to their co-operative which organised the coffee growers on Mount Meru. He later wrote a book about his experiences, entitled *The Freemen of Meru*, published by Oxford in 1967. He had considerable climbing experience, and amongst other things had been actively involved in the early ascents of the immense vertical rock faces in the Yosemite region of the Sierra Nevadas in the western United States. Ax was a great talker and very articulate, so that by the end of our expedition David and I knew just about everything about him and his philosophy of life. David Goodall was British, northcountry like myself. Although we lived in very close contact for two exacting weeks on the mountain, where we were totally interdependent (in fact, he saved my life), he remains an enigma. He was working as an agricultural officer in Kenya, and before that had done his National Service in the Parachute Regiment. He was very tough, totally dependable, and excellent company, but he exemplified the Yorkshireman's motto "Hear all, see all, say nowt."

We got together and made detailed plans. Late September was agreed on as the time and we all obtained leave from our work. We had all the necessary equipment except ice pitons, long narrow steel spikes to drive into hard ice as safe anchor points when climbing. These we ordered from the UK. I had a small Black's mountain tent big enough for two men, but as weight was going to be a critical factor, we decided to make do with it. Since we were going to be on the mountain for two weeks all our food would have to be carried, so that it would have to be carefully chosen and finely calculated. Tins were out of the question. Our basic bulk food were porridge oats with dried milk and sugar, plus hard biscuits. For protein and fat we took bacon and biltong, and instant coffee was our beverage. In the absence of fresh fruit and vegetables we took Vitamin C tablets, and for quick energy dried fruit and glucose tablets. We calculated precise amounts of everything, weighed it all out, and packed it into canvas bags that Sylvia made up for us. My old well-tried Primus stove and a supply of paraffin provided for our cooking. Even with food and equipment pared to a minimum we were still going to have very heavy loads to carry, with tent and sleeping bags, ice axes, crampons, pitons and hammers, slings and clips, rope, minimal spare clothing, food and fuel for two weeks. We decided there was no point in lugging this lot unaided through the forest, and so I asked the Mangi of Machame from where we planned to start, if he could find us a few porters to help us carry our gear up onto the Shira Plateau. This he very kindly did for us.

The route we planned would go from west to east. We would ascend to the Shira plateau first, and climb all the Shira peaks. The 12,000 feet altitude (about 4000 m) would enable us to acclimatise quickly before tackling the major problem of the Heim glacier. The route onto the Shira from Loldorosi that I had used in 1953 was long and time-consuming. A start from Machame would yield a more direct route, and we trusted to the porters knowing a way through the forest. Once on the Shira the porters would leave us and go back down, leaving us with a weighty transport problem. We would tick off all the peaks there, namely the Shira ridge, Shira dome, and the Platzkegel. The Heim was our great unknown, and we did not know the nature of the problems we would encounter. Ax had persuaded someone with a small plane to fly him past the glaciers and ice-walls, and he managed to get a good photograph of the Heim from fairly close quarters, which was to prove of great assistance to us. Once up the Heim, assuming we succeeded there, we would go over the summit of Kibo, and then down to the saddle between Kibo and Mawenzi. From a last camp below the latter we would make our last ascent — of Mawenzi, and then get down to Marangu.

We eventually left Machame on 20th September with five porters who knew the forest trails. We felt light-hearted and unburdened. We were glad of the latter for our route made no concessions and went up very steeply, following a ridge between two deeply entrenched river valleys. The forest was very beautiful, and since we had guides, we could relax and appreciate our surroundings, without having to concentrate on route-finding, and hacking our way forward. In the forest in 1953 I had been too concerned with route finding to bother much about aesthetics, while in the Ruwenzori forests, the overpowering wetness and mud could only offer pleasure to a sheer masochist. There is much wildlife in the Kilimanjaro forests, but one hears more than one sees. On our first night out we slept in the forest, always an intriguing experience with all sorts of strange noises, rustlings, scuffles, thuds, grunts, whistles and the odd trumpeting of a distant elephant. We were charmed by the very beautiful black and white, long haired colobus monkeys, which we often saw swinging in the trees, overcome with curiosity as to who and what we were. Late on our second day out we were surprised and pleased to emerge from the forest, and to see before us the final slopes leading up onto the plateau. This was the point where the porters were to leave us, but very sadly our parting was less than amicable.

When I came to pay the porters, they claimed we had pushed them too hard so that they had done in two days what they would normally consider three days' work. In consequence of this they wanted three days' pay. I pointed out that there were flaws in their argument, because Europeans did not come this way, and therefore they had no precedent on which to base their claim. I had no strong feelings however, and was prepared to come to some compromise or even to pay them what they wanted. A haggle was normal procedure and we settled down to it. However, Ax who spoke but little Swahili, asked what was going on. I told him, whereupon the Protestant Work Ethic raised its formidable head. "Like hell," said Ax, "tell them they get two days' pay for two days' work, period." I had to communicate this dour message to the men, and it immediately put their backs up. Haggling does not involve or welcome bald statements or firm positions. I was caught in a fix. I sympathised with the men, but I did not want to antagonise my friend with whom I was to spend the next two weeks in very close contact. The porters would not give an inch and eventually went down empty-handed. Some weeks later however, I was able to arrange payment for them. I found this little contretemps rather ironic — the radical American being less accommodating than the imperialist Briton.

From this point we took it fairly easily for a day, carrying our loads to a point high on the eastern side of the plateau, where we camped. We were acclimatising nicely, and the next day we made a complete circuit of the Shira, climbing all the peaks. We were not carrying any loads, but it was a long, exhausting day, though very exhilarating. From our camp in the evening we had a fantastic view out over an immense sea of clouds, through which in the distance Mount Meru thrust its sharp summit like an island in a vast ocean. Behind us reared the imposing rock and ice slopes of this side of Kibo, which slowly turned from gold to deep red, and finally a forbidding grey as the sun went down. We shivered and crawled into our cramped tent.

Our next objective was to get to the foot of the Heim glacier. This involved a long upward traverse over masses of broken rock and scree, followed by a descent into and climb out of the barranco, or deeply glaciated trough, which runs out below the Great Breach Wall. This was another long hard day, but we were now fully acclimatised, in good fettle, and moving well. We reached our goal in the late afternoon, and the crucial challenge of our expedition. About 3,000 feet (1,000 m) of steep ice reared upwards and curved out of sight far above us. It looked forbidding. The whizz and hum of flying ice and rock debris from above quickly drove us against the ice front below a protecting rock-wall, where we bivouacked. I felt butterflies in my stomach as one always does before a challenging venture.

Next morning we were up and off before dawn. We knew where we had to go. From Ax's photograph we had seen that the major defences of the Heim were two lines of ice cliffs about a third of the way up, and come what may, we had to find a way through these. We moved up steadily, and soon noticed without much enthusiasm, that there was no snow on the ice. We were on bare, hard ice, and very soon we had to don our crampons (steel spikes which are strapped to the sole of one's boots), and rope up. We reached the lower ice wall and traversed upwards and to the left across a very steep slope, aiming for the top of a small projecting rock buttress which split the wall. Here catastrophe almost overtook us. David was leading, cutting steps in the ice as he went. I was in the middle, with Ax bringing up the rear. We moved singly, of course. David had reached the rock buttress and was well belayed, or anchored to the rock with the rope. I was moving towards him when I caught a crampon spike in my sock and pitched forward and down. I was brought up sharply by a taut rope, and found myself dangling half upside down, with a fine vertiginous view downwards. A cool, steady, and very reassuring voice came from above, "Don't worry lad, I've got you." David had whipped in my rope and held me before the other rope had tightened up on Ax who was still very precariously perched on the wall. At the same time Ax had sensibly let go his slack as he saw David's prompt action — a case of perfect co-ordination that only experience can produce. I sorted myself out and climbed up to David. Very unfortunately I had lost my ice-axe, and felt very rattled, feeling I had let the others down badly. There were no recriminations, however. We climbed to the top of the buttress and held a council of war. A formidable ice climb towered above us, and we now had only two axes between the three of us. But we did have a good supply of ice-pitons, and decided to go on. This was perhaps a foolhardy decision, but since in the event we succeeded, it was the right one.

That night we bivouacked on the top of the buttress which was just big enough to take our tent once we had built up a platform with lumps of ice and rock. It was a cramped and uncomfortable spot, but we seemed to be out of the main trajectory of the flying debris of late afternoon. For the most part it whizzed harmlessly by, and we felt reasonably safe.

The following day we faced another crisis. David was snow-blind through not wearing his dark glasses. He could not go out, so Ax and I reconnoitred the route ahead. We found a good line on steep but sound ice, to the top of another buttress which was slightly more commodious than the first. We then climbed down back to the tent, to find that in our absence a flying piece of ice had ripped a hole in the tent wall. After a second night on our cramped site, we followed the route we had worked out on the previous day. David's eyes were much better but we could only move slowly. With only two axes we had to adopt a special mode of progress. Whoever was leading went ahead. After about thirty feet he drove in a piton and belayed to it. He then tied his axe to the rope and lowered it to the second man, who then ascended to join number one. The third man then came up and led through on the next pitch, and the sequence was then repeated. We handled the axe with the utmost care, for we knew that if we lost it we would really be in trouble. To have attempted to move more quickly would have been sheer lunacy.

The next ice-wall looked impressive as we studied it in clear weather in the late afternoon from our second camp. We worked out what appeared to be a feasible route. Next morning, however, we were enveloped in thick mist. We moved off nevertheless, climbing steeply and hoping we would not meet any impossible obstacle. Halfway up the wall we landed in a very beautiful ice-cave where we could rest. Further progress seemed problematic, as the roof of the cave overhung, and the walls to left and right were vertical. Ax solved this problem in splendid fashion. Leaving his heavy pack in the cave, he hacked out steps to the left and upwards, and climbed out of sight over an ice bulge. His rope inched out and fragments of ice flew past. Tension was relieved when a cry of triumph floated down to us. The slope had eased off and he had been able to drive in a piton and belay to it. He hauled up his pack and we followed. We still could not see anything, but we presumed we had mastered the wall. We just went on climbing upwards, pitch after wearisome pitch. As the day drew to a close we were literally nowhere, or so it seemed, on a vast ice-slope in poor visibility. All we could do was to go on climbing in the hope of reaching some place suitable for a bivouac, before nightfall. It was with some relief that we found a place of sorts. The slope began to ease off slightly, and on its convex bend a lurking crevasse appeared. We hacked at the lower lip to form a narrow platform just big enough to take the tent. We could only guy it fore and aft, and hammered in pitons with safety lines to ourselves, and crept into the tent. The two outer men hung in bulges over space, on one side the free void of the open slope, on the other the dark unknown depths of the crevasse. We fervently hoped that the stitching of canvas wall to groundsheet was sound. A wind got up, and we could not risk lighting the primus as the tent was flapping wildly. We went hungry and drinkless. Sucking ice didn't help much, and with dry mouths we could not eat dry biscuit. We consoled ourselves with the thought that if we had been forced to spend the night out on the ice, that wind in sub-zero temperatures would have been very trying.

Next morning our troubles lifted miraculously. It was a brilliantly clear morning, the slope eased off, and there was firm snow on the ice at last. We could move together. We were on a vast slope which curved out of sight below us whence we had come. In the clear air we had a breathtaking view directly out over the immense plains of northern Tanganyika. These huge isolated East African volcanic peaks stand proudly alone, and from their upper slopes there are no rivals to encumber and clutter the free surrounding space. We felt that we were literally on the roof of the world, and as success seemed within our grasp we felt a tremendous sense of elation. More mundane matters were also on our minds, or rather our stomachs, and we halted at the first convenient place, a lonely rock outcrop, and cooked a big feast of bacon, and pints of hot coffee. Life was good! We finally camped that night amongst broken seracs or ice pinnacles at the top of the Heim, and next morning we moved easily up to the highest point of the mountain, Kaiser Wilhelm Spitze or Uhuru Peak as it is now called, at 19,340 feet (just under 6,000 m). We felt the whole of Africa was spread out at our feet, rolling away into infinite distance.

Reluctantly we continued our trek, and shot down the abominable screes of the tourist route of ascent, to reach the Kibo hut. We had arranged with the Marangu hotel to have a box of food sent up with a porter, and left at the hut to await our arrival. This we found and eagerly broached. There were tins of meat and vegetables, fruit and chocolate, which we quickly organised into a minor feast. After eleven days on hard tack and using vast amounts of energy we were ravenous. At the hut were four young British army officers on leave from Kenya. Being young and enormously enthusiastic they had come up too quickly and were suffering badly from mountain sickness. They turned two shades greener as they watched us wolfing our food. We felt sorry for them, but some time later we were equally sorry for ourselves, as gluttony took its toll. Our innards rebelled against the untoward loads we had suddenly plied them with. Nonetheless we crossed the saddle, and made our last camp below Mawenzi more or less recovered from our excesses.

After our success on the Heim, tension eased off a little, and we felt a sense of anti-climax. Our muscles began to stiffen, but our resolve loosened. Getting up Mawenzi required a stern mental effort, and we had to really drive ourselves up to the summit and back to our camp. A final sense of achievement was our reward.

All that remained was to get down off the mountain. I had told Sylvia the probable day of our descent, but the Heim had delayed us a little. Imagine our great joy, when after jogging down for hour after weary hour, our legs like lead and our minds in neutral, we came round a bend and saw my landrover standing waiting with Sylvia sitting in it. She had driven up the appalling track as far as she dared, and had waited all day, just hoping we would appear. She earned our undying gratitude. That night we got cleaned up, had a wonderful meal, and slept like babies. Next day we went our separate ways. I have never seen David again, but have seen Ax on several occasions, and some years later we climbed together the active volcano Oldoinyo Lengai. He is now retired and living in California.

IX

Life in Lushoto quickly settled back into its routine. Once our daughter Philippa had arrived I had to revert to going on safari alone. An event occurred however, which disturbed the relatively peaceful tenor of our lives, and gave cause for concern when one had to go away on duty and leave one's family at home. Looking back on that time, it was perhaps a very mild foretaste of the appalling disease of terrorist violence that now afflicts so many people worldwide, when decent law-abiding people can nowhere feel safe from the acts of deranged and homicidal maniacs that society at large seems quite unable to control. A convict with a long record of violent assault and robbery had escaped from Tanga prison, and somehow had got hold of a sten-gun and ammunition. This man, a Luo named Osale, terrorised much of Tanga province, appearing from nowhere to rob and murder. Unfortunately he came up into the Usambaras, and we had to take a variety of precautions that I have already referred to, such as collecting arms from outlying homesteads. I borrowed an ancient .45 calibre revolver from the police but did not have much faith in its efficacy.

One night at about 1.30 am we thought our turn had come, when there was a loud and insistent banging on the front door. I got up, told Sylvia to get under the bed with Philippa, and approached the door, revolver cocked. I was relieved however, to hear the agitated voice of Inspector Yusuf, our Indian officer in charge of Police at the time. He brought news that old Dr Suffrin, whom I have mentioned earlier, had sent a note down to the police station by runner, saying that his house had been broken into by Osale and an Mshambaa henchman whom he had picked up, named Paulo. The note was written in a perfectly steady hand and stated simply as follows:

To O/c Police Lushoto

You will be interested to hear that Osale and Paulo have just broken into my house and threatened my life. They have now gone.

R. Suffrin.

We took four constables and went up to the lonely house in

a police landrover. After parking quietly down the approach road we moved towards the house with some circumspection. On entering I found the old man sitting in an armchair by his fire, and reading. I remember the title of the book — *A History of the Tudors*. He was mildly surprised to see us, and said that a day-time visit would have been quite in order. He was perfectly relaxed, and told us what had happened. From his description it was clear that his assailants had quite failed to ruffle his composure. He had told them to take what they wanted, and then go away and leave him in peace. He was a recluse, and his house a mild shambles, containing little of any value. There were piles of books and old copies of the *Times* stacked everywhere. In spite of loud threats, the good doctor had remained unmoved, and his unwelcome visitors had departed, no doubt vaguely disturbed by the old man's lack of fear. There was nothing we could do. Our birds had flown and so we left, with Dr Suffrin's warm thanks for our concern.

We got a number of false alarms, and reports of Osale's presence at particular places. One day we were following up one of these, and were approaching with extreme caution a house in whose environs the villains had reportedly been seen. We were flitting from tree to tree, rather like children playing cowboys and Indians, when the white-haired head of the occupant poked out from the kitchen window, and said in a mildly puzzled voice, "Can I help you, do you think?" I doubt if I have ever felt so utterly foolish, but the episode dissolved into laughter all round, and we were all invited in for a cup of tea.

Eventually Osale and Paulo were caught. A police patrol, acting on information received, ambushed them at Mtae. While trying to flee, Osale was shot dead, and Paulo wounded. The latter was taken to the Lushoto hospital where I had to see him. The police wanted what was called a "dying declaration" which only a magistrate could take. Though there was no apparent reason why I should be, I felt sorry for this by now pathetic figure. He was dying, and he stammered out to me the whole sorry tale of his movements with Osale, and what they had done together. That was not a very pleasant task for me. When the dust had settled, I gave my revolver back to the police, but before doing so thought I would try it. It wouldn't fire, and inspection showed that the firing pin jammed and did not reach the round in the breach. I presume the police adjusted it in due course.

Many less serious and disturbing events brought variety to the routine of life from time to time. The digging of deep holes was a mild local disease in the Usambaras. Many people were firmly convinced that before the Germans left during the 1914-18 war they had buried their valuables such as gold and jewellery. Others believed that gold or precious stones could be found. Legally one had to have a licence to search for these things. A prospecting licence was relatively easy to obtain, permitting a search for geologically based materials. Also obtainable how-ever, was a licence to search for "treasure trove", and in this case the applicant had to specify what he or she was looking for and where they expected to find it. Some people, of all races, applied for the latter, but most preferred to keep their ideas and insights to themselves, and break the law. It was a highly secretive business. It was not uncommon for people walking in their gardens in the early morning, to find deep holes dug the night before by persons unknown. This was especially common in the vicinity of old German houses. It was really quite uncanny how such deep holes could be dug in such a short space of time, and so quietly.

Some prospectors also had peculiar ideas and did things which were quite unrelated to the local geology or to any application of scientific principles. I was once on safari out on the Umba steppe, the huge plain between the Usambara mountains and the sea, when I came upon a European with a gang of labourers who were excavating a very deep hole like a mine shaft. Their method was horrifying. On top of the shaft was a very crude windlass made of rough logs. On this was wound a rope, to the end of which was attached a bucket. Apparently the labourers drilled holes in the bedrock at the bottom of the shaft, with hand tools of course, and were then wound up one at a time in the bucket. The blasting *fundi* (Swahili for expert) then went down, placed his charges, and lit his fuses. He then stepped into the bucket, shouted to his colleagues on top, who then wound him up on their slow and cumbersome contraption. The blaster looked quite normal, not what one would expect of a sort of *kamikaze* fanatic. Maybe he was just short on imagination. When the charges had gone off and the dust had settled, they went down again and removed the debris bucketful by bucketful. They said they were looking for rubies. I was amazed and intrigued, but had to tell the European in charge that this was quite ridiculous and he had better wind up the operation. He was not pleased and must have cursed his luck that this interfering DO had come wandering in this remote spot and found him at work.

Before we departed from Lushoto in mid-1958 our daughter Philippa was baptised by the Bishop of Zanzibar at our St George's church, a very happy event. A short time before this, an infant of the Twining family had likewise been baptised there, and water from the Nile had been obtained for the purpose. Some was left over and so Philippa also was christened with this supposedly precious fluid. We were not sure what the precise significance of Nile water was in the context of Christian baptism, but it all sounded frightfully impressive, and we did not demand Usambara water.

When we eventually left, our little daughter was blessed by a very different rite. We left from the small grass airstrip at Mombo below the escarpment, where a Dakota called once a week en route to Nairobi. Chief Kimweri and all his *wazee* (elders), devout Muslims all, came down to see us off. Kimweri paid special attention to Philippa, and insisted on wheeling her around in her carry-pram. Before we boarded the plane, all these dignified old men gathered round us to offer up prayers for our journey, our future and our small daughter. We were very moved, and the other passengers waiting on the aircraft, must have wondered what on earth was going on. It was for us a fitting climax to three very full and happy years spent amongst the Shambaa people in their beautiful but troubled homeland.

Chapter Five

Bukoba

Much have I travelled in the realms of gold,
And many goodly states and kingdoms seen.

Keats, On First Looking into Chapman's Homer

I

Our leave in Europe in 1958 was a very pleasant one. It was a special occasion in that I was taking home my wife Sylvia and daughter Philippa, to introduce them to my family. We also travelled widely in Germany, which Sylvia's family had to leave in 1937. In due course however, we were eager to return to Tanganyika, and were quite excited when we learned that we were to go to Bukoba, on the west side of Lake Victoria. I knew the area well of course, from my first tour, but it would be completely new to Sylvia.

I was to be posted to special duties, rather than to routine district work. The task I was to undertake was firstly to try to elucidate why the Haya people were unable or unwilling to extend and improve their cultivation of robusta coffee, and secondly to investigate the feasibility of mounting a social development-type publicity campaign to try to persuade them to change their attitudes. I was instructed to report first to the Social Development department headquarters at Tengeru near Arusha. The head there was Horace Mason, whom I have mentioned in Chapter 4. I was to be instructed, or rather indoctrinated as the letter put it, in the philosophy and methodology of social development as enunciated by Mason, who had become something of a guru.

This work that I was to do in Bukoba sounded both exciting and demanding, and I looked forward to it. Indoctrination by Mason most certainly did not appeal to me. I am at heart a very English pragmatist, with a deep distrust of theories, dogmas and philosophies, and those who perpetrate and perpetuate them. I intended to go to Bukoba with a very open mind, to try to get to know the people, try to comprehend the problem, and report on it in my own way. However, to Tengeru I went as instructed. As I had surmised, my three weeks there were a total waste of time, though it was pleasant enough living near Arusha in the shadow of the great mountains. Sylvia did not accompany me to Tengeru, but stayed with her parents near Tanga. She was expecting our second child, and we wanted to avoid all the worry and bother of temporary accommodation and frequent moving. She and Philippa joined me eventually in Bukoba when I had found somewhere to live there.

I finally escaped from Tengeru, and travelled by bus to Dodoma, thence by train to Mwanza, and across the lake by steamer to Bukoba. It was rather like my first trip along much of the same route way back in 1951. Now I was accompanied by my border collie Mackie, and having acquired fluency in Swahili, I could chat to all and sundry en route.

I arrived in Bukoba to a less than enthusiastic welcome. People on special assignments tend to be viewed with alarm and suspicion by colleagues in routine posts, who purport to be terribly busy, with no time to spare for those engaged on esoteric tasks. I made the obligatory courtesy calls on all those whom I knew would be offended if I did not so call on them, and then set about the job of finding somewhere to live. At first I camped in an empty house at the Rwamishenye Girls' School but then found an ideal place for my purpose, away from town and the government offices. Out in the Bukara chiefdom was the agricultural research station at Maruku, which as luck would have it, was headed by Bill Mitchell who had been one of the agricultural officers in Lushoto when we were there. He offered me the use of an unoccupied house on the farm, and I gratefully moved in. Sylvia and Philippa came to join me, our household effects came from Lushoto, and our car arrived from the UK. While on leave I had bought a Standard Vanguard saloon, a rugged no-nonsense car which was to give us excellent service. Maruku was a quiet place to live and perfect for my work purposes.

The Maruku research station's primary concern was with improving the propagation and cultivation of robusta coffee, and it was doing excellent work in this field. It was concerned also with other aspects of agriculture in this north-western region of Tanganyika, and especially with the banana, the staple food crop. There were a number of similar establishments in other parts of the country, notably the arabica coffee research station at Lyamungu near Moshi, and the cotton research station at Ukiuguru near Mwanza, in the major cotton growing area of Sukumaland. All these had been established in the early years of British administration, though they built on earlier pioneering work done by the Germans. Without the work of these centres, the great expansion in the production of coffee and cotton, and of agricultural produce generally which was taking place in Tanganyika in colonial times, would not have been possible. It gives the lie to the mischievous falsehood propagated by our critics, that nothing was done for the African peasant cultivator, but only for the European settler. A recent quotation exemplifies this fallacy:

"... because of the colonial practice which ignored the African farmer, who produced at a subsistence level only, while all services were geared towards the white farmer.'' (*Ecoforum* Vol II. 2 April 1986. p.12)

Maruku's work, as a case in point, could only have been for the African farmer, as there were few, if any, Europeans growing robusta coffee in Tanganyika.

It was very interesting to me to see the techniques and methods available for greatly increasing coffee yields, which had been evolved by agricultural research. I was also aware that the growers were unenthusiastic to apply these. In other words the fruits of research were not being used despite diligent extension work by the department of agriculture and the Bukoba Native Co-operative Union (BNCU). Part of my task was to try to get to understand why this was so.

II

I have already referred in passing, in Chapter 2, to Bukoba district and its people. I must now go into a more detailed description to assist understanding of the work I had to do there. Bukoba is a large district of about 5,950 square miles (15,410 sq km), with a population in 1957 of 367,962 people. It is by no means uniform in its physical characteristics, and this has affected the distribution of the population. Close to the lake and for a relatively short distance inland the north-south striking Bukoba sandstone outcrops in a series of eastward-facing escarpments. These can be seen clearly behind the town of Bukoba itself, hemming it in close to the lake-shore. Long gentle dip-slopes mark the western flanks of these outcrops. Farther to the east is an elongated basin-like zone occupied in part by Lake Ikimba, which is drained northwards by the Ngono river, a tributary of the Kagera river, and thus a Nile headstream. Beyond this again the country assumes a more open, rolling aspect which continues as far as the Kagera river in the north-south section of its course, which forms the boundary with Rwanda. The underlying rocks are ancient sedimentary and meta-sedimentary formations which on weathering yield rather poor sandy soils. Climate also shows a progressive change westwards, and particularly so in the key element of rainfall. Close to the lake the rainfall is good and reliable, and quite well-distributed through the year. Bukoba town has a mean annual rainfall of about 55 inches (1,400 mm) and no month is wholly dry. The lake shore is an unstable atmospheric zone, and violent thunderstorms, often accompanied by strong winds and torrential rain are common. Westwards the rainfall decreases sharply, and the Lake Ikimba area has only about 30 inches (800 mm) per annum. Temperatures are equable, showing very little change from month to month as might be expected so near the equator (1°2' S). Maximum temperatures rarely reach more than 30° C (86° F), and minimums seldom fall below about 18° C (64° F). Due to the unpromising parent material, very long exposure over time to high temperatures, and leaching by heavy rains, the soils are generally poor to very poor, and are lacking in essential nutrients for plants. The natural vegetation was woodland, as in Biharamulo to the south, but human beings have long since removed most of this.

This environment is pleasant enough to live in, neither too hot nor too cold, and is humid enough to sustain strong plant growth, but rather like Usambara it is deceptive. This is not a land flowing with milk and honey, and people have had to diligently apply themselves to its improvement. In such efforts the Bahaya people had been reasonably successful, and even within historic times they had changed radically their economic use of the land in response to calamitous natural occurrences. By the mid-twentieth century however, they seemed to have reached an impasse, as I will explain.

Like most other peoples, the inhabitants of Bukoba district are of composite origin. They are referred to today as the Bahaya, their country as Buhaya, and they speak a language known as Luhaya, which is one of the great group of Bantu languages. The major stratum of the population are cultivator-pastoralists, who are sometimes known as the Bahamba or Banyambo, though these terms are imprecise. At some time in the past, possibly about three hundred years ago these people came under the dominance of an invading pastoral people from the north known as the Bahima. A clan of these intruders, known as the Bahinda, established their hegemony and became rulers of a series of small states or kingdoms. These remained the basic political and administrative structures of the Haya polity until 1962 after independence, when all traditional rules were removed, and their by then residual powers abolished under a new rigidly centralized government based in Dar Es Salaam. Intermarriage has taken place over time, so that the racially distinct characteristics of the Hima have become merged in the mass of the population, though certain physical traits are still visible in some of the former ruling families. They are tall, slim when young, long-visaged, and have a natural elegance which often appears as arrogance.

The aspect of the land and the economy of the people in the mid-nineteenth century were well described by the explorer Speke in his book published in 1867, *Journal of the Discovery of the Source of the Nile*. The political economy at that time was based on cattle as the cement of social and political relationships, and as the foundation of the ruling group's power and prestige. The end of the nineteenth century brought catastrophe in the form of the great rinderpest (a killing disease of cattle) and smallpox, which decimated both cattle and people. Later came the upheaval of the 1914-18 war. Probably the major element in this catalogue of disasters was the virtual disappearance of cattle from the scene. The people were forced to fall back solely on the cultivation of the soil as their main means of sustenance. This was not simply a change of a purely economic nature, but ultimately had great social and political consequences. The ownership or rather the control of land became as significant as the ownership of cattle had been in the past. The kings or *bakama* as they are called, were not slow to realise this, and they succeeded in maintaining their traditional control, partly by the creation of large fiefs known as Nyarubanja estates. These they allocated to their relations and supporters. Many ordinary people became tenants on these estates and had to render tribute to their lords. The system was a sort of feudal one, though one must not carry any European analogy too far. The whole people meanwhile were selecting the most promising land for their agricultural settlements, and the pattern emerged of "islands" of banana plantations in a "sea" of *rweya* grasslands. Homesteads tended to be dispersed within the plantations and slowly fertility was built up under the shade of the bananas by the use of household refuse, vegetation wastes, and manure from the few cattle which were still kept. In the improving soils other food crops like beans were grown. Robusta coffee had long been known to the Bahaya. They chew the raw beans as a stimulant, and it is still a courteous gesture to offer a handful of beans to a guest. In this century, coffee was eventually to become of very great importance as a source of cash, and it has been planted extensively in the shade of the bananas. Though cattle had ceased to be the prime source of wealth as they had been in the past, small numbers were kept, and hand-fed in the same way as the Chagga keep them, as a source of milk and valuable fertiliser.

With intelligent adaptation to their changed conditions, and persistent effort, the Bahaya thus survived calamity, and established a productive and sustaining new life-style. The great good fortune of high coffee prices brought them the bonanza of a high cash income, from which many other developments have flowed.

The rapid emergence of a cash-oriented society, with coffee as the major source of new wealth inevitably led to the build-up of new stresses and strains within Haya society at large. Nyarubanja became a much resented institution and the slow modification and rationalisation of this became a major preoccupation of the administration as I will later describe. A new type of person began to emerge, who acquired prestige and power through entrepreneurial activities such as trade, especially in coffee, and in transportation. Such people were impatient of control, and they very much resented the still very strong traditional authority of the *bakama*, which the British administration supported under the system of Indirect Rule. They were also often supported by a new class of educated people, clerks, teachers and the like, produced by the expanding school system. Trouble was inevitable, and trouble duly came, first in 1937 when riots or near riots occurred in a number of areas. There was a mixture of grievances and motives involved, from resentment at government orders to cut out diseased coffee trees, the exactions of Nyarubanja landlords and attempts to rationalise the coffee trade, to envy of the power and wealth of the *bakama*. A typical instigator at one end was Clemens Kiiza, a coffee trader, and another was Ali Migeyo, an archetypal congenital grouser and trouble-maker (whom I later got to know quite well). To claim as some historians and others do, that these troubles represented a first stirring of nationalism, of peasant resistance to colonial exploitation and misrule is utter nonsense. Put at its starkest, it could be interpreted as the beginning of attempts by a newly emergent class or group of embryo capitalists to acquire power for themselves and in their own interests, and so to displace traditional authorities. Naive patriotism, local or national, was hardly a driving force with such men, though they may have flaunted it as a banner. They were the early precursors of the sorts of new élites which by incompetence, mismanagement, corruption and self-seeking interests have brought many African countries to their knees, betraying the hopes raised in the minds of the common people as they campaigned for "independence".

Success in re-adjusting to their environment then, brought prosperity to the Bahaya, but also a multitude of new problems and stresses, as people sought to re-adjust yet further their societal and political affairs to accord with new demands and imperatives. This was the situation in which I was to become deeply involved during the three years we spent in Bukoba from 1958 to 1961.

III

The task I was allotted in late 1958 when I arrived in Bukoba gave me an ideal opportunity to get to know something of the

Bahaya at grass-roots level, and to gain some understanding of their attitudes and drives. The place where we lived, Maruku, was in the centre of the Bukara chiefdom, close to the lake coast and very typical of the banana-coffee culture at its most developed level. I spent my time wandering around on foot, chatting to all and sundry from Mukama Daudi Rugomora to employed labourers from the surrounding poor districts like Biharamulo. Rugomora was a typical Hinda, tall, elegant, always immaculately dressed in a well-cut suit or a smart club blazer and flannels, with a distinctly authoritative bearing.

One way in which I managed to inveigle myself into local society was by assisting in communal monkey-hunts. Vervet monkeys, or *tumbili* in Swahili, were regarded as vermin by the Bahaya, for they were partial to bananas, and they damaged coffee trees. They were hunted by gangs of men with packs of dogs. The technique was to drive the beasts up isolated trees, and then knock them down with stones for the waiting dogs to pounce on and kill. This was a rather hit-and-miss business, and often the quarry escaped. A shot-gun greatly raised the success rate, and as I had a gun, I offered to assist. Thereafter I was in great demand. This monkey hunting was exciting, sometimes too much so, and one thing I always insisted on was that when I was involved, mine was the only firearm present. I didn't want guns going off accidentally all over the place in the general fracas. We would gather at some appointed place, fan out and advance, with the dogs in the van. As soon as monkeys were seen, a shout would quickly concentrate our forces at the critical spot, and thereafter we would try to encircle the tree in which the animals had taken refuge. I would be called upon to blast away into the trees with the general idea of killing the prey. This was not as easy as it may sound. The foliage was usually dense, my eyes were not as sharp as those of my companions, and shooting vertically upwards at a small target hidden in dark foliage with a bright sky beyond was difficult. Everybody was shouting, pointing, and gesticulating at the same time, and this bedlam by no means aided concentration. Excitement reached fever pitch when dead or wounded monkeys came tumbling down through the branches to be pounced on by the dogs. In many ways it was a gruesome business, but the little beasts were a real pest, and my joining in their hunting was furthering my own work. The hunts were usually followed by free beer. This created rather delicate social problems, for I did not like the local beer or *pombe*. My stomach is not the strongest, and in Moshi once I was very ill after drinking local beer. The problem was amicably solved by the very relaxed Bahaya who simply had a few bottles of tusker lager on hand (which they also like themselves). During these contacts I was tactfully and unobtrusively putting the odd question to people on their coffee and other things, and so building up an impression of their attitudes. My work was not confined to Bukara only. I also journeyed to other chiefdoms and sub-chiefdoms to address the councils. These latter were by that time fully elected, and the councillors were very articulate in debate and discussion of everything that concerned them. I managed in this way to visit all parts of the district and thus got to know it quite well in a short space of time.

I spent four months at this interesting work, and just at the end of this period our second child was born. That was quite an exciting event. Maruku was about fifteen miles out of town. Sylvia had no problems with her pregnancy, and planned to go into the local hospital, have her baby and leave again. The hospital did not cater for Europeans with their supposedly high demands in the way of facilities, and so they were not welcome. This is another hoary fallacy to be demolished — that the colonial governments only provided medical facilities for the officials and their families, and did little or nothing for the local people.

One morning Sylvia woke me with the warning that we had better start getting ready to go into town that day, but that there was no immediate hurry. I was quietly shaving when the situation changed drastically. Sylvia said things were developing fast, and we had better get going at once. I got her into the car and drove into town at a reckless speed, with my wife curled up in agony on the back seat. As we arrived at the hospital, by great good fortune we met one of the nursing sisters who immediately took Sylvia into a room with a bed in it. I went back to the car to get some things, and as I returned to the room some two minutes later, a lusty baby's yell broke on my astonished ears. We had made it in the nick of time. Julian was a bonny nine-pounder. Sylvia walked out of the hospital that same day and went to stay with friends in town. I went back to Maruku to organise our move into Bukoba where we were henceforward to live. Ron Neath, the district commissioner, wanted me as his first district officer, and so I returned to my normal role in district administration.

Before assuming my new duties I wrote my report. My conclusions were brief and succinct. I tend to agree whole-heartedly with the instructions said to have been given by Churchill to persons who had ideas they wished to put to him: "Your views, on one side of foolscap, pray." It is not only great men like Churchill who are not prepared to wade through long rambling assessments, hedged about with "ifs" and "buts" and "perhaps", and so if one wants one's ideas and suggestions to be read and taken seriously, it is as well to be brief and to the point. This is probably why academics as a class make very poor advisers and consultants to working executives and policy-makers who have no time for prevarication and equivocation.

My main conclusion was that the Bahaya were reasonably content with their lot, or at least saw no point in extra effort whose utility in terms of additional income they thought would be slight, or not required. Such an attitude is of course sensible and rational, and accords with the most basic economic prin-ciples. As a concomitant to this, and also in view of another thing I had learned about the Bahaya, namely that they had a sharp intelligence nicely spiced with a touch of both cynicism and scepticism, I said I considered that a social development mounted publicity-cum-propaganda campaign would be a waste of time and effort. All the ballyhoo would simply wash over the Bahaya who would treat it as so much eyewash and something of a joke. My report went in, and nothing further was heard of the matter. Mason never communicated with me again.

It had not been any part of my remit to suggest how the problem of the stagnation of coffee production in Bukoba could be solved, but it was certainly a matter which worried everyone. The growing of robusta coffee had been very strongly encouraged by the British administration after the 1914-18 war, and the Bahaya had responded with enthusiasm, realising that its production was very profitable indeed. They developed the growing of the crop with even more alacrity than the Chagga had taken to growing arabica coffee. It was not grown at the expense of their major food crop, the banana, however. Their care of this crop was exemplary and they grew over twenty varieties, the majority for cooking, and the rest for beer-making. In Usambara we had tried to introduce Haya methods of banana cultivation to the Shambaa but alas with little success, and I often wondered why this was so.

As I have already mentioned, the rapid growth of a strongly cash-oriented economy based on the production and sale of coffee, and the great increase in the value of banana-coffee land, created new strains in Haya society. Dissatisfaction with prices and the dishonesty of traders were ubiquitous and inevitable, and in the nature of things almost insoluble. It was not a result of colonial policy as many have tried to argue. We struggled with the problem and as a move to try to address the major grudge against dishonest traders we introduced marketing co-operatives. This was successful and the Bukoba Native Co-operative Union (BNCU) was formed in 1950. Unfortunately this did not prove to be a final answer to the growers' dissatisfaction, for over time the co-ops themselves became corrupt, after the demise of supervising colonial service co-operative officers at independence. The government of independent Tanzania abolished all co-operatives in 1976 and replaced them by state crop-buying authorities. These in turn proved to be hopelessly inefficient, and in 1982 co-operatives were re-introduced.

Other measures were carried out in Bukoba to try to stimulate increased production. Of major importance was the work of the Maruku research station, linked to a vigorous extension effort mounted by the agriculture department and the BNCU. Large nurseries of new coffee seedlings were maintained from which growers could obtain new stock, and skilled pruning teams were available to assist growers. In short a great deal was done to help the Bahaya improve their coffee. This sort of problem is of tremendous significance at the present day. Agricultural production in independent Africa has not only stagnated, but has also in some countries including Tanzania decreased since the 1970s. Answers to the questions of why the decline has taken place and how it can be halted and reversed are fundamental to African advancement.

IV

Bukoba town where we were henceforward to live until late 1961 is a pleasant place. Situated on the lake-shore, it has an equable climate, though the frequent violent thunderstorms can be frightening. The town is located on a wide bay flanked by headlands to north and south, and there is a large island out in the bay. It is an important lake port, with regular services to the other ports of this great lake. The establishment of shipping services on the lake in 1903 was of critical importance to the Bahaya, for it enabled them to send their coffee across the lake to Kisumu port on the Kenya side, whence it was taken by the Kenya-Uganda railway to Mombasa for export to world markets. There was also a small airfield which in the 1950s was served, like Musoma, by the Caspair round-the-lake service linked to Nairobi.

Bukoba had a club, the first station we had been in with such an institution. There was a club at Moshi but we had no contacts there during our short sojourn. The colonial club figures prominently in the literature of empire, and it has thereby acquired a less than attractive reputation. The conventional image is of a place to which the Europeans retreated to play their games, or just relax, or drink their sorrows and homesickness away, and above all "escape from the natives". As usual, the received image is a travesty of the truth. I speak as one who was never greatly enamoured of club life, and spent little time in clubs. One very common criticism made of the club as an institution is that it was a hot-bed of racism, and did not allow non-whites to be members or even in some cases guests. This is in many ways a misinterpretation. Most clubs were British only, and alien persons of whatever race or colour were not welcomed. My wife who was not born British can testify to this. Her family was not allowed in the Tanga club until well after the war, by which time insular attitudes were beginning to crumble all round. We British tend to be very insular, and place enormous value on what we choose to call privacy. It is not that we despise or feel superior to foreigners or outsiders, but simply that when relaxing we like to do so in familiar company. Even within our own society we have the same behaviour patterns, with our Old Boys Clubs, Regimental Associations, and the like. Nor would you be welcome as an intruder in a Working Men's Club in a northern town. We like to be insiders in our own small circles, and so tend to resent outsiders whom we regard as intruders. It is an attitude which has its good points, but which is terribly open to misunderstanding, and in the colonial context, has been made to look awful.

We were members of the Bukoba club, and played the odd game of tennis and golf, but apart from natural predilections, and a preference for the company of our own family and a small circle of friends, we were too busy raising a young family to have much time to spare for socialising. By 1961 we had three children under the age of five years.

In 1958 the population of Bukoba town was about 3,500, of which a sizeable proportion was of Asian origin and engaged in trade. The European population was almost entirely official. Although still part of Lake Province, and thus under the provincial commissioner at Mwanza, the west lake area was in the process of being hived off as a separate province with its own PC. First it had a resident deputy PC, and then in 1960 it finally became separate and was known as West Lake Province (it is now known as Kagera Region). All the technical branches of government were well represented, and included Agriculture, Education, Forestry, Water Affairs, Survey and Lands, Veterinary, Medical and Prisons. There were two resident magistrates, a revenue officer and a town clerk. Some technical officers tended to harbour vague resentments against the administration whom they were wont to imagine had superiority complexes. I found such attitudes at best pathetic, at worst stupid, but they were facts of life of which we had to take note. A DC or even more so a DO had to tread warily when dealing directly with officers of provincial rank in their own departments. Bukoba was a big station, and the bigger and more important a station was, the more complex the web of human behaviour patterns became. I often longed for the rustic simplicities of Biharamulo, or Musoma.

The district office staff was very strong. Besides the DC, we had five DOs, and a woman administrative assistant. There was also a district assistant, responsible for technical things like roads, buildings, vehicles etc; and a big staff of clerks. We had no magisterial work to do, as the resident magistrates took care of all that. Similarly the revenue officer attended to all treasury matters.

V

Bukoba district was an excellent example of the unfolding in practice of long-standing British policies of colonial development. Cameron's concept of Indirect Rule through existing traditional authorities, which he had introduced in Tanganyika in the 1930s, was never conceived solely as an attempt to maintain the *status quo* or as a cheap way to maintain law and order, and collect taxes. The ultimate purpose was to create sound institutions of local government, as a natural growth from the existing traditional authorities with which people were familiar. It was to be an organic growth. The dynamic core of the policy was given strong impetus after the 1939-45 war when British policy became explicitly concerned with internal political development, towards eventual self-government. In terms of this policy local government was regarded as an ideal training ground and foundation for a later evolution of politics and government at the national level. Progress could not be uniform everywhere since the different parts of a large country like Tanganyika showed tremendous variation in natural resources, state of economic development, and political awareness. It is not the British way to attempt to impose uniformity or a strongly centralized system, and our policy was to coax the people of each district along the road of development, just as fast as they were able and prepared to move. From what I have already written so far about my experiences in four districts, namely Biharamulo, Musoma, Lushoto, and Moshi, the reader will have appreciated something of the nature of the great diversity which existed. Biharamulo was very poor, and the people only just beginning to be interested in education. Musoma was a congeries of different peoples and cultures with widely divergent interests, which created problems in securing agreement on policies and basic aims. Lushoto was bedevilled by traditional conflicts which were hampering development, and which without firm external control would have led to a degeneration into near anarchy and stagnation. Moshi was wealthy with a sound resource base, where traditional and more modern political and economic conflicts showed signs of being resolved in favour of the fostering of common interests, and a very strong local government structure was emerging. The DC in Moshi was an adviser only, and he had to consider very carefully any intervention he might be inclined to want to make.

Bukoba was very similar to Moshi in many ways. Both the Haya and the Chagga peoples had the banana as their staple food crop, though the Chagga also grew a lot of maize. Both had a valuable cash crop in coffee, the robusta variety in Bukoba and arabica in Moshi. Both had welcomed the introduction of co-operative growers associations, and had developed strong institutions in the BNCU and the KNCU. With the wealth derived from coffee both districts had been able to afford to create good social services such as schools, clinics and an extensive road system. Both peoples were divided into a number of separate chiefdoms with strongly entrenched traditional rulers, the *bakama* in Bukoba, and the *wamangi* in Moshi. But, with our guidance and encouragement both peoples were moving away from purely traditional forms of local government under chiefs, sub-chiefs and headmen, and by the late 1950s they had fully adopted a system of democratically elected councils structured on a pyramidal system which culminated in a strong central council body, the Buhaya Council in Bukoba and the Chagga Council in Moshi.

In Bukoba I was intimately involved in the final critical stages of this political development, which formed the background to most of my work there as a district officer and from 1960 as district commissioner.

It is worth examining briefly some of the background to these developments which took place in Bukoba before I arrived there in 1958. I have briefly alluded to the early history of the Haya people and their traditional system of autocratic rule by *hinda bakama*, and I have also mentioned the stirrings of discontent which had already been felt. This latter was to some extent only a surface phenomenon, and there was not yet any powerful groundswell of popular disenchantment with the traditional rulers. In the 1950s the administration set in motion a determined attempt to begin the democratisation of the local government structures. This was very sensible, and was based on the realisation that as education and literacy spread, and with it a greater political awareness, there were enough potent sources of discontent and disruption within Haya society, to lead to serious trouble unless people in general could feel free to discuss these things openly, and find democratic solutions to them. Some of the major problem areas were *inter alia* the Nyarubanja system of land tenure; land matters generally, including the question of female ownership of land; the coffee trade; and the role of traditional cults in society.

The administration proposed to institute popular elections to *gombolola* (sub-chiefdom) and *lukiko* (chiefdom) councils, and introduce an elected element into the Buhaya council. Naturally the *bakama* opposed these moves, and with their great power and influence they were able to orchestrate strong popular opposition. It must be remembered that the bulk of the population were not educated clerks, teachers, traders etc, but were rural conservatives with a very strong attachment to their inherited traditions. In short, a very resistant, strongly entrenched inertia had to be overcome to get things moving. There is nothing so strong as an idea whose time has come however, and by the time I reached Bukoba in 1958 the administration had succeeded in establishing a structure of elected local councils. The *bakama* and *bami* (sub-chiefs) were still however automatically chairmen of the *lukiko* and *gombolola* councils, and in the Buhaya Council the *bakama* were still top dogs, and one of their number was always chairman. The final step to full democracy came in 1961, with new elections, followed by the elevation of commoners to chairmanship of all the councils at every level, including the Buhaya council. I was by then district commissioner, and thus deeply involved in these developments which I will describe in due course.

VI

I became first district officer in Bukoba in April 1959, and subsequently served in the district administration until November 1961. I travelled widely in the district, and soon found that the car we had purchased, though tough and willing, was not really suitable for working safari, especially in the remoter parts of the district where the roads and tracks were rugged. Sylvia also needed a vehicle when I was away up country. We therefore bought another landrover. We had little cash available and so we bought from Sylvia's father an old specimen which after years of arduous estate work was being boarded. For this we paid £75. It was sent up from Tanga by train and lake steamer and duly arrived. It looked very old and battered, but I went to work on it. The only thing I had to replace was a clutch plate, and though it leaked oil through every seal I calculated that it would be cheaper and certainly less time-consuming if I just kept putting oil in, rather than embarking on major dismantling and parts replacement. In fact it gave me two years of sterling service, and though I drove it on the most dreadful roads and tracks, it never once let me down. When we left in 1961 I sold it to a grateful Muhaya for £75.

I used to travel very light in Bukoba, with only my district office *tarishi*, an ex-askari named Johannes. I remember once meeting a United Nations expert with his retinue, in a fairly remote part of Ihangiro chiefdom, at Nshamba. He was a forestry specialist, a Belgian who had worked in the Congo (Zaire) for many years. He was in Tanganyika to carry out a survey for FAO of the timber resources of the territory, and assess future requirements. When we met at Nshamba he expressed great surprise at my mode of travel; battered ancient landrover, no servants, and only one assistant. The conversation went thus:

"You are the district officer, aren't you?"
"Yes."
"Do you always travel on official duty like this?"

"Yes, of course."

"Surely you must have an armed escort, or at least carry a weapon?"

"Good heavens, no, whatever for?"

"Officials in the Congo would not travel like that."

"But this isn't the Congo!" was my only reply.

My *tarishi* Johannes asked me afterwards what the strange European had been arguing about. When I told him what had transpired he was highly amused, and thereafter often repeated the story.

A major task which faced me immediately in 1959 was a very large backlog of local court appeal cases, numbering 167 and growing daily. The Bahaya were top of the league of litigious peoples, measured by the number of cases they sent to the highest court of appeal in the land, which sat in Dar Es Salaam and was presided over by a High Court judge. I had already had experience of their closest rivals for this dubious distinction, the Chagga of Moshi, and the Kuria of North Mara and Musoma, and so I was in some sense prepared for the task which faced me. In hearing these appeal cases in Bukoba I had the invaluable assistance of a written record of Haya Customary Law. This had been produced by Hans Cory, the government sociologist, who had also recorded the laws of some other peoples. This record was in no way a codification, but simply a record of what he had discovered from discussions with *bakama* and elders over a long period. In using this record I came across variations in practice, or arguments on points of interpretation, but it was of enormous usefulness. Almost all the cases I heard concerned land, as had been the case in Moshi, and to a lesser extent in Lushoto.

To set this work in context, I must say something of the Haya system of land holding and their agricultural practices. As I have earlier pointed out, land in most African societies is not generally thought of as being susceptible to private ownership. Tribal authorities, such as chiefs, or elders in less hierarchical societies, were responsible for allocating rights to use land, or to use grazing in pastoral societies. In Bukoba the *hinda bakama* had controlled grazing and had established complex systems of obligation and vassalage through this and the allocation of cattle. As already mentioned, the drastic consequences of the natural calamities which struck these people at the end of the last century turned them from a mainly pastoral economy to one based mainly on the cultivation of the soil. Land became valuable in so far as it could support food crops, especially the banana. Land *per se* was not scarce, since there was plenty of unimproved infertile *rweya* grassland. The only crop which could be grown on most of this land is the bambarra nut, but so poor is the soil, that a twelve-year fallow is required between crops. Better areas could be found, but fertility had to be built up slowly over a period of time. So good land was scarce, and good improved land carrying bananas was doubly so. The pockets of better land became covered with the banana groves that yielded the staple food. These areas became even more valuable once robusta coffee acquired a market value and became a ready source of cash. The permanent nature of the occupancy of these lands created a type of freehold ownership, and the holdings are known as *kibanja* plots, very similar to the Chagga *kihamba*. By mid-century such plots were being openly bought and sold. Quarrels over the inheritance of land, conflicting claims on ownership within families, the often disputed right of women to sell land, the frequently obscure nature of land boundaries, were all common causes of legal action. Since I have mentioned the fact of female ownership of land, some further explanation is necessary, in view of the almost universal belief in the inferior status of women in traditional African society. Haya women do not fit too well the received image. They tend to be very independent. One less commendable result of this was that many of them became prostitutes in towns and cities throughout East Africa. They used to come home with quite large earnings from this profession, and they often invested this in land, their right to do this being eventually legalised by rules promulgated by the Buhaya council. I hasten to add that not all Haya women who travelled were prostitutes. While at Maruku we employed a young woman named Mwamina to help with the children, and she stayed with us for seven years, accompanying us to Morogoro, Mwanza, and finally to Tanga.

To return to land disputes. Nyarubanja was a festering sore, and the root of much litigation. As such it requires more explanation. As I have mentioned earlier, Nyarubanja estates had been created by the *bakama* when cattle ceased to be a potent means of cementing and sustaining a network of political obligations and linkages. The allocation of land became a new means of consolidating and extending their power. These Nyarubanja holdings were very lucrative, for the tenants were obliged to pay tribute to their landlords in the form of produce and also free labour. Over time, as tenants improved their holdings by careful manuring and mulching, and as coffee became an important cash crop, this tenant status became increasingly resented. The British administration made two major attempts before the 1939-45 war to get some sort of order into the system, and remove its worst abuses. District Commissioner Baines in the 1920s tried to get all Nyarubanja tenancies listed and authenticated. This was only partially successful, for though some people obtained their right as freemen to the land they occupied, undoubtedly the *bakama* and their henchmen succeeded in registering as tenants many who were not such. One source of discontent was removed however, with the abolition of tribute in the form of labour. In the late 1930s District Commissioner Fairclough made a further attempt to improve matters. Once again landlords and tenants were registered, and again some tenants secured release from that status, but the system itself remained in being, and basic resentments continued. After the war, the continuing rise in population, and the big increase in coffee prices had the effect of greatly increasing both the demand for improved land, and its value. Against vehement opposition from the landlords, the administration persuaded the Buhaya council to frame new regulations under which the origins of the Nyarubanja tenancies were strictly defined, and means provided for persons denying their tenant status to contest it in the local courts. The landlords organised themselves well in fighting these rules. They sent petitions to the Governor, to the British government, and to the United Nations. They complained that the Tanganyika government was riding roughshod over traditional practices, and thereby causing great distress amongst the Haya people. As late as 1960 I had to write a long defence of our actions, to counter yet another UN petition. After independence the new government abolished Nyarubanja at the stroke of a pen, something we would never have dared to do, partly because of the rumpus it would have caused, but also because of our respect for the rule of law. Ironically a certain type of observer has in subsequent years branded the perpetuation of the Nyarubanja system as a typical example of colonialist support for the oppression of a downtrodden peasantry by a corrupt ruling élite, under the execrable system of Indirect Rule!

The task of trying to cope with the huge backlog of appeal cases was a hard one. It was not something I could do simply by sitting in my office for long hours. I had to get out to the *gombolola* courts where the cases had arisen, and where necessary see and hear witnesses. My earlier rule of always visiting the land at issue had to be abandoned temporarily, unless it seemed to be absolutely essential. In time, once I got the work under control, I was able to resume that practice. The work was mentally tiring. I would go out to a particular *gombolola*, and over a period of two or three days try to hear as many as a dozen cases. I would have the record of the lower courts, usually written in terrible hurried handwriting, and in often bad Swahili. From this I had to get a good grasp of the issues in a case before hearing the appellant. I would then have to decide how much of the original material to re-consider, and which witnesses if any to cross-examine. If there were tricky points of customary law involved, these would have to be discussed by my two assessors. In all this I was under the psychological pressure of dealing with wayward human beings, of trying to recognise liars and false witnesses, and of seeking to disentangle truth from falsehood, and of doing all this as quickly as possible. Total concentration was required to get to the heart of the matter and reach a decision. At the end of a long day I used to feel absolutely exhausted. Sometimes rather peculiar aspects of customary law would come up, and while older people might accept these, quite often younger folk could be very sceptical. One of these was the custom known as *bisisi*. This allows for the relationships between sexual intercourse and childbirth, but leaves the time factor out of consideration. This means that the first child born to a woman, maybe several years after a husband's death or even divorce, is regarded as his son, with all that this entails in terms of inheritance rights. The ramifications of this in quarrels over the inheritance and ownership of land may be imagined. Another but rarer type of case involved religious cults. I remember one or two cases where rights over land were claimed on the grounds that the claimant was of a family who were traditional keepers of a shrine. By extension, claim was also made to the surrounding land for present-day utilitarian purposes, namely the growing of bananas and coffee. It seemed easy to be cynical about such claims, but I found in practice that considerable emotional heat could be generated. I had to be careful, especially as in one or two of such cases my elderly assessors seemed to be uncomfortable, and reluctant to express a clear opinion.

Nyarubanja cases always aroused a lot of local interest. I had to be very circumspect in accepting the record of the lower courts, for the *bami* (sub-chiefs) were of the same class as the landlords, and were often under great local pressure, so that skulduggery was an ever-present possibility. In these cases I was often in the same position as I had been at Buhemba in Musoma, when Van Maltitz's pigs had got into the local's maize *shamba* — both sides thought I might favour the other. Solomon's simple if drastic remedy was seldom possible. Key evidence in these cases was documentary, a piece of paper signed by Baines or Fairclough who had wrestled with Nyarubanja in the past. Quite often these documents were faded, torn, and falling apart, but their value was great to the owner thereof. If the person producing such a document was not its original owner however, but claimed to be an heir, then the question of the legitimacy of such a claim had to be thrashed out. Nyarubanja cases were never simple. Valuable ownership rights were at issue, and the landlords were often wealthy men of substance. I think it was an unspoken or implicit testimony to the incorruptibility of the administration that I was never offered a bribe, nor was pressure of any sort ever brought to bear to try to influence my decision. We were trusted, of that there is no shadow of doubt. Sometimes however, that trust could be betrayed in minor and less tangible ways. It was easy to feel impatient, and one of my predecessors clearly found this work irritating and time-consuming. He got into the habit of writing very cryptic judgements such as "*Nakataa rufaa hii*" or "*Nakubali rufaa hii*" meaning simply "I refuse this appeal" or "I allow this appeal". This was extremely unwise and simply sowed the seeds of further trouble. I sometimes had to reap the harvest by having to go over such cases again to satisfy some poor baffled fellow who didn't know what to make of such brief pronouncements and thought he had in some way been cheated.

So far as district court work went, we were fortunate in having two resident magistrates who handled all the work. Needless to say they were kept very busy. One onerous task did arise for us from time to time, however. Where the death penalty had been passed on any person, an appeal to the Governor for clemency could be permitted. Usually the file in such a case would come to the DC with a request for background information, and an indication of local sentiment. I once had to deal with one such case in the Bugabo chiefdom. I requested the *mwami* of the area to arrange for a public meeting at the village of the convicted man, and along I went on the day appointed. The man had killed his father after a quarrel about money, and there appeared to be mitigating circumstances in that a fight of some sort had occurred. When I arrived at the village I was surprised to find a large crowd gathered and it did not take long for me to realise that they were in an ugly mood. I briefly explained the purpose of my visit, but much of what I said was drowned in shouting, and cries of *"Wacha upuzi, anyongwe huyu"* — "Stop this foolishness, he must hang". They had somehow got the notion into their heads that I had come to tell them that the murderer was to be spared. Eventually I succeeded in soothing their savage breasts, and I made sure they understood that I was simply seeking their opinion or feeling in the matter, and this they were expressing very clearly. Very obviously they thought the killing of a father by his son was a most heinous offence for which there was only one punishment. I did not linger there. It had been a most unpleasant experience, and I have seldom seen such mass vehemence. It was almost palpable, and very disturbing.

All district officers at all times had to deal with a multitude of unofficial disputes and complaints. We were well staffed in Bukoba so that the load was shared, and the DC himself could usually avoid much of it as he had a secretary to hide behind. The corridors of the district office were never empty, and out on safari there was never a shortage of petitioners of one sort or another. One or two individuals were regular visitors, and some made a business of acting as intermediary, bringing complaints on behalf of other people, or acting as a mouthpiece for a "client". One such was Ali Migeyo who had been a thorn in the flesh of district officers since the 1930s. One DO, something of a wit, had nicknamed him "Ali Matata", a sort of *nom de guerre* as he put it, for *matata* in Swahili means "trouble". In my time he was quite an old man, but he still had plenty of fire in his belly.

He was willing to take up the cudgels on anyone's behalf, and was totally impervious to any form of rational argument. Since it was seldom possible to agree with what he wanted, his visits would often end in a stream of invective about rotten colonialists and all their damnable works. I found him rather entertaining, and because I was always prepared to give him a hearing, I became his favourite whipping post. I like to think that we eventually developed a sort of grudging respect for each other. When TANU came on the scene, Ali was naturally an early member, and became a leading light locally in the organisation. He was not really literate however, and he was old, so that the young men of the movement didn't have a lot of time for him. His ultimate fate I suppose, was that of all old soldiers, though I wouldn't be surprised if he became in time the subject of a popular myth, a Robin Hood of the Bahaya.

One notable festering dispute occupied the administration over a long period of time, and was very resistant to solution. It involved the local Muslim community. I was not deeply involved before I became DC, as Ron Neath dealt with the matter himself. Two factions were concerned with the relative importance of the *adhuhuri* and *ijumaa* prayers at the local mosque. From what I could gather, the *adhuhuri* or full prayer was favoured by the conservatives who were strong in the rural areas, and the *ijumaa* by the more progressive element who were dominant in the town of Bukoba itself. Inevitably Ali Migeyo was involved, and helped to keep things on the boil. Unfortunately the dispute did boil over into physical violence in which the police had to intervene on a number of occasions. Neath tried to organise a final solution by getting the two parties to agree to his inviting the chief *khadi* of Zanzibar, a noted authority on Muslim law, to come to Bukoba to arbitrate the dispute. This learned man came and listened, and as the days of his visit went by, he became visibly more dismayed and disenchanted looking. He eventually departed, leaving behind him a ruling which laid down under which circumstances either prayer rite should take precedence. Needless to say, after a brief spell of peace, the quarrel began again, this time over the correct interpretation of the *khadi's* ruling. I suspect, that as with my Somali friends in Moshi, the dispute was in reality a form of entertainment, a continuing source of excitement and diversion. The affair finally landed in my lap when I became DC myself. I was desperately busy at the time, with many important matters in the final year leading up to independence, and I decided to give the Muslims short shrift. I summoned all the elders to a meeting in my office, and got them all seated round a large table. I then told them that I had no intention of listening to them since we had done this endlessly in the past. I further reminded them that we had obtained learned advice from a leading lawyer of their faith, but his ruling also they had chosen to ignore. I then simply told them that any more trouble in the form of physical violence and disturbing the peace would not be tolerated, and would be sternly dealt with. I then dismissed them. The meeting had taken fifteen minutes. A period of relative peace followed, but I am sure that they must to this day still be in dispute, with the ghost now of Ali Matata still stirring the pot.

VII

The second major task which fell to my lot as the senior DO, was to supervise the operations of the Buhaya council treasury, or the *buhanika* as they called it. Supervise is probably the wrong word to use in this context, as my work was much more in the nature of being advisory, though I did function as an auditor. The treasury was a large and wealthy one, and was partly decentralized in that each *lukiko* (chiefdom council) had its own subordinate treasury. The *lukikos* in turn had sub-treasuries at the *gombolola* (sub-chiefdom) level, which were mainly revenue collecting points. Revenues were derived from a graduated local poll tax, court fees, school fees, beer licences, market fees etc. Recurrent expenditure included a very large salaries bill, for everyone from the *bakama* down to the lowliest messenger; upkeep of buildings and roads; maintenance of vehicles; minor public works; debt servicing, and much else. Capital expenditure included new building works, schools, courts, offices, new roads and bridges, new vehicles such as cars, lorries, road graders, and again much else. Large items of capital expenditure could attract loan finance from the central government, which maintained a fund for the express purpose of assisting native authorities and district councils.

Regular auditing of *gombolola* accounts was carried out by DOs on safari. The *lukiko* councils were mainly my responsibility, whilst the central treasury at Rwamishenye was my major concern. On the accounts of the latter I carried out a regular monthly check with the treasurer. The latter was a very competent and dedicated man named Anatoli Rugabandzibwa. The work we did was not a sort of paternalistic inspection, as the Bahaya were well past that stage of development. What we were involved in was a partnership in a co-operative educational and training operation.

One notable development in the control of the treasury which we successfully introduced was a system of internal audit. A small group of good experienced treasury clerks were selected and trained in regular simple checking of *gombolola* and *lukiko* records of revenue collection, expenditure vouchers, and ledgers. They then toured the district on this work. It was not an easy task for these people. They were to some extent resented, and had to face pressures and resist temptations that a district officer as an outsider never had to face as he inspected accounts. On the whole, however, the system worked well, though one totally unlooked-for outcome was a strike of council employees which was almost certainly initiated and organised by a small politically motivated group within the internal audit cadre. Being peripatetic they were able to advertise and spread their cause fairly effectively. The envy and petty intrigue common to rural small-scale society anywhere, and certainly well-developed in rural Africa — and beautifully summed up in the Swahili word *fitina* — together with the close network of mutual obligation within the extended family, inevitably makes for trouble when transferred into modern administrative and executive structures. Such things are at the root of much of the petty corruption which bedevils African bureaucracies at the present day. It was certainly beginning to be a problem in Bukoba, and the creation of a system of viable checks and balances was a major concern.

The financial affairs of the council were guided by its finance committee of which I was an *ex-officio* member, though present in a purely advisory capacity. The days were long past when the DC or his representative could dictate to the council or its committees what they should or should not do. In my work with the finance committee I would tactfully point out that perhaps a certain course of action or some proposed expenditure might be unwise, or might possibly be in contravention of some central government policy. Anything I said had to be fully supported by reasoned explanation, and long argument or discussion over most matters was normal. The members of the finance committee were not simple unsophisticated peasants, but were canny men of the world. Some of them were successful traders and businessmen, while others had long experience in the co-operative movement. Most of them spoke good English, but business was always conducted in Swahili. Sometimes when an argument got heated they would lapse into their vernacular Luhaya, when I would have to gently point out that I could not follow the thread of the discussion in that language. I remember one of the co-operative officers in Bukoba who was a Welshman, telling me that once he was at a co-operative society meeting where the committee members persisted in using Luhaya which he could not follow. He quietly sat through the discussion until they wanted some advice from him, whereupon he replied in Welsh. He made his point, and thereafter Swahili was used. I had no such stratagem to fall back on, though I doubt if my Haya colleagues would have understood Lancashire dialect had I chosen to use it. In any case the situation arose but rarely.

A major financial task each year was the preparation of the

annual estimates of revenue and expenditure. This was a lengthy and time-consuming business. It began with discussions in the *gombolola* councils who decided what they wanted in the way of new schools, clinics, roads, staff etc. These requests were then filtered through the *lukiko* councils who cut out a lot of requests, weighed the needs of the subordinate *gombololas*, and eventually presented a consolidated proposal for the whole chiefdom. The central treasury staff framed draft estimates on the basis of all the information available to them, and these then went to the Finance Committee. The draft would include very tentative proposals for increased taxation or for loan finance. The finance committee considered this draft at length, and took into consideration not only what could or could not be afforded. They also had to try to balance what the various parts of the district were to get, and a good deal of lading and teeming was involved in this process. The committee men knew they had to be careful, for the final proposals had to go before the full council where they would be examined very carefully and debated at length. The process was typical of democratic local government procedures anywhere. In this process again my role was purely advisory. The whole business in Bukoba was a far cry from Biharamulo, just 120 miles to the south, where the DC, with the treasurer in attendance, carried out the whole exercise himself, down to the last detail such as calculating exactly which council employees were due for salary increments, or how much to allocate for the purchase of new stationery. The DC had to do the job until such time as the council had the staff and the competence to take on the work itself. Between these two extremes of Bukoba and Biharamulo were other district authorities at various intermediate stages of progress towards the almost total responsibility for their own affairs that the Haya had achieved.

A major item of expenditure during my time in Bukoba was for a brand new council headquarters. This comprised a council chamber, with attached committee rooms, and new suites of offices for the secretarial and treasury staffs. The Bahaya were very conscious of their position as one of the most advanced peoples of the country, and they intended that the new headquarters should reflect this. A large firm of architects with branches in Nairobi, Kampala and Dar Es Salaam were commissioned to work out the design, and the building contract was awarded to the Italian Construction Company of Dar Es Salaam. An enormous amount of discussion in finance and executive committees went into the design, and the young supervising architect, a Mr. Walsingham, who came up regularly, was kept on his toes by the councillors. Frequent requests to change this or that had the man on the verge of breakdown on a number of occasions, and I felt very sympathetic towards him. When the main building was almost complete, a councillor named Munseri broached the idea of adding a high clock tower to the complex. This had never been considered in earlier discussions, but it was taken up with enthusiasm. Vainly I pointed out that it would be very expensive and would serve no useful purpose. At this I was rebuked by Munseri who reminded me that "a thing of beauty is a joy forever". This elegant tower, this vertical component standing on top of Rwamishenye hill would be a visible mark of Haya pride in their achievements. There was no stopping it. The tower was designed and built at great extra expense, and indeed it did look very splendid. The whole complex of new buildings when complete was most impressive and satisfying. The council chamber must rival or even outclass that of many a national assembly. It is panelled throughout in beautifully grained wood, with large zebra-skin covered insets around the upper walls. The seating for the councillors is arranged in a wide semi-circle facing a raised dais on which the *bakama* are to sit. Below the dais are tables and facilities for the supporting administrative staff. At a higher level above the main doors is a large visitors' gallery. The lobby outside is spacious and again beautifully panelled, with high polished solid timber doors giving access to the chamber. The whole concept speaks of a dignified pride, and there is nothing cheap, nasty and brash about it at all. I am very gratified to have played a part in its achievement. The official opening was a lavish affair. Nyerere was invited and came. He looked thoughtful, as well he might.

Haya self-confidence received another fillip in 1960 when one of their number, Laurian Rugambwa, became the first African cardinal of the Roman Catholic Church, a historic event of some significance. Rugambwa was a product of the White Fathers diocese of the west lake area. He had been trained for the priesthood, and showing great intellectual promise, he had been sent off to Rome for long periods of study and training. He was a most impressive looking man, tall, very handsome, with a powerful well-cut face, and he carried an air of natural authority. At the same time he was very gentle, and very easy of approach. When he returned to Bukoba as a cardinal, the reception he was given was tremendous, huge numbers of people crowding into the town to attend a big open air welcoming ceremony at the largest open space the town could muster. It was not only Roman Catholics who came, but people of every religious persuasion. The government joined in of course, and both the PC and the DC were at the airfield to greet the cardinal as he stepped from his plane. A large official reception took place in the evening. There are now other African cardinals, but to the Bahaya, in the natural order of things, the very first was one of their own.

VIII

The two houses we occupied whilst in Bukoba were both close to the lake-shore, and the second, which was the official DC'S quarter had a situation which was superb, right on the back edge of the beach. The interest of this position was not only aesthetic, however. There were many hippo in the lake and they used to come out at night and wander around foraging for food. They made gardening something of a risk, for they were partial to any fresh and tender thing they could find, and once removed in a night a crop of carnations we had been carefully nurturing.

Shooting hippo was strictly forbidden, and they had free access to the town at night, when they were often to be seen in the lights of car headlamps. By unwritten law they had right of way. Sometimes they would come out on the beach in the daytime, and we often watched Mackie, our collie, chase them back into the water. He used to circle them as if they were sheep, and then get them moving. They didn't know what to make of this, and generally set off at a gallop along the sands with Mackie in full pursuit. It is amazing how fast such a large ungainly beast can move, and they used to hit the water without slowing down, with a tremendous smack and vast clouds of spray. It was also a pleasure to sit out having tea or a beer later in the evening, and watch a family of hippo disporting themselves in the water just offshore. My mother once wrote from England clearly worried after we had described the antics of our hippo. She hoped they would not gobble up one or other of the children as they played on the beach. We reassured her that this was extremely unlikely.

Living near the lake was not however all undiluted pleasure. I have already mentioned the high incidence of severe storms along the lake coast. Oddly enough, these were almost always in the small hours of the morning or just before dawn, and not as conventional wisdom would have it regarding equatorial weather, in the late afternoon. They were not however, conventional storms, but must have been associated with a sharp temperature gradient that built up between cool land and still warm lake at night. Huge whirling waterspouts were not an uncommon sight out on the lake in the early morning light. Sometimes these small concentrated storm centres came ashore and did a lot of damage before dying out. I have seen clear-cut swathes of destruction cut like roads through the banana plantations by these tempests.

A real pest associated with the lake, was the lake-fly. This is a tiny flying insect, actually what the entomologist calls a chironomid midge. The larvae live in the mud on the lake-bed, and then the pupae rise to the surface and the insects emerge in huge dense clouds like smoke. Tales were told of fishermen being caught in these and suffocating to death. The clouds of midges used to drift inland on the wind and come to rest in the foliage of trees, in mosquito gauze on windows, or inside houses if they found an opening. There they quickly died to leave a smell as of dead fish which would hang around for several days. Some people used to collect them from the trees and pound them into a sort of cake for cooking and eating.

While on the subject of edible insects I must mention the termite ant which emerges as part of its life cycle as a flying insect occurring in large swarms. This creature has a fat body about an inch long which the Haya regard as a great delicacy, as did several Europeans whom I knew. These insects are known by the Haya as *nsenene*. They are usually eaten lightly fried, but they can also be dried and stored. Whenever the *nsenene* appeared in Buhaya, all work ceased and the whole population turned out to collect them. I once had to postpone a council by-election in Bugabo because nobody turned up to vote. The *nsenene* had appeared.

There were plenty of fish in the lake, but though there were Haya fishermen, they were not so active as the Luo, say on the eastern side of the lake. The best fish for eating is the tilapia which is delicious, and we used to buy them on the beach at three for a shilling. Neither meat nor milk was plentiful in Bukoba so we welcomed the fish. The local fishermen used long seine purse nets which they set out from the land. Their method was to paddle out in canoes to set the net well out from shore, and then bring back the lines. After an interval they would then haul in the seine purse to the shore, which was a long and arduous task. They usually did this at night, and as they worked they chanted. A single drum would tap out the rhythm of both the song and the work which it measured and paced. It was a pleasing sound to hear above the ceaseless lapping of the waves which formed the endless background to our lives there. At full moon we would sit out on the stoep to watch the shadowy forms of the men at work. Sometimes, however, the romantic element palled, especially when a fractious child could not sleep, and one's nerves were on edge. All we longed for then was blissful silence.

Another large expanse of watery wilderness was up-country in the swamps of the Ngono river. Here were extensive marshlands with masses of papyrus reeds and other aquatic plants, which extended after heavy rains. A huge population of water birds of every sort and description congregated there, and a small group of enthusiasts used to go out very early on Sunday mornings to try their luck at potting a few geese or ducks. We had to wade out to small islands to use these as vantage points, and as we had no dogs and had to retrieve our own birds, we used to get soaked to the skin. It was good fun however, and the environment was surpassingly beautiful, a luxuriant mosaic of greens, blues, greys, and whites of every conceivable shade and tone, all sparkling fresh in the early morning sunlight.

IX

Eventually the time came when we could think of taking some local leave. I was keen on some more mountaineering, and Mount Kenya, by then free at last from Mau Mau dissidents, was a big attraction. My situation was now very different. I had a wife and small children to consider, which apart from anything else, made any risk to life and limb more than a purely personal concern. Clearly I could not just go off for a month and leave the family. We compromised. I would spent two weeks on Mount Kenya, with a promise not to do anything unduly risky, and then I would join my family at Sylvia's parents' house on the coast at Tanga, where they were by then retired.

I had no great ambitions on Mount Kenya, but simply wanted to wander around it, and if possible reach its summit peaks, by a known route. I had no specific companions available, and so wrote to the Kenya Mountain Club in Nairobi to see if they could put me in touch with someone planning a trip to the mountain. They very kindly put me in touch with a party who very obligingly said I would be welcome to join them. We were a mixed party, a forester, a geologist, a demographer, a missionary doctor, and myself. We met at Nanyuki at the foot of the mountain and right on the equator. From Raymond Hook, a local farmer, we hired mules to carry our gear up the mountain. His farm was more like a zoo than a farm. He had successfully crossed zebras and donkeys, and bred a variety of wild cats which he tamed and sold as pets.

Mount Kenya is a long extinct volcano. It is much older than Kilimanjaro which still has residual volcanic activity in its inner crater in the form of fumaroles or steam vents. Kenya's central peak area is surrounded by very extensive rolling plateau-like country resembling the Shira plateau of Kilimanjaro, but much bigger. This moorland zone has a number of delightful small lakes or tarns on its surface. It is also dissected by a number of deep glaciated valleys which give access to the upper alpine zone of bare rock, snow and ice. The apex of the mountain is a superb rock peak which has twin summits known as Batiaan and Nelion, named after two Masai leaders or *laibanani* of the nineteenth century. This peak is in fact the plug or filled vent of the ancient volcano, which has longest resisted erosion.

A number of rocky ridges splay out from this central peak area, and on these are found a number of subsidiary summits, such as Point Piggott, Point John, and Point Lenana. Some small residual glaciers remain on the main peak, while below it lies the still quite large Lewis glacier. The first ascent of the main peak was made in 1899 by the British geographer Sir Halford Mackinder with two Swiss professional mountaineers. Since then many routes of varying degrees of difficulty have been climbed and recorded.

Our route of ascent through the forest zone and across the moorlands was gradual and very pleasant, for there was a well-worn path rather like the one of the tourist route on Kilimanjaro. As the mules were carrying all our gear we could loiter and enjoy the magnificent scenery. My companions were also anything but spartan, and the food supply was plentiful. Compared with what I was used to on mountains it was positively exotic, with such things as tinned spring chicken to titillate our palates.

Once we had reached the alpine zone, our first serious outing was to make a complete circumambulation of the central peak area. There were no technical climbing problems involved in this, but it was a long hard day. It was clear and sunny and we had splendid views of this truly magnificent mass of rock and ice. We then went on to the Firmin hut by the side of the Lewis glacier. From there the doctor and I made an ascent of the twin main peaks. We crossed the Lewis glacier, and climbed to the crest of one of the subsidiary ridges. From there we climbed a massive buttress and then traversed right across a very exposed face. This was not technically too difficult, and it led us into a shallow gully which we followed up to the summit. It was a clear day, warm and sunny, but there were great masses of cumulus clouds drifting around which cast enormous shadows over the landscape below us, which stretched out to infinite horizons all around. We spent about half an hour on top and then began the descent. One advantage of descending steep rock, is that one can do this very speedily by abseiling or rappelling, that is sliding down a doubled rope. In no time at all we were back at the hut after an excellent day's climbing.

Our next venture was to make an attempt on the south face of the main peaks. We walked to the foot and made a bivouac amongst some gigantic moraine debris. That same day we reconnoitred the route up the lower glacier, and cut steps to save time the next day. Unfortunately I felt awful, and the sound of flying debris from above didn't improve my mood. I went down, and not long afterwards the other two followed me. The attempt was off and I was not sorry. Two days later we went down off the mountain. En route we met a party going up, one of whose members, we were to learn later, was killed in a fall while climbing the main peak.

I had enjoyed the trip, and had climbed the central peaks of the mountain, but I felt under a cloud throughout the expedition in some way hard to define. Trying to rationalise this I have come up with a number of reasons. The trip had no specific objectives, no new route to tackle, and therefore we lacked a sharp cutting edge which the easy approach and exotic food further blunted. My family responsibilities discouraged risk, and I was nervous on that account. More distressing still, a climber was killed on the mountain just after we had left, and I have often wondered if one can pre-sense tragedy. Most real and tangible however, I was far from fit. I know now that this was due to bilharzia or schistosomiasis. I had been swimming regularly in the lake, and had almost certainly augmented the population of parasitic worms I had picked up from the same source in my Musoma days.

Once off the mountain I motored down to Moshi where Sylvia and the children had been staying with the Veits at Machare up on Kilimanjaro. We went on down to Tanga for an idyllic ten days by the Indian Ocean. I then had to get back to work, but the family stayed on for a while longer. I split my journey at Arusha, but then motored non-stop to Bukoba via Nairobi and Kampala, a 650-mile stretch. Much of the journey was overnight and I shall never forget the section from Eldoret high up on the Kenya plateau downhill to Tororo on the Uganda border. There was a tremendous electrical storm raging over Uganda which went on for hours, and I was driving down towards it. The whole horizon before me was continuously alive with lightning which illuminated towering cumulo-nimbus storm clouds. A distant drum-roll of thunder was continuous background music. This was nature at her most dramatic, and to me, sitting alone in my car, it seemed like a private performance. I sat back in my car, and just rolled slowly downhill, absolutely spellbound. I hit the rainbelt beyond

Tororo, and thereafter drove through a continuous light mist as
the rain evaporated immediately off the warm road. But for the
continuous lightning I would have had to stop, for the mist simply reflected back the light of my headlamps.

X

It was not long after our return from this leave that I was
saddled with a responsibility that I was neither expecting nor felt
entirely prepared for. Ron Neath was moved up to a secretariat
job in Dar Es Salaam, and I was appointed district commissioner
in his place. Bukoba was near the top of the half dozen or so
most important districts in the territory, and I was a fairly junior
district officer on my third tour. The task seemed daunting but
there was naught else to do but get on with it.

It was shortly after this promotion that our third child was
born. As I pointed out earlier, the hospital did not welcome
Europeans (Julian had been an emergency) so Sylvia had her
baby at home. Justin was born at 9.45 am in the middle of one
of our storms, with the wind shrieking round the house, waves
crashing on the beach, and thunder rolling around. David
Brooke, the medical officer, got to us just in time, and an-
nouncing the birth of a bonny bouncing boy asked what he was
to be named. "Justin" I replied, to which the medical wit retorted, "As far as I'm concerned, he's justout." Later that day
friends came round to see mother and child, and they brought
some champagne. They insisted Sylvia have some, which she
did, being partial to the stuff. She then fed Justin, who thereafter
relapsed into such a deep slumber that we began to get worried.
He eventually came round, apparently none the worse from what
we supposed was a bout of secondary inebriation. He has never
looked back since.

In tackling the task of DC, I was very fortunate in having five
excellent DOs to share the burden. David Connelly was first
district officer, and took over the Buhaya treasury work, while

Ken Ranyard, Humphrey Taylor, Alfred Njunde and Ian Plant shared the other work. Ian Plant came as a brand new district officer (cadet) in the year immediately preceding independence, so his career was short. I'm sure it was sweet, for he got married whilst in Bukoba.

One thing I found very quickly was that as DC, I got precious little chance to get out into the district myself. My presence was required at committees on this or that; the Buhaya council took up a lot of time; the PC was always wanting information on what the Bahaya were up to; and all sorts of people just had to see me on some matter of desperate importance to them. I had an excellent secretary in the person of Mab Sutton, wife of the town clerk, and she was an excellent filter, shielding me from petitioners whom she guessed I would find unwelcome. These she steered to one of the DOs. Sitting in my office I often heard her tell someone that the DC was out, and I wondered what would happen if someone had just peeped round the door to check. I used to walk to the office, so there was no tell-tale car standing outside to confound my deceitful but very understanding secretary.

Unable to get out much myself, I did introduce a new procedure. This was a systematic monthly programme of DO visits to *lukikos* and *gombololas* throughout the district. A consolidated programme of touring involving all DOs was drawn up and circulated each month. Each DO knew where he would be going and when, and the officials out in the district knew whom to expect. This could be and indeed was criticised as a late imposition of close direct administration, but I did not view it at all like that. Our task was educational in the broadest sense. All the local administrative officials were learning their jobs by doing them. A learning process functions best when there is an assistant or instructor on hand and readily available to lend help and advice. Mistakes and wrong directions can be checked in time. I firmly believed we were partners in development, and as DC I was able for a short spell of time to put my ideas into practice. It worked and was appreciated, but we were rapidly overtaken by events.

Obviously politics, both local and national, occupied a good deal of my thinking and my time. TANU was strong in Bukoba. Its activities were inevitably closely intertwined with local Haya politics which had deep roots in the past, and these affected the party machinery. The old guard of local politics fought a rearguard action against the young men who saw their chance for early advancement in the national movement. Ali Migeyo with his long history of bloody-minded intransigence was an obvious candidate for party leadership. But Ali was a "one-off" personality, a rugged individualist who didn't fit easily anybody's concept of party unity and discipline. The old guard who in their youth had been firebrands, had mellowed somewhat and many had worked hard within the framework of evolving local political institutions which we had created in Buhaya. Some were valued councillors, or committee men in the BNCU.

Some of the new wave men acquired an exaggerated sense of their own importance and could be rather pompous. They could be either amusing or irritating depending on the situation in which one crossed swords. If they blocked an important initiative they could be a great nuisance. On two occasions I remember the pomposity of one of them being delightfully pricked. It was in each case at a provincial team meeting, attended by all DCs, provincial technical officers, and invited politicians. On one occasion one of the latter was berating us, saying we knew nothing of hunger and starvation (there were no starving Bahaya, and the gentleman in question was very fat). One of the DCs retorted, "My dear fellow, I have been very near starvation on several occasions." (He had been in the Burma jungles during the war.) The second occasion was even better. One of the politicians, annoyed at some remark by a DC, exploded, "Sir, you are a relic of outworn British imperialism." The reply came at once in a patient drawl, "You know, Sir, I have been yearning for years for someone to call me just that."

In 1961 we were in the period of so-called Responsible Government, as a prelude to full Independence which came in December of that year. Nyerere was Prime Minister. One of my major tasks in this period was to supervise new elections to the Buhaya council, and to the lower level *lukiko* and *gombolola* councils. This was no mean undertaking. The run-up to these elections was a worrying time. The young guard in TANU really got the bit between their teeth, and were dead set on winning control of the whole local government structure of Buhaya. This created stresses which I have already hinted at. I suggested to the PC, Ted Martin, that incipient trouble might be circumvented if certain innovative preliminaries to the elections could be agreed and acted upon. I pointed out that any realistic view of events indicated that TANU was on the crest of a wave and was going to win all the seats on the councils. I then referred to the local stresses within TANU and suggested that the party might organise a sort of preliminary election to choose its candidates, thus letting the voice of the people, and not just the party caucus, be heard. The PC forwarded my ideas to the Chief Secretary of the government in Dar Es Salaam. The reply came back that the Prime Minister (Nyerere) wondered if the DC of Bukoba was proposing what approximated to the mechanisms of a one-party state where the single party chose its candidates for simple approval of the people. The note of heavy sarcasm was unmistakable. It is interesting to note in retrospect that in due course TANU did introduce the one-party state, and the party did introduce the practice of more than one TANU candidate standing for election, as a means of trying to democratise the process of elections within a single party system.

Fortunately the elections of 1961 passed off peacefully, and my worst fears proved to have been unfounded. The young enthusiasts of TANU won power as expected, and at the first Buhaya council meeting after the election, the Bukoba branch party secretary Samwel Luangisa was elected chairman. The *bakama* were unceremoniously demoted, their surface power now very much atrophied. As district commissioner I also stepped down, and joined the council officials below the dais. I was asked by some people if I felt this as ignominious or a loss of face. My answer was a clear negative. This was surely the fruition of years of grinding toil by my predecessors, to reach the goal of fully representative and democratic strong local government.

I was able to strike up an excellent working relationship with Luangisa, as I had already in full measure with the long standing Buhaya council secretary, Sospater Zahoro, an absolutely first-class person and excellent administrator by any standard.

My advice and assistance were continually sought, and the council's business continued to be conducted with good sense and decorum. The main policy-making body of the council was its executive committee, on which the *bakama* retained representation. This met regularly in its sumptuous quarters in the new building, and I attended all its meetings in an *ex-officio* capacity. This could be very tedious and time-consuming. I was used to such meetings, of course, having attended all the finance committee meetings for two years, and before that in other districts countless council meetings of one sort or another. Africans tend to be very unpunctual, something which they will admit to being conscious of, though many young men of my acquaintance are beginning to talk of "African time", a peculiarly negative defence to a fair criticism. Executive committee meetings were always scheduled to start at 9 am but we rarely got a quorum before 11 am. Thereafter however, the meeting would go on without a break often until well into the evening. Agendas were long, and discussion generally detailed and tedious. Africans again do not like division, so that the device of voting is unpopular and rarely resorted to. The alternative is to carry on a discussion until some form of consensus is reached, often from pure exhaustion. By this means nobody loses face, and all are responsible for the consequences of any decision. This is in many ways a wise way of proceeding — if time is of no consequence, as indeed is the case in a pre-industrial society. My patience and good humour were further tried by the fact that in Bukoba I suffered from acute hay fever. Sitting through endless meetings with a thick head, streaming nose and smarting eyes was very trying.

There was one exception to the generally smooth and tolerant ingress to the council of many new, young, and potentially impetuous councillors. A number of them had an ingrained suspicion that the council administration was corrupt, that financial affairs were conducted in the interests of a small influential minority, and that "brotherisation" was rife. This term of "brotherisation" was very much in vogue, and was used to mean the appointment and promotion of family members and friends of important officials. A small committee of new councillors was formed to look into this matter, and was charged with uncovering such malpractices. Very wisely the administration gave the committee every assistance in its work. In spite of diligent burrowing, nothing of substance was brought to light, and the impetus of the drive slowly petered out.

Finance was a very large issue, and the first estimates prepared after the election gave rise to a lot of discussion and heartsearching. Naturally the new men wanted to spend money on local services to demonstrate their concern for development and to prove their new power and influence. New brooms want to sweep clean the world over. This enthusiasm had to be bridled and steered into constructive channels — no easy task. I wrote a long paper for the council which set out some simple and basic economic principles, sketched the state of development in Buhaya at that time, and warned of their excessive dependence on coffee whose price was falling, while production was stagnant. I drummed in the fact that they could only spend what they then had available, that future needs had to be carefully assessed, and that whatever they planned to spend in future would have to be raised by new taxation. The paper was given wide circulation, and certainly had a sobering effect. The budget which was finally approved was in general a sensible one.

In 1961 we were visited by both Nyerere and his principal lieutenant Rashidi Kawawa in their official capacities. All was sweetness and light, at least on the surface, and it certainly was with the administration. I suspect however that Nyerere was uncomfortable in places like Bukoba or Moshi, where there was a very strong sense of local identity, and where the development of strong local government institutions was far advanced. Both were to demonstrate plenty of evidence of this in the years following independence. It is worth noting that new elections were held in 1963, two years after independence, and independent candidates won control of the council, with TANU men swept aside. Clearly the Bahaya had emerged as a people with a strong faith in democratic principles, and with a determination to apply them. However, the TANU controlled central government could not tolerate independent opposition, and it dissolved the council. A similar pattern of events unfolded in Moshi. Finally in 1969 the government swept away all local councils in a drive towards total and rigid centralization.

If only we had had the time to establish in all districts throughout the country the sort of strong institutions we had fostered in Bukoba and Moshi, before full national independence was granted, subsequent history might have been very different. Unfortunately we lacked both the political will and faith in our policies, and so abdicated. The consequences at the present day are deplorable.

Independence was set for 9th December 1961, but we departed on leave before that date. The Buhaya council gave us a great send-off. A big party was organised one evening, and I was publicly thanked for the work I had been able to do with them. They draped me in a huge traditional bark-cloth blanket as a token of respect and thanks — we still have this as a treasured possession. Lots of group photographs were taken with the committees and officials, and a very good time was had by all.

We were not sorry to be leaving before Independence Day, for

I had no desire to see the Union Jack lowered. There was no trace of chauvinism in my attitude. I simply felt that we were irresponsibly abdicating from an unfinished job. Even Nyerere had not originally envisaged getting independence before the early 1970s. In any case we had no intention of leaving Tanganyika, and we returned after our leave in early 1962. We stayed on until 1969 as I will describe. And as I write this in 1987, we are still working in Africa.

PART 2
Expatriate Teacher

Akufaaye kwa dhiki, ndiye rafiki.
(He who stands by you in time of need, he is truly a friend.)

Swahili Proverb

Chapter Six

Transition

He either fears his fate too much,
Or his deserts are small,
That dares not put it to the touch,
To gain or lose it all.

*Montrose, **My Dear and Only Love***

I

Our leave in late 1961 to early 1962 was a winter one. Enjoying the cold weather we anxiously awaited news from Tanganyika of what was going to happen to us. There were some vital questions on our minds to which we needed answers urgently. Would I be kept on as a district commissioner, or would I be pensioned off and have to start searching for a new career elsewhere? In fact we heard nothing, and simply returned to Tanganyika after our leave to try to find out there what our lot was to be in the immediate future. A visit to the secretariat in Dar Es Salaam was frustrating. Nobody seemed to be very sure about anything. A lot of people had left while others were preparing to leave, so that someone returning from leave and eager for work was rather an anomaly. We stayed at a hotel in town. It was there that we witnessed an amusing scene, a delightful example of the sort of transitional state we were all in. We were having a drink in the bar one evening preparatory to going in for dinner, when a young man without tie or jacket strolled in and joined a group of people who were sitting chatting and drinking at a table. I think most people who were in the bar recognised the newcomer as Oscar Kambona, one of Nyerere's principal henchmen, and a minister in the new government. Unfortunately the maitre d'hotel, a large immaculately dressed Swiss gentleman, did not recognise him and, accosting him in a less than wholly courteous manner, requested him to leave as he was improperly dressed. Kambona laughed rather sardonically and stayed where he was. His accoster, seemingly oblivious of the hush that had descended on the hitherto noisy scene, persisted in his request. The barman's eyes were almost popping out. As it happened, a gentleman who was a leading light in the Dar Es Salaam establishment was present, and he broke the tension. He strolled up to Kambona, and said with a loud laugh, "Oscar, my dear chap, let me lend you a tie". He also whispered something meaningful into the ear of the hotel official, who paled a little, and quickly left the scene. If he had not done so he would almost certainly have earned for himself a one-way ticket out of the country.

Eventually we were informed that we were to go to Morogoro district where I was to take over from Tony Lee, who was leaving the service. Morogoro was just 120 miles due west of Dar Es Salaam so we would not have far to travel. We arranged for our stored effects and car to be sent to us from Bukoba, and we set off for our new station. In fact we knew from rumour and more substantial clues, that British DCs and DOs were due for replacement by TANU appointees in the not-too distant future, so that our stay in Morogoro was likely to be short. Nevertheless we moved up there, and went through the motions of taking over the district, as though nothing had changed. Morogoro district is large, about 1,450 square miles in extent, with a population in 1961 of about 280,000 people. The township was quite large too, with a population of about 25,000. In many ways the district is similar to Lushoto, including as it does a large area of mountains, the Ulugurus. It had been the scene in the 1950s of the Uluguru Development Scheme, which as I pointed out in Chapter 4, was less than successful and was abandoned early. Serious erosion and land degradation were continuing problems.

I was to be DC there for just three months, eventually handing over to a very junior DO, Stephen Sandford, who would have as his immediate superior in my place an area commissioner. The titles "district" and "provincial" were abandoned, and replaced by "area" and "region", and the posts to which they referred taken over by local political appointees who were TANU party officials. As it happened, the new regional commissioner of the eastern region, resident in Morogoro, was none other than Selemani Kitundu, an old friend from Musoma, now quite high in the TANU hierarchy. He greeted me in a very friendly fashion, but was obviously slightly embarrassed as I had known him in his less elevated earlier life as a fisherman and trader. I deferred naturally to his now senior rank, and we had no problems.

Even when the new policy of replacing us with political appointees had been announced, no immediate order to move came. The whole changeover was carried out in a very relaxed and leisurely manner. Doubts as to our future were eventually dispelled by a personal letter from Nyerere, which I still have. It seems he addressed similar letters to a number of DOs and DCs. In these letters he praised our work in the past, and informed us that our services were still urgently required in the fledgling state, though not in district administration which had to be politicised. He begged us to stay and work in the country and offered us employment in such roles as resident magistrates, as senior administrators in the ministries in Dar Es Salaam, or as most of us were graduates, as teachers in the expanding school system. I chose the latter, as offering the best opportunity for a new and permanent career in life, and certainly as the most interesting. Permanent work as a magistrate, or pushing paper in a Dar Es Salaam ministry did not appeal to me at all. I communicated my decision to the government, and awaited events. It took several weeks before any order to move came, and in the meantime I carried on as DC of Morogoro, in a sort of peculiar limbo.

During this period of waiting I did have one interesting task to perform. The new government was confident that it had the enthusiastic support of the populace at large, as indeed it did, and it was decided to enlist this in a great drive to step up agricultural productivity. DCs were instructed to tour their districts and at meetings with the people record their considered targets for increased cultivation and crop production. It seemed a rather naive operation, but it was not for me to question it, and as far as I was concerned it offered a splendid opportunity to get out on a long tour of the district, which I gratefully seized. The weather was wet and cold, and the roads quagmires in which we got bogged down on several occasions, but I enjoyed it immensely, and by and large we achieved our purpose. That was my last safari as a district commissioner, and I must admit to having felt pangs of regret as it ended. These didn't last for long as I eagerly looked forward to the challenge of a new career and adapting to our new status in life.

The end of my first career perhaps should have been traumatic, but in fact it wasn't. I had reached a stage in that career when I would have been burdened henceforward with endless paperwork, committees, and the necessity to behave generally in a manner befitting the Queen's representative in a chunk of her imperial possessions. I remembered Jim Rowe's complaints of the burdens of office when I had appeared before him as a young, fresh district officer cadet back in 1951, and I was not enamoured. I had enjoyed tremendously my years as a district officer, and my brief spell as a district commissioner, and for these I was very grateful, but I was not sorry at the prospect of a change. In the event my expectations of my new career were to be satisfied in great abundance.

II

Finally our move came. We were to proceed to Mwanza on Lake Victoria, and join the staff of the Bwiru Boys' Secondary School. We loaded our longsuffering Vanguard car with as much as we could pack on to the roof rack and into the boot, and three adults, Sylvia, Mwamina, and myself, with the three children, and Mackie our collie, squeezed inside. We decided to take an adventurous route and see more of the country. This took us down to Dodoma, then on to Singida where we stayed in an empty house, one of the many there. Most British officials had left, and the place had a depressing atmosphere, with once well-tended gardens looking wild and unkempt. From Singida we crossed the Wembere steppe by a rough bush track, no road having yet been built at that time. From Shinyanga we were on gravel road again, and we went on to Mwanza.

It was dark when we reached the town after a long and very tiring journey. It was also pouring with rain. Murphy's law held good and just outside the town we got a puncture. I got soaked to the skin changing the wheel. When we finally reached the school which was quite a way beyond the town, we found that nobody was expecting us, so that we had to go back into town to try to find lodging somewhere. It was hard to be cheerful but we survived.

At Bwiru we had to camp for a while in a tiny house until something larger became available, so it was some time before we could unpack our belongings which had come from Morogoro. I was given teaching responsibilities in Geography and English. As the school only taught up to Cambridge Overseas O level, the work was in no way arduous, and so I had an easy breaking-in to my new profession. The staff was mixed, with local, British and American teachers. By great good fortune I was not the only ex-district officer on the staff. The other was John Cleverley who had also opted to stay on in Tanganyika as a teacher. He was older than me, and had gone through the war as a fighter pilot, and had flown Spitfires in support of Tito's partisans in Yugoslavia. He had an interest in rock climbing, and together we explored our surroundings, which offered plenty of sport. The school was located amongst a series of rocky granite hills, which made the place very picturesque, especially as the lake lay below us in full view. Here there were problems galore for the rock enthusiast, and we thoroughly enjoyed ourselves until one day disaster struck. We were trying to climb a large granite face, the lower part of which was unfortunately holdless. About twelve feet up however, there was a small ledge, and this I tried to reach by the technique of rushing at the face, and placing my right foot against it to catapult myself forward and upward. As I did this I felt a severe blow on my ankle. I thought perhaps a snake had struck me, but as I twisted into a sitting position on the ledge I noticed that my right foot was hanging limply and felt very numb. Somehow I got down and we took off my boot. The problem was revealed as a ruptured achilles tendon. With John's help I got off the hill and was taken to the Mwanza hospital where Mr. Patel the surgeon stitched up the tendon. For the next six weeks my leg was in plaster, with knee and ankle tensed at an angle. I was given a pair of crutches designed for a dwarf, and so could only hobble around with difficulty.

1962 was proving to be a less than auspicious year. Sylvia in particular was unhappy in Mwanza, especially as her mother was very ill at the time. I also felt unsettled, and so I requested a transfer to Tanga, with Sylvia's mother's sickness as a reason. I got a non-committal reply, and so we decided to cross our Rubicon. In the Christmas vacation we packed up and moved, lock, stock and barrel to Tanga.

We drove south to Tabora where we stayed with the Ranyards who had been with us in Bukoba. From there we did some cross-country travelling to reach Babati on the Arusha-Dodoma road. Here we spent a few days with Sylvia's brother Klaus who was farming in the Kiru valley. He had taken a lease on a parcel of land that was part of a large area that had been cleared for large-scale cultivation by the Germans pre-1914, but then later abandoned to revert to bush and infestation by the tse-tse fly. In the late 1950s the British administration had decided to reopen the land which the local people did not seem to be interested in. The object was to drive back the tse-tse and bring potentially productive land into cultivation. Klaus had been employed in the sisal-growing industry, but wanting to set up farming on his own account, he had applied for and been granted a lease. He had driven up from Tanga with a tractor and trailer laden with his worldly goods, and had moved on to the totally bush-covered land, where he set up camp. He didn't have long to wait before local people came asking for work, and he was able to build up a small labour force with which he started to clear the land. He allowed each man to build a house and cultivate his own plot. The land teemed with buffalo, and by hunting and shooting these Klaus was able to keep his men well supplied with fresh meat. He had no labour problems. This was tough pioneering in the old style. Within a year they had cleared enough land to plant and harvest a crop of maize, and to begin planting permanent crops such as coffee and paw paw. A small house with mud-brick walls and a corrugated iron roof was built and round it a garden with flowers and vegetables flourished. It was here that we stayed on our journey to Tanga. The situation was magnificent, tucked up against the huge wall of the Rift Valley, and about thirty miles south of Lake Manyara.

From Kiru we carried on to Tanga where we stayed with Sylvia's parents in their small retirement house down the coast on Mwambani Bay. I set about the task of getting a post in one of the two government secondary schools in Tanga, and first went to see George Hornsby, the headmaster of the Tanga Boys School. He was something of an eccentric extrovert and greeted me brusquely with the questions "Who are you?", and "What do you want?" I told him and as soon as he heard I was an ex-district officer he exclaimed, "I'll have you, leave it to me." Next day he went to Dar Es Salaam and into the Ministry of Education to demand my posting to his school. As he wasn't the man to take no for an answer, the matter was agreed forthwith. I was posted to the Tanga School. Our gamble had paid off, and to Hornsby we are eternally grateful. We spent six very absorbing years in Tanga, leaving reluctantly in 1969 to return to the UK.

Chapter Seven

Tanga

With scents of coral where the tide recedes,
With thunderous echoes on deserted strands.

Grimble, *A Pattern of Islands*

I

Tanga lies in latitude 5° south on the East African coast, almost equidistant between Mombasa in Kenya to the north, and Dar Es Salaam to the south. It is Tanzania's second port and for years handled the bulk of the country's main export crop of sisal, whose major growing area lies in its hinterland. Its population in 1967 was just over 61,000. Of Arab-Swahili origin, the town had been developed by the Germans as the railhead and port for the potentially rich agricultural region of the Usambara and Pare mountains, and the Kilimanjaro-Meru massifs to the north. They had pushed a railway line as far as Moshi and Arusha.

The township of Tanga lies on the south side of a wide bay which is the outlet to the sea of two rivers, the Sigi and the Mkulumuzi. In the middle of the inner bay is an island with the lugubrious name of Toten (meaning "the dead" in German), given to it because it was used as a cemetery in the past. The far north side of the bay has extensive mangrove swamps alternating with low raised coral cliffs and wide sandy stretches. Quite large areas of low-lying swampy ground inland of the coast made the area very malarious in the past, until the Royal Navy during the last war put in an efficient drainage system which greatly reduced the breeding grounds of the Anopheles mosquito. The

186

outer bay is protected by a screen of fringing coral reefs, either awash at high tide, like Fungu Nyama reef, or elevated well-vegetated islands such as Yambe and Kerenge. To the south and north are other bays, Mwambani and Manza respectively, but they do not offer such good sheltered anchorages as does Tanga Bay.

The East African coast generally is a region of enormous fascination, and the Tanzanian part of it has not yet been despoiled by badly planned and poorly controlled mass tourism as it has in Kenya to the north. Its history is a long and rich one, for the region has had links with other parts of the world from the earliest times. As early as the first century AD a Greek work, *The Peryplus of the Erythrean Sea* was produced as a pilot's manual for the coast, and it was in this that the name of Azania was first used, a name rather improperly taken over now by South African black nationalists for their country. From across the Indian Ocean trading ships came from Arabia, the Persian Gulf, India and China. They utilised the seasonal alternation of the monsoonal winds, from the north-east in winter to bring the ships, and from the south-west in summer to take them back. This traffic continued into modern times, and while we lived in Tanga we loved to go and see the big dhows which had been beached for careening and maintenance, a most romantic sight.

The Arabs were the most significant of the peoples who came to this coast. They established important trading settlements and towns, such as Mombasa in Kenya, and Kilwa Kivinje in Tanzania. From the contact of the Bantu vernacular languages of the coast and Arabic emerged the Swahili language, a rich and flexible tongue with an extensive literature of prose and poetry, much of it, alas, still in the Arabic script. Much later an Arab dynasty from Oman on the Arabian peninsula established itself on Zanzibar island, and from there extended its rule over the mainland coast, with trading routes extending far into the interior, to the highlands of present-day Zimbabwe, the Great Lakes of the Rift Valley, and to Lake Victoria and the headstreams of the Nile, a truly vast area.

In the sixteenth century came the first Europeans in the guise of the Portuguese, whose daring mariners came round the Cape of Good Hope and up the coast, to establish a hegemony over the whole Indian Ocean trading region. They in turn built their trading posts and forts, the most magnificent example still extant being Fort Jesus at Mombasa, still proudly standing after three centuries' severe wear and tear from war and climate. The Portuguese faded in their turn, and were overcome by the resurgence of Arab power and enterprise coming from Oman. Finally in the late nineteenth century came the Germans and the British to establish control over the whole coast and far into the distant interior.

The rich fabric of history is all about one on the coast, not yet having been submerged and crushed by a modern uniformity of life-style and culture. Islam and the Swahili language create a powerful cultural inertia and give a sort of unity to the great variety of peoples, a variety daily visible in the great range of physiognomies and colours of the people around one. In many ways the past intrudes. In my research work along the coast (of which more later) I often found fragments of Indian and Chinese porcelain, and on Kerenge island off the coast I found ancient Arab tombs hidden in thick, almost impenetrable bush. The annual visit of the big Arab dhows seemed to us like history reaching into the present, as indeed it was.

In the 1960s when we lived there, Tanga town was a thriving town and a busy seaport. The peoples of the coastal villages to the north and south were very attractive folk, in that they displayed, and probably still do, a remarkable degree of what could be called cultural integrity. Solidly Muslim and Swahili speaking, they are very conservative, and seem satisfied with their distinctive way of life. Such people tend to be branded by the eager, development-oriented person as sluggish and backward. A book on Tanganyika published in 1962 described them unkindly and pompously as "poor and sapped in vitality by the heat". Though seasonal drought can be marked, rainfall is generally good. The coconut grows well and yields nutritious food, and the fruit when it has been dried can be sold for cash. Cassava grows well under the coconut palms, and milk cows can be raised successfully. The sea is an unfailing source of protein-rich food. Not too much effort is required to live a comfortable life, with time available for such civilised pursuits as sitting in the shade gossiping with one's neighbours. Local crafts are well-maintained; the fishing canoes or *ngalawas* for example are locally made and maintained in a way which cannot have changed for ages. Society is by and large open, and outsiders who are Muslims do not find acceptance difficult. Our house servant Ramadhani, an Mluguru who came with us from Morogoro to Tanga, settled down at Mwambani when we left and is still there, a real Mswahili now.

II

When we first arrived in Tanga we lived with Sylvia's parents who had built a small retirement bungalow at Mwambani, six miles down the coast from Tanga town. It lay just back from the beach above a low coral cliff, and around it they had planted a fine lawn and masses of colourful bougainvillea bushes. At the back was room for a small vegetable garden and chicken-run. A borehole yielded reasonable water. All around were the coconut groves of the local people who were very friendly and showed no resentment at this foreign intrusion into their midst. Their *ngalawas* were daily drawn up on the beach in front of the house. The only drawback to this was when they careened their boats by burning shark oil under them, for this had a rather unpleasant smell. In front of the house lay the wide expanse of Mwambani Bay defined at its oceanward edge by the coral islands of Yambe and Kerenge, and a connecting submerged reef. The breaking surf could be seen as a long white line along the horizon, and its low distant roar, carried on the wind, was a continuous background sound. The inner bay was shallow, and large expanses of sand and mud were exposed at low spring tides. This was a magical place where we spent many happy hours, and to our children, now grown up, it remains a cherished memory of a childhood paradise.

Once I had joined the staff of Tanga school I could apply for government quarters, and we were very fortunate to be allocated a house with a fine situation on Ras Kazone, a headland jutting out into Tanga bay and marking roughly the divide between the inner harbour and the outer more open sea. The sight and sound of the sea was the background to our lives, and from our front stoep we could watch the big ships coming and going, and hear the deep throb of their engines. This was our home for the six years we spent in Tanga. It was two miles out of town, and I purchased a bicycle to get me to and from school daily.

Tanga school where I taught for two years was probably the oldest secondary school in the country, having been founded by the Germans in 1892. It was right in the centre of the town and had no space for games etc. It was also very hot and noisy, and eventually in 1966 a new school was built to replace it on a pleasant site outside of the town. The old school where I taught consisted of an imposing main building which was double storeyed and was occupied by the administrative offices and some classrooms. Flanking this was a line of single storey classrooms which opened on to a central space, part of which had been used for newer buildings such as laboratories and craft rooms. On the far side were the dormitories, kitchens and dining room. All the buildings were completely innocent of any form of modern air conditioning. Protection from the tropical heat and humidity was afforded by thick walls with large openings, shaded by long overhanging eaves. In wet and windy weather this situation was not ideal, but the bother we had then was the lesser of two evils.

The staff of the school were a mixture as at Bwiru, of local

My wife Sylvia with the peak of Kibo in the background.

Philippa, Julian and Justin with Kilimanjaro in the distance.

Sunday morning market scene in Lushoto township.

Masai cattle crossing Ruvu river, January 1955.

The south face of Kibo, Mount Kilimanjaro.

View from high up on Shira Plateau, Kilimanjaro; Mount Meru in the distance.

On the Uhuru peak of Kibo, after making the first ascent of the Heim glacier. From left to right: Ax Nelson, author, David Goodall.

The central peaks of Mount Kenya at dawn. We climbed the face lit by the sun.

Central Kalahari landscape in summer, with rainstorm approaching.

The inner crater of Lengai.

Bushman child in central Kalahari, with model of wheeled vehicle. He must have been very intelligent to conceive and build this model, as he can have seen very few vehicles in his young life.

Rock outcrop, Makgadikgadi - a natural Stonehenge.

On Sua Pan, with Kokonje Island in the distance. Note the clothing on a cold winter day.

Some members of our cave exploration team, Tanga Caves.

Stalactite formations in Drotsky's cave, Gcwihabe hills.

Massive sinter flow formations in Tanga cave.

Tanganyikans, British, and American teachers. They were all enthusiastic and competent, and good colleagues. Our headmaster George Hornsby was a British eccentric and he sometimes puzzled the Americans. He could be rather abrasive at times, and his rendering of Peace Corps as Piss Cops didn't exactly endear him to some of them. Some of the Americans also had problems of adjustment. One of them told me that before leaving the USA he and his colleagues had been indoctrinated with the idea that they were going out to save Tanganyika from the depredations of years of British colonial misrule. He was led to imagine from all this something akin to a Central American banana republic. On arrival, what should they find but as he put it, an efficiently run, clean, peaceful country full of cheerful happy people. This was a surprise to which he and others were still adjusting. A black American colleague had real problems arising from the fact that though black-skinned like the locals, his culture, language and habits were the same as his white compatriots. One day after he had a slight accident in town, he expressed exasperation, saying half jokingly, "You know, John, the best thing your great-great-grandpa ever did was to get my great-great-grandpa out of this goddam place."

Our students were all Africans, since this had always been an African school. They came from all over the Tanga region, and also from further afield. We were primarily a boarding school, so that there were few day boys. This meant that the staff had boarding duties in addition to teaching responsibilities, but these were by no means onerous. The boys were mainly Shambaa, Pare, Chagga, Bondei, Zigua, but all spoke fluent Swahili, because of British language policy in education. Its universal use in Tanganyika sprang from a vital decision made in the department of education in the 1920s, that Swahili should be the sole language of instruction in the primary schools, and English in the secondary schools. In Kenya and Uganda the vernaculars were used, with divisive consequences which are still very much alive. Our students' English was also good. It was the language of instruction in the secondary schools, but I was able to mix both languages in my teaching where I thought it to be appropriate and convenient. Hornsby did not like this, and bluntly pointed out that the school was not a forum to demonstrate my fluency in Swahili, but a place where the students' fluency in English had to be cultivated by every means. He also discouraged the boys from speaking Swahili or their own vernaculars when in school. This was probably a wise and sensible requirement in education terms. Hornsby himself spoke fluent Swahili.

We taught to Cambridge Overseas O level and as at Bwiru my responsibilities were in Geography and English. The former was no problem, and I enjoyed trying to communicate my own enthusiasm for places and peoples to the boys. In English I was given classes in English literature, and this also I thoroughly liked. Youngsters from a mainly oral culture, unspoiled by television, and even in those days by radio, showed an eager liking for, and appreciation of, literature. Shakespeare's plays were greatly appreciated once the initial unfamiliarity with the language was overcome. All was grist to the mill. Chaucer was popular too, though we had to read him in translation into modern English. A book which never failed to excite was Orwell's *Animal Farm*. The allegory of this cautionary tale went right home to boys from politically active backgrounds at the tribal and village level. I remember with pleasure many lively class discussions of character and human behaviour revealed in the books we studied together.

My new career was not proving a problem at all, and I soon realised that the decision to launch myself into a career in education had been a sound one. In the twenty-five years that have elapsed since those early days I have had no cause to change that opinion. The profession of teaching is not alas, highly regarded generally at the present day in western society, and particularly in Britain, though it still is in more traditional and less "advanced" cultures. I remember once in Tanga having to give a pep talk to a young British graduate teacher who was just finishing a two-year contract, and was going home without much enthusiasm for his future. He said he could not understand why or how I could have chosen to take up teaching as my new profession after my earlier "more elevated" (as he put it) profession. I tried to explain my thoughts on the matter, which were rapidly developing at that time. The gist of these was that teaching in reality is a profession where one wields enormous power and influence. This lies in the wide-open opportunity one has to guide and mould young malleable minds at their most impressionable stage of development. This should be an inspiring challenge, but so often it is not seen in this light at all. I have often been asked how I stand the "sheer boredom" of teaching "the same thing" to fractious juveniles and adolescents year in year out. This is such a narrow view. Good teachers change and modify their material continuously, both to keep pace with developments in their discipline, and to adapt it to the particular group or class which is being taught. More important however, is the fact that the objects of one's efforts are, being human, infinitely variable and a continuously shifting challenge. It is a sobering but not unpleasant thought, near the end of a period of many years spent in teaching at various levels, that many hundreds of people out there in the world are remembering one directly in many of the things they are doing, or are acting and behaving according to ideas and precepts one planted as seeds or embryos in their minds long ago.

My young friend brightened up somewhat after our talk together, and seemed more hopeful about his future. I hope he stayed in teaching for he was a personable young man who was capable of a major impact.

Late in 1964 Hornsby was transferred from the Tanga School to the much bigger Karimjee School, which was also in Tanga. Shortly afterwards he engineered my transfer there also. This large school had been built by the wealthy Indian community. The Karimjee family with large interests in sisal and in commerce generally, were the major benefactors, a fact recognised in their name being given to the school. It was constructed to a high standard, doubled storeyed with big roomy classrooms, excellent science laboratories, adequate staff facilities, and a large assembly hall. It catered for well over one thousand pupils. Originally intended solely for the Indian community, it had been opened to all race groups after independence, and was eventually absorbed into the state system completely. In due course pettyminded chauvinism had its way, and its title was changed to Usagara school, Usagara being an old name for the Tanga region. The school was organised on the British pattern, and taught to Cambridge Overseas O and A levels. A large sixth form catered for the A level work. Most of the pupils lived in Tanga, but the sixth form drew pupils from all over the country, and a boarding house was located in the old Park Hotel in town, which had been purchased and modified for this purpose.

I now had a much heavier teaching load, and was responsible for Geography teaching throughout the school. I had two assistants to share this task, but nevertheless there wasn't much spare time left each day, and I said good-bye to the pleasant and relaxing task of sharing the delights of English literature with my students.

The Karimjee school was a fascinating place, if for no other reason than its quite remarkable racial composition. We were Africans, Arabs, Americans, Europeans, Indians, and even one or two Chinese. Morning assembly was to me a most impressive affair. Hornsby ran it on the British pattern, and the central event each morning was the recital in unison of the school prayer. This requested God's blessing on ourselves, our school, and the nation. There we were, Christians of several denominations, Muslims likewise of varied persuasions, Hindus, Sikhs, and others of no specific religion, and black, white, brown, and yellow in colour, all praying to a common God. I often used to glance around during this performance, to see examples of the various groups, eyes tightly closed and clearly deeply concerned with what they were doing. There was never any comment I know of, nor certainly any protest against this practice, and I found it a very moving and encouraging daily ritual. I do not recall, either, any examples of racial or religious animosity during my years at the school, though instances of gentle leg-pulling were not uncommon. I remember when the Chinese and Indians were squabbling about their common frontier in the Himalayas, and the Indians were getting rather the worst of the encounter, overhearing a Chinese boy taunting an Indian. He was saying, "Indian soldiers with British officers were very good, but look at them now." Which was a far more subtle remark than simply boasting of Chinese prowess. On another occasion I remember a very pugnacious Punjabi on our staff, lecturing some bewildered American colleagues. The Americans at that time were making some gaff on the international scene, and our Punjabi was telling his US colleagues that really the American government ought to send its diplomats to London for some decent British training.

I had not been long at the Karimjee school when an event occurred that reminded me of my changed status in life. I was quietly cycling to school early one morning when I was stopped by a TANU Youth League member who demanded to see my bicycle licence disc. The Town Council were carrying out a widespread check on licence avoidance of varying types, and had enlisted the TYL to assist. I had no licence. I tried to get around this embarrassing difficulty by arguing that I had to get to school, and was being unnecessarily delayed, but to no avail. I tried feigned anger, pleaded, cajoled, but it was no use. Had I pretended not to understand my young friend, I am sure I could have got away with it, but seeing that I spoke his language he took the opportunity to lecture me, and berated me for my sins. I had to abandon my bicycle and walk to school. I was cross at first but then on reflection amused; the high and mighty district commissioner of yore had indeed come tumbling down from his pedestal, not with a bang or even a whimper, but with a gentle thud. As later in the day I queued up to pay my licence fee and retrieve my bicycle, I mused on the intriguing ironies of life.

III

During this time secondary education in Tanganyika was being expanded very rapidly, and the Dar Es Salaam campus of the University of East Africa was also developing. Large numbers of expatriate teachers were being recruited, mainly from Britain and the USA to make this possible. I hope that one day their vital contribution to Tanganyika and the other East African countries will be properly acknowledged.

The British administration has been subjected to considerable criticism for its alleged lack of attention to educational development during the colonial period. Much is ignored by such critics who seldom think very deeply about the basic problems which were faced by the colonial governments when they took over large slices of African territory, and began the task of turning them into the embryo nation states which eventually fledged themselves as independent nations in the second half of this century. There was no system of education in the territory which ultimately became Tanganyika and later Tanzania. In the Muslim areas of the coast there would be Koranic schools, while in the interior each tribe or group would have its own system of initiation into the culture, history, and practices of the society. There were many tribal groups each with its own language, and there was no lingua franca to give a common means of communication. Swahili was only used along the main trade routes into the interior. Nor was there any organised system of administration or communications, nor a unified economy, all of which are the necessary foundation for an organised system of public education.

To set about creating a full system of education from primary school to secondary, and on to university in such a situation was a formidable and long-term task. The British took over Tanganyika in 1918, and in the forty-two years to 1960 a system of education using the common languages of Swahili and English was established successfully to the point where the crowning element of a national university could be created. The Germans had laid the foundations of this great endeavour by setting up the very first schools and spreading the use of the Swahili language.

It is instructive and salutary to list some of the stages which were necessary in this long process. Firstly, local teachers able to teach in the tribal vernaculars had to be identified and trained. There were no expatriates fluent in these languages, very few of which had been recorded and written down. The recruiting and training of these first indigenous teachers must have been a difficult task requiring vision, patience and dedication. The language difficulty would have been formidable, but also in those days education was not valued by the people at large. In areas like Biharamulo as I have described, as late as 1951 education was only just beginning to be valued and sought after, and that only for boys.

Those first indigenous teachers were the seed from which a large crop of primary teachers were in time produced. In time from them, and from the product of their efforts came the secondary teachers and so on. This process of its very nature had to be slow. It could not outpace the steady development of society, economy and polity which was taking place: the spread of communications, the establishment of a common system of law and administration, the growth of a cash-oriented economy, and with all this the slow realisation by the mass of the people of the nature of modern material culture, and the necessity of education to make its attainment by the many possible. That all this was achieved in less than half a century is amazing, but is seldom acknowledged.

Another major criticism is that our education system produced an élite educated according to western European standards. It is true that much attention was paid in Tanganyika to the education of the sons of chiefs. But secondary education had to be started somehow, and the sons of the traditional rulers were obvious early choices, and readily identified and captured. In time secondary education was provided for pupils from all strata of society. This process was able to accelerate after independence because the foundations had been well and truly laid.

The British administration did tackle very actively the problem of creating an educational system capable of inculcating many of the skills needed in the rural environment in which the vast majority of the people lived. This was based on what was called the Middle School. These were developed in all districts. The curriculum included a large element of material relevant to rural life, and all such schools had large agricultural plots where the students could learn and practise better agricultural methods. The most academically inclined pupils who showed aptitude for more advanced studies were identified to go on to secondary school. Criticism was inevitable and came in full flood, the most frequent one being "You are distinguishing between African and European education". Of course the problem of preparing young people of varying abilities and aptitudes for life and work at all levels of society is well-nigh insoluble and is not a product of colonial government, nor is it limited to developing countries. Our inheritors face the same problem and are being no more successful in solving it. Once education is seen to be the key to wealth, influence, status, comfort and escape from the grinding monotony and drudgery which is often associated with rural life, then everybody wants it. All parents want their offspring to have the chance of following the golden route from primary to secondary school, and if possible to university, and so on to wealth and status. Even in our western society, only now are we perhaps beginning to see a possible end to this intractable problem, which can only come when everyone, scholar, craftsman, artisan, labourer, executive manager, or whoever, can earn enough with or without a higher education, to live a comfortable secure life, with all the trappings of material culture available to all who want them.

Nyerere, wearing his idealist hat, tried after independence to counter élitism in the educational system by having posted in every school for all to see and read, a quotation from one of his speeches. In this he compared those young people fortunate enough to be enjoying a secondary education, with the young men of a famine-stricken village. The community pooled their remaining food supplies and gave them to the young men so that they would have sufficient strength to journey afar in search of food and help which they could then bring back for the relief of the whole community. He went on to say that if those young men simply took the food, and used it to secure their own survival, without thought for their people, then they were abject traitors. The analogy with school students was then drawn. They had to use the education which society was giving them, not merely to further their own careers, but to enable them to work for the good of the whole community. I knew many fine dedicated young people who really took this parable to heart, but alas there were many more who did not, and they were the majority. One of Nyerere's biggest mistakes has been to believe naively that idealism and altruism alone can inspire and drive common humanity. One must at the same time acknowledge his own genuine sincerity, honesty and incorruptibility.

As a school teacher I was no longer in direct touch with political affairs, at local or national level, and can comment therefore only in very general terms as an ordinary person on the receiving end of the results of political decision making after 1962. The initial years of independence were undoubtedly a period of widespread national enthusiasm, and the new government was able to use this to accelerate the strong forward momentum already imparted to the country by the colonial experience. The civil service still worked with reasonable efficiency, and was still able to cope with the level of activity required of it. Education was expanding rapidly, and the co-operative movement created by us on a sound footing was enthusiastically encouraged by the government. Shops and stores in town and village were still well-stocked, and people could afford to buy. In the districts the removal of the traditional chiefs, and the disappearance of impartial dedicated district officers was creating problems for the common man. This I learned from local people I knew well and communicated with, especially in the Usambaras, my old bailiwick. The redress of minor grievances felt by ordinary people was becoming difficult, a small but significant cloud on the horizon.

The first major crack in the fabric of the new order came with the army mutiny in 1964. People were stunned and frightened. Events in the Congo were fairly fresh in people's minds. Nyerere and his major henchmen, with the exception of Kambona, did not behave as leaders should behave in such circumstances, and in fact Nyerere cravenly fled into hiding. TANU was quite unable as a supposed mass party of the people to overcome the soldiers by the sheer weight of organised popular feeling. If a British force had not been providentially in the area, and able to step in and restore order quickly and with minimum fuss, there is no knowing what might have happened. It was a very worrying time, and I doubt if Nyerere has ever recovered from the shock and humiliation.

Eventually in 1967 came the Arusha Declaration, Nyerere's blueprint for a people's socialism. It marks a great turning point in Tanzania's post-independence history. The State was to take control of what his proliferating radical advisers called "the commanding heights of the economy". Banks, industries, the wholesale and retail distribution systems were to be taken over and run by the state. Private ownership of property was out of favour, and individual enterprise was discouraged. Hailed as a blueprint for popular mass progress when it appeared, many of the policies and actions which it engendered have served to gravely hinder economic development, and since the early 1970s the country has suffered progressively worsening economic and social conditions. The effects of this did not begin to be fully felt until after we had left the country in 1969, and I do not wish to comment further on these matters at this point. Suffice it to say that on successive visits back to Tanzania since 1969, we have seen ample evidence of decline, and of frustration and disappointment on the part of the common people. The evidence of our eyes has been confirmed by the comments of friends, both African and European.

In the decade of the 1960s however, all this was in the future, and by and large that decade was a happy one, and Tanzania was an exhilarating and satisfying environment in which to live and work. One still felt as one did in colonial days, that one was building a new nation.

IV

One advantage of the teaching profession which became apparent to us was that it gave time for other activities in the school vacations. In 1963 we used the long vacation to good effect. I still hankered after the mountains, and so we planned a trip up north to stay with Klaus on the farm. My plan was to leave the family happily ensconced on the farm, while I made an attempt on the ascent of Oldoinyo Lengai, an active volcano in the Rift Valley south of Lake Natron. I was in touch with Ax Nelson again, and we planned the expedition together. My initial problem was how to get fit and to test my leg which had not had any hard usage since my achilles tendon had been stitched up. Once we had settled on the farm I embarked on a drastic programme of exercise. I rose early each morning, and climbed the rift wall by a narrow track, carrying a rucksack filled with heavy rocks. After a week of this with no untoward effects, I put phase two of my plan into action. This involved climbing a mountain called Hanang, about thirty miles to the south. This is a fine mountain rising to over 11,000 feet (3,400 m), and is an extinct volcano which stands proudly alone to the west of the Rift Valley. It is off the beaten track and little known, and few people have ever climbed it.

I left the farm very early one morning and drove to Katesh where there is a local authority headquarters. I introduced myself to the clerk there and asked if there was anyone around who knew the approaches to the mountain, and who would like to accompany me on an ascent. A young man wrapped in a coloured blanket volunteered and off we set. He knew the area well, and under his guidance we negotiated the car over ever narrowing and steepening tracks until it was prudent to go no further. We then set off up a prominent ridge and made good time. After about an hour of forcing our way through dense and often thorny bush we emerged on to a slope covered with short grass and herbs, with bare rock appearing here and there. This was very pleasant going. My companion spoke just enough Swahili to enable us to converse with reasonable ease, and as the slope was not too steep, we chatted as we climbed. When he learned that I was a teacher my friend was quietly impressed. But he was a courteous and self-contained person and accepted without comment my explanation of why I liked climbing mountains. It was a warm and rather hazy day and much of the distant view was obscured, but as on all the great East African isolated volcanic peaks, the sense of infinite open space all round was very real and exhilarating.

After about three hours' steady going we had reached a long narrow ridge leading to the summit which was about a mile further on and perhaps a thousand feet higher. Here trouble started. My right knee seemed to give up the struggle, and would not bear any weight being placed on it, a peculiar feeling. I carried a stick and limped on for a while, but it became apparent that reaching the summit might not be possible. We sat down, and shared the sandwiches, fruit and water that I carried. We considered our situation. My friend wisely advised retreat, but he was not driven as I was by an irrational urge to get to the summit, the day's objective. Having made his point he just sat quietly and awaited my decision. I needed someone to offer cogent rational arguments in favour of retreat and so smother my sense of being weak and infirm of purpose. I tried to go on, but it quickly became apparent that simply to get down was going to require a considerable effort of will. A sufficiently ego-satisfying challenge thus presented itself, and we therefore retreated. My friend was salvation itself and without him I would have been in a real fix. With him and my stick to lean on I limped and hopped along and we slowly descended. We eventually got back to the car. I dropped my saviour back at the village, and paid him in cash and compliments for his excellent company and invaluable assistance. I arrived back at the farm after dark to a worried household.

After a couple of days' rest the knee seemed to right itself, and I was thus able to go ahead with the attempt on Lengai. I arranged to meet Ax where a track takes off northwards from the Arusha-Dodoma road towards Engaruka. Ax brought with him his two teenaged daughters, and Peter Badura-Skoda, a friend from Arusha whose landrover we travelled in. Together we journeyed past Engaruka and on to the wide open grassy plains to the north. We could see our objective looming up on the horizon, and just drove over the grassland towards it. We camped that night under a solitary thorn-tree near the foot of the mountain.

Oldoinyo Lengai is the only presently active volcano associated with the eastern branch of the Rift Valley system. It is one of a group of mountains of volcanic origin known as the Crater Highlands, the best known member of which is the Ngoro-Ngoro crater, a huge open caldera teeming with wildlife. The landscape in the vicinity of Lengai is fascinating, with a moon-like surface dotted with old craters and small cinder cones, almost all of which are now clothed in a cover of short grasses, though there are one or two bare rock-rimmed small calderas. This is the heartland of the Masai who graze their herds over these immense plains, and depend for dry season water supplies on permanent springs in the highlands. The name Oldoinyo Lengai is the Masai name for the mountain and means literally

"Mountain of God". It is feared by these pastoral people, for its eruptions in the past have spewed out hot ash and dust which have damaged their pastures and poisoned their water-holes.

The slopes of the mountain, composed of relatively unconsolidated volcanic ash, and lava, are seamed by deep radial gullies cut by heavy rains. Between these are broad ribs which narrow progressively upwards. We selected one of these for our ascent, and drove the landrover as far as we could towards it over some horrendous gullies, and as far up the basal slope as possible, until a boiling engine and wheelslip indicated that we could go no further. From that point we set off on foot, loaded with sleeping bags, food and water as we intended to bivouac on the summit overnight. I was worried about my knee but it behaved well and gave me no untoward trouble. This was the strangest mountain I had ever climbed. The slope was steep and sometimes composed of soft ash, sometimes of hard crusted ash, and every now and then a steep little outcrop of hard lava had to be surmounted. It was a bizarre, wild, disrupted and shattered landscape, dominantly grey in colour, but with streaks of russet, yellow and brilliant white in places, with here and there patches of vivid green where hardy plants had begun to colonise this unpromising environment.

When we reached what had appeared from below to be the summit, we found ourselves on the lip of a large hollow, well covered by wiry grasses, and on its far side another slope rose steeply. The dense sward of grass and herbs was an amazing sight, and it gave us a pleasant camping place. This must have been a relic of an old earlier crater long since filled in, while the slope before us was the outer wall of the presently active centre. We quickly dumped our loads and climbed the far slope. The sight which met our eyes from the top was breathtaking. We were on the edge of a large circular crater, about six hundred yards or metres in diameter, with near vertical chalk-white walls. The white colour is due to the carbonate-rich nature of these Rift Valley lavas which are known as carbonatites to the geologist. The floor of this crater lay about 600 feet or 200 metres below us. It was quite flat, but in the middle were a series of spatter cones built up of ash and thin lava flows. From these came an occasional puff of fresh hot ash. Half way down the slope below us was a sloping terrace seamed by wide cracks from which were issuing jets of sulphurous steam whose strong smell of rotting eggs drifted up to us. A dull rumbling, bubbling sort of noise fell on our ears, rather like the sound of thick porridge boiling in a large pot, while every now and then a loud burp erupted, as of a thick bubble bursting. We were eager to descend into this cauldron, but we held our enthusiasm in check, considering that it would be much wiser to make our attempt in the early morning when the air would be cool and the sun low in the sky, and we would have a full day in front of us. We retreated to our camp in the hollow, and spent a rather restless night, keyed up for the morrow's enterprise.

Next morning we were up betimes and off with the dawn. We descended into the crater by a route we had decided on the previous day. It was a matter of slipping and sliding in knee-deep ash and climbing down little cliffs of lava, avoiding the steaming cracks which lurked in our path. Once at the bottom we tested the nature of the crater floor with some trepidation; it seemed firm and cool, but like Agag we trod delicately, and couldn't help wondering what awful things lay beneath the crust of hardened fresh lava, for that was what the floor consisted of. We reached the spatter cones and ventured to the edge of an open vent. The heat was terrific so that we could not get too close. We then climbed over the cones and peered inside. There was a chaos of scattered solid lava chunks, and masses of ash, clearly the result of explosive violence. Over one vent was a curious and arresting structure. It was a sort of lipped hood rather like a monk's cowl. Where the face would have been there was a gaping void which looked like the entrance to Hades and probably was. Hot air, puffs of ash, and dull rumbles issued forth. The cowl must have been formed of coagulated steam-borne ash. As we retreated from this intimidating place we were momentarily terrified by a loud burp, and a swooshing sound behind us. We spun round as one, to see a cone we had just traversed round, in the last stage of disintegration and collapse. This served to lend speed to our retreat.

Back at the foot of the wall we were faced with the problem of ascent, to which we clearly had not given sufficient attention before descending. The heat was now intense. The equatorial sun was high in the heavens, and beat down vertically into the pit we were in. The white walls caught this and reflected it so that the light was dazzling. The terrestrial heat source into which we had ventured added its considerable quota of thermal energy. We felt we were being baked alive. How we got up that slope I know not, but somehow we did, slipping and sliding, often thigh deep in bitter-smelling ash, and clawing at every piece or outcrop of firm hard lava that presented itself. We arrived at the top hot beyond belief and desperately thirsty. To quench our raging thirst and re-hydrate ourselves we had about a gallon of luke-warm water, which was totally inadequate. We had planned to spend a second night on the mountain, but this was now out of the question, and so we went straight down, reaching the landrover in the later afternoon. Never did water taste so sweet as that we had left in the vehicle. That night we camped again under our thorn-tree, and departed the next day, exploring one or two of the small cones and craters on the way out.

The mountain as it was in 1963 on our visit is no more, for in 1967 there was another major eruption, and to judge from air photographs I have seen since, it appears that our crater has been filled in by that event. Our visit had been for us an enormously impressive and mind-stretching venture. We felt we had been privileged to be allowed to reach out and touch something utterly primeval, outside and beyond the human scale of things; a very moving and humbling experience.

V

A major element in our life at the coast was inevitably the sea. The use of boats for sailing, and exploring the reefs were common activities. Most of the people of the coastal villages are involved in fishing. Their principal craft, the *ngalawa*, is a long, narrow dug-out canoe, with a raised prow. To cross-pieces on this hull are lashed two blade-like outriggers inclined at a slight angle to the vertical. A single short mast carries a big boom to which a large triangular sail is attached. The clew of this is controlled by the helmsman who sits aft by a tiller lashed to a simple rudder. These craft can only sail before the wind, or on a broad reach, a fact which allied to the nature of the local winds, governs the time of fishing. Along a coastline the wind is normally off the land to the sea at night, and strongest shortly before dawn. By day a breeze develops off the sea, and strengthens as the day warms up. The fishermen sail out to their grounds with the dawn land breeze, returning late in the afternoon with the sea-breeze. Quite often the wind in the afternoon can be strong and steady, and the *ngalawa* is then to be seen at its best, scudding in at high speed, with the crewman balanced out on the windward outrigger, leaning back on a line from the mast. An exhilarating sight indeed.

These craft are not very comfortable to anyone not born to them, as one has to sit crouched and tightly wedged into the narrow hull, more or less unable to move. But it was interesting to sail in a craft whose basic design cannot have changed for centuries. We sailed in more modern craft from the Tanga Yacht club. Here there was a variety of boats, but the pride was a fleet of Ospreys which had been built in the carpentry workshop of one of the sisal estates. These were eighteen-foot long hulls normally sailed by a crew of two, though in strong winds a third crew member was required to man the trapeze. These were very exciting boats to sail especially in the season of the north-east monsoon, when a strong steady northerly wind known locally as the Kaskazi, blew. Within the outer reefs, and protected from the heavy ocean swell, one could get these craft up onto a long planing reach, and attain very respectable speeds. With all three crew braced out at full stretch this could be very exciting, especially for the crew on the trapeze. Accidents could happen, but were seldom serious. Masts and booms were known to snap, and sails could be ripped apart. A more potentially dangerous mishap once happened to me. I was out on the trapeze when a very careless helmsman capsized the boat towards me. I found myself under the mainsail, struggling to free myself from the trapeze harness. As I was wearing a life-jacket I could not dive to get clear of the rigging once I had got loose, and had to blindly grope my way out. By great good fortune I was able to disentangle myself and come up for air, my lungs just about bursting. I had enough breath however to curse the helmsman roundly. On another occasion I was again out on a trapeze when a vast marine creature, probably a manta ray, slid past, just breaking surface. My instinctive reaction was to spring inboard, to the helm's intense displeasure, as he almost lost control. It was his turn then to berate me. Not all marine creatures are so alarming when seen at close quarters, and one of our greatest delights was whenever a school of porpoise or dolphins took position by our boat to accompany us for a spell. For pure perfection of motion I can imagine nothing to compare with these beautiful creatures, gliding effortlessly through the water, then leaping and rolling, or with a mere flick of the tail accelerating miraculously away at amazing speed. We also had sharks of course, but there were no cases of people being taken, at least whilst we were in Tanga. There was an amusing, if rather macabre story told about sharks, however. One day a human arm was washed up on the beach, and the police had to be informed. Enquiries ensued, to reveal eventually that some minion at the hospital, which was close to the shore, whose task it was to see to the incineration of amputated limbs, was instead selling them to fishermen as shark bait. The arm in question must have come off the hook, and got lost.

A tropical coral reef is a place of awe and wonder, and we spent much time exploring our reefs, goggling in shallow clear water, or wandering over the exposed surfaces at low spring tides. Spring tides occur with the full and new moons, and have a much bigger range than the intervening neap tides. Sylvia became an ardent shell collector, particularly of the many varieties of cowry. Searching for these small shells is best done at night, as one can then see more in the concentrated pool of light thrown by a torch. Some reefs were accessible from the shore, but the best were out at the far edge of the bays, and these we could only reach by sailing out to them. On one such expedition we came very near to drowning. We were keen to get out to the Kerenge reef at the oceanward extremity of Mwambani bay, and one night at new moon spring tide Sylvia and I went out with two medical men who were also keen collectors. Tony Hodges was our surgeon and owned a Lightning sailing boat on which he also had an outboard engine fitted. The other members of the party were Dr. Tom Sweeney and his son.

We got to the reef without any problem and anchored the dinghy fore and aft, with a hurricane lamp hung up in the rigging as it was a dark night. We then set off to explore the reef. In this activity we became as usual very absorbed. A reef at night is utterly fascinating, every square inch seemingly alive and moving. It is hard to imagine a more totally fecund environment where life seems so riotously active. After a long time I was the first to realise that the tide was rising fast, and I sought to alert the others who were spread all over the reef. Eventually we came together and made for the boat whose lamp we could see. We were soon wading knee deep in rapidly deepening water, and Tony dashed off ahead to try to get to the boat which seemed to be swinging violently at its moorings. The four of us who remained linked arms and pressed on, with the water soon up to our chests, and large marine creatures leaping and splashing around us. Then the boat light disappeared, and we could neither see nor hear anything but the sound of the heavy surf breaking on the reef. Eventually to our very great relief our boat hove out of the darkness, and we were able to clamber aboard. As I hauled myself up, my feet were already no longer in contact with the bottom. We had just made it in the nick of time. Tony related what had happened. When he got near to the boat it was swinging in deep water, and he had to swim to it. He then had to retrieve his two anchors, then start the outboard engine, and at the same time try to control the boat in a steep sea and freshening wind. Then his lamp fell and went out, but he got the engine going, and headed for where he guessed we were. He guessed right and so found us. We were four miles offshore, and I doubt if any of us could have managed to swim that far if we had lost the boat. Oddly enough I do not remember feeling particularly frightened at the time, though as we sailed back to port, we were all rather silent. Thinking back on this episode however, I have felt distinctly uncomfortable. It had been a close call, and due to crass carelessness.

VI

Whilst we were in Tanga we were able to fulfil a long-standing ambition to penetrate the remote country of southern Masailand. This is an extensive area lying between the northern mountains, and the Ugogo region far to the south, and from the Ruvu or Pangani river in the east to the Arusha-Dodoma road in the west. Tracks there were few and far between. From the high Usambara escarpment we had often gazed out over this land beyond the Ruvu, and itched to explore it. Now we had the time and the opportunity, and we made two three to four day trips there. Here are vast plains of open savanna grassland and mixed woodland, with bold rocky outcrops or kopjes giving frequent vertical variety to the rolling landscape. This was the home of large herds of wild animals, including elephant, and of course the Masai with their livestock. It was an unspoilt wilderness known to few people apart from the Masai, and officials of their district, and it was a rewarding experience to wander through it. Of particular interest were the wells where the Masai water their stock, at such places as Naberera and Ngasumet. Some of these wells are very deep, and their excavation must have taken a great deal of effort. Often a deep cutting gives access for the cattle to a lower level where a long trough is cut from the rock. From this a vertical shaft opens to the water below. The means of raising the water to the trough level is most interesting. At the water level a young Moran fills a leather pannier-like bucket with water and flings it up to a colleague standing at the higher level who empties it into the trough and then throws it forcefully down into the pool, where the first man retrieves it full, to repeat the whole process. This is very hard work, especially for the man at the bottom, but the young men do it with perfect co-ordination and a rhythm that is a joy to watch, their lithe muscular bodies swinging with perfect timing to the task. The thirsty cattle are kept under perfect control, and released in small numbers to descend to the trough, drink, and ascend again. Once more I was impressed with the amazing rapport between man and beast which these people display.

After our Lengai expedition, with my limbs seemingly whole again, my thoughts began to turn to big mountains once more. Ax Nelson was still in Arusha with the Meru Co-operative, and together we planned to attempt the ascent of the Kersten glacier on Kilimanjaro. This lies just to the east of the Heim glacier which we had ascended in 1957. It had been climbed once, by a pair of young German climbers from Munich, in 1962, and they had taken two days of actual ascent on the ice. To join us we also recruited Dennis Gower who was an instructor at the Outward Bound Mountain School at Laitokitok on the northern Kenya side of the mountain. Dennis is a fellow Lancastrian and a member like myself of the Manchester based Rucksack Club. While we were on the mountain Sylvia and the children stayed with relations and friends in Moshi and Arusha.

To get to the foot of the ice-wall we planned to ascend, we used a route worked out by Ax who had been spending a lot of time on the mountain. This route went straight up from Kibosho, and thus well to the east of the earlier routes I had used in 1953 and 1957. It proved to be a quick if rather steep route, and by using it we reached the upper slopes and our destination in a day and a half's hard going. If we succeeded on the Kersten we intended to descend to Laitokitok, to Dennis' home base. We were a competent, experienced, and mutually compatible trio, and we should have had no great difficulty in climbing the Kersten. Regrettably I let the party down. I felt decidedly weak, and quite ill when we got above 15,000 feet. To have attempted a severe ice climb in my condition would have been worse than foolhardy. We debated what to do. One alternative was to abort the whole venture and go down at once, but this I refused to countenance. Instead we ascended by the Great Breach, an easy if long rock climb up 2000 feet of interminable slabs and ribs of rock, which divides the southern ice wall of the Heim and Kersten from the glaciers to the west. Once up the climb we camped in the crater of Kibo. Throughout the climb I had been moving on willpower I suppose, but the next morning when I tried to stand up I just fell down again. I was disoriented, dizzy, and suffering from nausea. I had climbed at this altitude often before, so this indisposition was hardly a normal case of altitude sickness. However, whatever it was, I had to get off the mountain, and as my friends certainly could not carry me, somehow I had to get up and walk. With some help I managed to do this, and we proceeded on our way. The rest of that day I do not care to think about. The weather was bad, with a strong wind and driving snow, and in this we crossed the crater, climbed the far wall, and descended the screes of the tourist route of ascent. We continued down towards Laitokitok, and in due course came down below cloud level. That night we bivouacked in a cave and continued our journey the next day, finally reaching our destination, to my enormous relief. I had been moving in a sort of disembodied dream world, and do not recall much detail of the descent. I had survived and was grateful for that.

Once back in Tanga, on Sylvia's insistence I went to see a doctor who passed me on to Richard Davis, who at that time was studying the chemotherapy of bilharzia or schistosomiasis in the Tanga region, under the auspices of the British Medical Research Council. He diagnosed a heavy infestation by the *mansonii* variety of the schistosome, and treated me with a new drug called Ambalal. This drug was a great advance on earlier treatments which had been unreliable and dangerous. The treatment was effective, and eventually I was pronounced clear of the parasites. I felt like a new man. At last my weakness on Mount Kenya and more recently on Kilimanjaro could be explained, and I felt happy to be assured that I had not been a case of premature senility or infirmity of purpose.

VII

Fit and well again I was soon full of energy and had to find something on which to expend it. My teaching work was interesting and absorbing, but I found that I had spare energy which sailing and exploring the coast, with the odd trip up-country, was not utilising fully. Fortunately two events conspired together to open up a whole new field of endeavour. One day I was chatting to Henry Hector, an American colleague, about the future and what we might do with it. In typical American fashion Henry suggested that I should get myself a "work ticket" as he called it, and go for a University job in due course. On my enquiring what this "work ticket" might be, he replied "Why, a PhD of course", and went on to point out there were a thousand and one things one could study and write a learned thesis on, in the Tanga region alone. I was mulling over this advice when another friend, Jan Junker, a Dane and manager of a local sisal estate asked me to go and have a look at a very strange gorge and some bizarre rock formations on his land. I went with him one Sunday, and realised that what I was looking at was what the geomorphologist call a karst landscape. This is an assemblage of characteristic landforms which include such things as underground cave systems, deep rocky gorges, and remarkable sculptured surface forms, which tend to develop on exposed limestone due to that rock's solubility in mildly acidic water. I already knew of the so-called Amboni caves which were a minor tourist attraction, located along the valley of the Mkulumuzi river not far out of town. I realised that these must be a related phenomenon. My interest was aroused, and Sylvia and I made several exploratory visits to the gorges. I was also able to fly over the area in a friend's light aircraft. The next step was to obtain air photographs of the area from the Department of Surveys and Lands in Dar Es Salaam. I soon realised that the whole outcrop of limestone over an area of about ninety square miles was seamed with secret gorges hidden in dense bush, and that there must be many underground caves as yet undiscovered and unentered by human beings. Pure curiosity and a well-developed instinct for and love of exploration drove me to spend an increasing amount of my spare time in probing this fascinating discovery.

Remembering Henry Hector's advice about the work ticket I enquired of the University College of Dar Es Salaam, which was a constituent college of the University of East Africa, if they would accept me as an MSc candidate, my intention being to carry out an in-depth study of the outcrop of the Tanga limestone. As I had a good honours degree from Manchester University I did not envisage any trouble, and indeed there was none. Professor Len Berry who was head of Geography and himself a geomorphologist kindly offered to supervise my work, which he proceeded to do over the next four years of my study in a very positive and uncommonly helpful way. On our next home leave in UK I went down to Oxford to see Dr. Marjorie Sweeting, a leading authority on karst studies, and she too was extremely helpful and encouraging. In due course she was external examiner for my finished thesis in 1969.

Although I had a degree in geography, my studies for that which included quite a lot of geology, had ended nearly twenty years previously. However, I had maintained my interest in the physical environment, and tended to regard myself as something of an enlightened amateur in the best Victorian sense. I soon became aware of large gaps in my knowledge, and of an acute need to fill these. This I was able to do as I went along. I bought a lot of textbooks, and wrote to authors all over the world for offprints of their recently published work in the field of karst studies. The limestone solutional process is partly climate controlled, so I had to brush up my climatology and meteorology, and teach myself some elementary statistics to handle the climatic data. The work went well, so much so that Len Berry suggested that I upgrade it to a Ph.D study. My work ticket was coming into sight.

The fieldwork area was literally on my doorstep, and any part of it could be reached by car or bicycle within a half hour or so. Weekends and free Wednesday afternoons when there was no school were usually spent in exploring, surveying and mapping the caves and gorges. I could not do this work single-handed or work alone. My wife Sylvia was always a great help and encouraged me constantly. I also invited senior students and colleagues to help in the work if they felt interested. Most people were put off by the idea of penetrating dense bush and gloomy unknown gorges, and even more by the thought of crawling into caves, and once curiosity was satisfied they didn't come back for more. Some stalwarts were however, very keen indeed, and we put together a core of genuine enthusiasts. Both African and Indian boys were involved, and Ken Spitzer, an American Peace Corps teacher of chemistry, became my chief aide. He was lean and laconic, and totally dependable in all circumstances.

It was evident that the whole of the limestone outcrop, apart from the Amboni caves, was totally unexplored. I could find no published descriptions apart from two short papers and part of a book, all of which deal with the Mkulumuzi valley and its caves. Careful questioning of the local people also drew a blank. They shunned most of the area which was of no use to them, and they regarded the caves with superstition. They would certainly have known of any outsider having investigated the caves and gorges in the past. In our subsequent explorations we never found the slightest sign of any earlier human ingress.

The task before us was to locate the position of the gorges and possible cave entrances on the air photographs, and then try to find these on the ground. Once found, means of entry had to be probed for. Thereafter we proceeded to explore as far as it was possible to go. The next stage was careful survey, and subsequent rendering of our survey data as maps. A photographic record was also built up of all characteristic features of the surface and sub-surface landforms. Samples of the different types of limestone encountered, and of the shales which were also present, were collected, labelled, and recorded. These latter were sent off to the Government Geological Survey laboratories at Dodoma, whose director very kindly offered to have my samples identified and analysed free of charge. Since karst landforms result from a solutional process, regular systematic sampling of cave waters had to be carried out. Sylvia and I spent many tedious hours collecting water from slow drips below stalactites and flowstone curtains in dark, dank cave interiors. We then had to analyse the water samples in the laboratory for calcium and magnesium hardness and level of acidity or pH, which is a handy measure of the water's aggressiveness as a solutional agent. Many mammal and reptile bones were found in sediment infills in the caves. These were carefully collected and sent off to the British Museum of Natural History in London where my good friend Dr. Anthony Sutcliffe organised their identification.

The work was arduous and slow, but never boring, and gradually we acquired a detailed knowledge of, and familiarity with, the whole area. In all, we found, surveyed and mapped over two miles of new cave passages, and completely explored the whole tributary gorge network of the Sigi and Mkulumuzi rivers, which cut across and through the limestone outcrop. My own task was not merely to explore and map, however. I was engaged in a scientific study, and had to describe the landforms, and try to explain their genesis, and set all this firmly within the context of an active current debate in the academic world on the nature of karst landforms and the processes responsible for their evolution. This involved a lot of hard thinking in addition to careful observation.

One thing that became apparent to us was that since this landform assemblage was close to a coastline where there was evidence of oscillating sea levels in the past, coupled with the fact that the caves were grouped at distinct levels, its development must be related to those sea levels. This fact made it necessary to enlarge the study, to identify, survey, and map all the evidence we could find of raised beaches, submerged channels, and other signs of changing sea levels along the coast and on the offshore islands and reefs. This material then had to be compared and correlated with our findings in the caves and gorges.

Those five years we spent carrying out this work were perhaps the best of my life. Teaching and exploration completely absorbed my energies and enthusiasms, and I was loyally supported and encouraged by my wife who shared fully in the work. I had no tiresome committees and boards to attend, no difficult touchy people to argue with or placate, no quarrels or arguments to settle, no antagonisms and petty jealousies to contend with. At school my students were keen and eager to learn, and class discipline was never ever a problem. Our exploration team was a close-knit band of volunteers, all keen as mustard, completely dedicated and ready to do anything I asked of them. We were black, white, brown; Christian, Muslim, Hindu and Sikh, but such differences were of absolutely no consequence whatsoever.

I am sure there are few human experiences which are quite so satisfying and fulfilling as working with such people in a common task. Our explorations certainly provided plenty of excitement. The limestone gorges and their flanking areas were full of dense bush, which was often difficult to penetrate. Numbers of wild pig inhabit these places and on them prey such beasts as leopard, the odd lion or two, and hyena. We didn't mind the proximity of pigs, but the others were more of a problem. However, there seemed to be a degree of mutual respect involved, and we usually, if not always, managed to keep out of each other's way. I met a leopard face to face on two occasions. On the first a companion and I were entering a cave opening from the side of a gorge, when the light from our headlamps was reflected back from two green eyes that were decidedly cat-like but very undomestic. We turned and quietly departed, but as we did so I felt the hair rising on the nape of my neck. On the second occasion I was slashing my way through a tangle of bush while climbing a rocky divide to reach a fissure on its far side. As I reached the top and peered over, what should I see but a spotty face, clearly curious as to the source of all the commotion, for it could not have caught my scent. As soon as it saw me it was off in a flash, having far faster reflexes than me. It was some minutes before my heart stopped pounding. Another less potentially lethal beast is the porcupine, of which there were many in the area. None of us had any great desire to tangle with this sharply armoured beast in a confined space, and fortunately we never did encounter one at close quarters. There were troops of monkeys in the gorges, but they simply screamed abuse at us from a safe distance. We rarely saw snakes, though they must have abounded, and we always carried anti-snakebite serum and syringes with us. On one occasion that I am unlikely to forget I was crossing very carefully a sharply dissected rock platform, when I was horrified to see a mamba sliding along the shallow fissure just below my feet. I suspect that as I was balancing very lightly on the knife-like edges, it had not sensed my presence. Fortunately any form of rapid movement which could have alarmed the serpent was quite impossible, and I just froze. The snake slid on and away. My rigid posture was quickly replaced by a gentle trembling, and I could feel my thumping heart pounding in my ear-drums. Insect life was very abundant, and the thick carpet of bat dung in the caves was a living moving mass. One of the most splendid cave denizens was the whip-scorpion. It is really a spider, and not lethal as its name might imply. It has articulated arms which when outstretched have a span of about six inches. We once got a fright when the light of a lamp threw a freak silhouette of one of these beasts on the cave wall opposite. Bats were present in large numbers, but we had no time to study them. There were clearly several species present, the largest of which were fruit bats with an eighteen-inch wingspan. It was perhaps as well that these seemed to have a single favoured home in a large open cave, which we tended to avoid. One particular aspect of the cave biology worried us. Bat dung can harbour the spores of an organism that carries a wasting fungal disease of the lungs known as pulmonary histoplasmosis. It was rumoured that beggars who had occasionally slept in the Amboni caves had contracted the disease. Fortunately in spite of often exceedingly close contact with bat dung in large quantities, none of us contracted the disease.

We were never bothered with human problems, because as I have said, the local people tended to shun the places we were interested in. I remember one amusing incident, however, when I nearly frightened an old man out of his wits. We were working in a cave quite near the limestone edge not far from the village of Kiomoni. On the low plateau above, the people sometimes cleared small plots to grow cassava. On this occasion I was down in a passage from which I saw an opening high above. Slowly I worked my way up to this, and I found I could thrust my head and shoulders through and out into daylight. I did this and saw an old man hoeing his plot nearby. Hearing me pushing and thrusting he turned, and saw a creature like a human being literally emerging from the earth. I shall never forget the expression on his face, which was compounded of astonishment, horror and sheer disbelief. He sat down gasping, whereupon I came right out and spoke to him. He then recognised me and got very cross, scolding me for doing a thing like that. A couple of cigarettes soon pacified him, and we chatted for a while as I tried to explain what we were trying to do down there in the bowels of the earth.

Our work in the caves gave us pleasure of a wide and exciting variety. First of all we had the sheer thrill of exploration and first-footing into unknown places where nobody had been before. During the first two years, for week after week we were making new discoveries. Many of the places we reached were of surpassing beauty. In this relatively high rainfall area, solution of the limestone is fast, but in the cave voids re-precipitation of limestone as sinter is equally rapid, and the caves are very finely decorated by sinter in a multitude of forms. There were stalagmites and stalactites, both regular and eccentric in form and shape, huge pillars, superb draperies and curtains, massive flows, and great tiers of gours or rimstone barriers, all of a multitude of colours varying from brilliant crystalline white, through many yellows, to russets and browns. We treated all this with the greatest reverence, taking only photographs away with us.

We also had much exciting sport, with straight free ladder pitches of up to sixty feet in length, some good free climbing, and tight crawls along tubes and constricted bedding-planes to satisfy the most ardent and masochistic of squirmers. To enter some of these very tight passages for the first time could be forbidding and required courage. There was always the possibility of getting stuck, and becoming, as some macabre wit once put it, "a permanent filling in a limestone sandwich". We were lucky in having a specialist in such places. He was a very thin Indian boy named Prasad. He seemed able to wriggle into anything, but alas, quite often nobody else was able to follow him on his perforce solitary reconnaissances. For the ladder pitches we made our own ladders of sisal line and hardwood rungs. These were heavy and unwieldy, and viciously awkward when wet, but they served our purposes. The heat and humidity were problems, especially in the caves. This was to be expected so close to the equator and at sea-level. Cave temperatures were usually in the region of 28°C and the humidity hovered around 80%. We sweated profusely and usually came out well plastered with mud compounded of cave earth, bat dung, and our own sweat. In a few hours underground one could lose several pounds' weight and generate a mighty thirst, both of which could be corrected by a few pints of good beer — religion permitting.

My own special satisfaction came from the maturing of my scientific studies. After four years' work I thought I had most of the answers, but getting all my findings and ideas down in a logical and convincing fashion was another full year's work, which I was just able to complete before we left Tanzania in early 1969. For this I was eventually awarded my PhD degree, and I was also able to publish several papers in good international scientific journals. I thus acquired a work ticket and some of the other essential credentials, namely publications, for entry to academia, though entry was not to be immediate. The other reward for carrying out the work to a successful conclusion was as a wise lady once put it, describing why she had carried out a PhD-type study rather late in life — "the satisfaction of realising that you know more than anyone else in the world about some small piece of it". My thesis ran to two hundred pages and contained a mass of detailed description, explanation and interpretation, with many maps, diagrams and photographs. Sylvia typed out the lot, seven copies in all, a real labour of love.

VIII

In 1968 the Tanzanian and British governments quarrelled over a number of issues, which included the Rhodesian problem.

One unfortunate result of this was that the British government cut off all aid to Tanzania. The effect of this on British nationals working in the country was that part of our salaries paid by the British government, together with education allowances, were cut off at source. We were in a quandary. Philippa, our daughter, was approaching secondary school age, and the two boys were not far behind. We had long ago decided that they would have to go home for their secondary education. Tanzanian schools were for Tanzanians, and we wanted continuity in our children's education once they were launched into the secondary phase. The only place where that continuity could be assured irrespective of their parents' movements, was at home in Britain, at boarding school. There was no way we could have afforded boarding school fees and cost of passages, without assistance, out of a local salary. Another factor was that I was at that time forty two years of age. A critical age. I had no idea for how much longer I could be employed in Tanzania, at school or university, and the longer I postponed a move elsewhere, the more difficult it would become to find reasonable alternative employment. Sylvia's parents and her brother Klaus had all died while we were in Tanga, so that we had no family ties in Tanzania to consider any longer. We decided therefore, with great reluctance, that we would have to leave in early 1969.

At least we felt that we had not wasted our time in Tanga, and that we had made some contribution to the new state in its early years of independence. In this regard my morale had received a satisfying boost when I received a letter from one of my sixth form students who had left after successfully passing his A level examinations. It was a simple letter of thanks, which I still have, a very special possession, worth more to me than the acclamation of multitudes or the plaudits of kings. (See p. 225.)

Our last few weeks in East Africa were happy ones, though tinged with sadness. We packed up all our goods and chattels and shipped them off to Britain, and then drove up to Kenya. There we spent Christmas with the Ranyards at Thika, where

Ken was then employed by the Metal Box company. I shall never forget going to a Christmas carol service at a little church up in the hills above Thika. The sun was setting as we arrived, and like a vision, to the north the snow-capped peak of Mount Kenya emerged above the clouds, bathed in a golden light. I felt strongly moved, and the service took on for me a sort of valedictory significance. The church was full of European farmers and their families, and the minister preached on the changing scene in Kenya, then at the end of an epoch. I thought back to Elspeth Huxley's description in her book *The Flame Trees of Thika*, of her parents' arrival in this very area in the early years of the century, and I wondered if the enormous contribution made to this surpassingly beautiful country by my countrymen would ever be fully acknowledged in the long perspectives of history, when short-term hatreds, envies and hypocrisies were long forgotten.

From Thika we drove back southwards down the main road to Arusha, and near Kajiado, quite early in the morning we were blessed with another unique vision. To the south the snow-capped Kibo summit of Kilimanjaro glistened in the sun, while to the north, well down on the horizon, Mount Kenya too was gloriously visible. We were entranced, and felt that these great mountains that I knew so well were honouring our departure; a foolish fancy no doubt, but what would life be without myths and fancies?

From Arusha we went on to the Ngorongoro crater, and then across the Serengeti plains to Seronera. Much was changed from my early days when as district officer of Musoma this had been part of my parish. There was now a good gravel road where once there were only dusty rutted tracks, and at Seronera where I had almost walked into two recumbent lions, there was now a full-blown tourist resort, enormously expanded from the few simple huts that Peter Bramwell had started to build in 1954. But the endless magnificent vistas of these great plains were the same, and from a camp near Lake Lagardja we were privileged to see part of the annual migration of the wildebeest, thousands of these animals slowly moving westwards over the plains towards the lake and water. Our children especially were thrilled. The mundane however, often interrupts one's reveries, and on the long climb back up to Ngorongoro we were brought back to practical matters. Our old Volkswagen *Variant* was approaching the end of its useful life, and found the gradient and the altitude almost too much to cope with. I sat tensed at the wheel, with my foot on the accelerator pedal flat on the floor, the engine revs gradually falling as the car moved ever more slowly upwards. We just made it, and we all heaved a big sigh of relief.

Once back in Tanga from our wanderings, we stayed for a final week by the sea out at Mwambani, enjoying the kind hospitality of Marjorie and Joe Lloyd. Sylvia had sold her parents' house, but not without difficulty, for the property market was at rock bottom. Socialist dogma was in full flood after the Arusha declaration, and everyone, citizen and expatriate alike, feared for the survival of the concept of private ownership of property. We sold the house in the end for £1,500. It was an almost new house, soundly built and roomy, with a fine garden and its own borehole water supply, and in a superlative position overlooking the whole splendid sweep of Mwambani bay. On the Kenya coast to the north it would have fetched ten times the price we got. Such is life.

Our final journey home took us first by air to Johannesburg in South Africa. There we hired a car, and drove to Cape Town, going via the Drakensberg mountains, Natal, and the south coast, a splendid and enjoyable journey. At Cape Town we boarded a ship for Europe. As we sailed out of Table Bay at sundown we were heavy-hearted and sad beyond belief. We thought we were leaving Africa for ever. Little did we know it then, but we were wrong, and much was yet to come. In two years' time we were back, this time to Botswana, where we were to spend many more very satisfying and fulfilling years.

Donatus A. Komba,
P.O. Box 52
Peramiho,
Ruvuma Region,
April 2nd, 1967

Dear Mr. Cooke,
   The poor background I had in geography together with the vastness of this subject took away from me all confidence of passing it in my exam. I must admit that, were it not for your excellent and unfailing guidance, I would not have passed that paper at subsidiary level, much less at principal level as I have done. So I take this opportunity to thank you most heartily for working with great diligence and dedication so as to get me and my classmates through the exam. It was your efforts rather than our own initiative which made us succeed.
   Even if I would fail my exam, I would still thank you because you taught us a lot more than geography. From you we learned and appreciated sincere devotion to one's work, clean habits and discipline in life, and punctuality. Whenever you entered our class-room, these four points came back to my mind immediately. I intend to remember them in my life and live up to them. I shall always look back to my stay at your school as one of great benefit to me. Now and then I recall with gratitude the educational re-creation you gave us as enthusiasts of speleology on Wednesday afternoons. I hope that your students of 1967 will derive as much benefit from your lessons as we did, and even more.
   Along with my vote of thanks for your assistance, I send you and your family my love and best wishes for a happy and prosperous life.

Yours most respectfully,

D. Komba.

Chapter Eight

Botswana

.... but something ere the end,
Some noble work of note may yet be done.

Tennyson, **Ulysses**

I

Our return to Britain in 1969 was initially exploratory, as we were not sure where we would finally decide to settle. We thought of Australia, New Zealand, Canada, USA, but eventually we decided to stay where I at least had some roots. I found a very good post as a schoolmaster at the Manchester Grammar School, undoubtedly one of the finest schools in the country, and with location settled we bought a house with the commuted pension from my Tanzanian service. Our children went into local schools. Philippa was just eleven years of age, and took a special 11-plus examination to determine to what type of school she should be allocated. She was given a place at the Marple Hall Grammar School for Girls. The boys went to the nearest primary school. It seemed we were settled, and certainly our friends thought we were. In reality we were not. I enjoyed my new work at MGS but somehow I felt prematurely retired and under-employed. Sylvia shared my unease and we began to scan the columns of the educational supplements for job advertisements overseas. Eventually in 1971 we saw a notice that the University of Botswana, Lesotho and Swaziland was expanding from its base in Lesotho and establishing campuses in Botswana and

Swaziland. Posts were advertised which included lectureships in Geography. We held a family council, and announced to the children that we were thinking of going back to work in Africa, and that if we did, they would have to go to boarding schools in Britain, and only come out for the holidays. There were no questions, only whoops of delight. I applied for a post, and after an interview at the Inter-University Council as it then was, in London, I was offered a three-year contract. As we needed greater continuity than that during the children's education, I asked if a six-year contract would be possible. The answer was affirmative and I accepted the post, which would be in Botswana. Our friends greeted the news with incredulity. Were we mad, giving up a secure job and home at our ages, for an uncertain and risky future in southern Africa? How could we explain? We couldn't, and didn't even try.

By great good fortune the Cheadle Hulme School, a very good direct grant grammar school with a boarding house, was close by where we lived, and all three children were accepted there, so solving a major problem. That settled, I left for Africa three days after the end of term at MGS. Sylvia followed in October. A new and exciting chapter in our lives was opening.

Our two years in Britain had been enjoyable and interesting. I have neither space nor inclination to write at length on the changes I observed in my home country after an absence of eighteen years, except to comment on some aspects of the educational system, in which I can claim a professional interest. In fact our children's reactions to their new schools were more revealing than any comments I might make. Philippa went to a good grammar school and was happy there. The boys were not so happy. They had been at a school in Tanzania run by Roman Catholic fathers, where discipline was firm, and the three Rs emphasised, though plenty of sport was provided for youthful energies. They liked it. Adapting to an English primary school proved to be difficult. They complained that discipline was slack, that unruly pupils were a nuisance, and that there was a lack of direction in their studies, with no encouragement to try to do well. They became bored and we became worried. If the school was typical of how the primary school system had changed since my childhood, then our worries were not just for our children, but for the country at large.

Manchester Grammar School was for me a most interesting and mind-broadening experience. The staff common room was a very stimulating and civilised place, full of men highly qualified in their several disciplines, and very dedicated to their profession, of which they were the cream. The boys were as sharp as needles, since entry was highly selective, and based purely on merit. When I was there, local authority councils in the Manchester catchment were still supporting bright youngsters who could pass the stiff entrance examination, but whose parents could not afford the fees, relatively low though these were because of the government direct grant system. The school thus had many capable boys from working class backgrounds. This situation began to change in the 1970s and is now alas no more. A Labour government removed the direct grant to the nation's great grammar schools such as Manchester, Leeds, Bradford, Bristol — the list is a long one, and they were forced, much against their inclinations, to become private schools, and thus inevitably middle class preserves. In the Manchester area labour-controlled councils ceased to offer support to poor boys at MGS and similar schools. If ever there was an offence perpetrated against working class people, these acts were just that, and committed ironically by a socialist government, blinded by mindless dogma and a perverted anti-élitism.

I was thus not impressed with the way education was developing at home, and I was not sorry to be leaving. Subsequent events under governments of both persuasions have offered no reassurance. The public system seems destined to deteriorate to the level of the lowest common denominator. Mediocrity is acceptable and the pursuit of excellence branded as anti-social except in the private schools. To make matters worse, the teaching profession, poorly paid and supported, and its status eroded, seems demoralized and in gross disarray.

Our return to Africa came as a great relief. We were back to where fundamental things loomed large; where poverty, ignorance, and disease were real dragons to be fought, and where economic, social and political development were mammoth challenges. We could throw ourselves wholeheartedly into a splendid task, namely the creation and development of a new university in a poor and newly independent country.

Before settling fully into our new location in Botswana however, I was presented with the totally unexpected chance to return to Tanzania for a brief visit. In October 1971 I received via my bank in the UK an invitation to the Tenth Anniversary of Independence Celebrations in Dar Es Salaam, as the guest of the government. I learned later that this was Nyerere's idea; that a selected band of former Colonial Civil Service officers should be invited back to the country to see how it had progressed since independence in 1961. A special aircraft was chartered to bring the group from the UK. I had to reply that unfortunately I was now in Botswana, and thus unable to accept the invitation, grateful though I was at receiving it. I also pointed out that as they should know, I had only left in 1969, and was thus aware of progress in the country. In very quick time a further letter came, enclosing an authority to *Air Botswana* to issue me with a return ticket to Dar Es Salaam via Johannesburg. The invitation was for a two-week stay, beginning and ending on a Wednesday. Unfortunately I could only travel at the weekend by the only airline flying direct from Johannesburg to Dar Es Salaam, which was *Swissair*. I thus missed the first stage of the reception planned for us ex-imperialists. This was for each officer to return to the district he was serving in at independence. I should thus have gone to Bukoba, which I would have loved to do. I heard later that a crowd had also gathered at Lushoto to greet me, in response to a rumour that I would be arriving there. I was touched and doubly sorry.

For the whole time of our visit to Dar Es Salaam we were treated as VIPs, with transport at each officer's disposal, and invitations to all the official functions during the celebrations. I met many old friends and acquaintances including Selemani Kitundu whom I had known since my Musoma days, and most recently in his role as regional commissioner in Morogoro in 1962. He was now Chief Political Commissar of the Tanzanian Defence Force, and resplendent in red-tabbed uniform. He greeted me with great warmth, much to the surprise of the Lesotho director of education who was representing his government, and who had attached himself to me as his guide and interpreter. The crowning event of the celebrations was the State Banquet at which Nyerere made a remarkable speech. In this, amongst other weighty matters, he referred specifically to the ex-colonial service officers whom he said he had invited back as friends. That was what he said we were in spite of the fact that we had served a system which they had striven to get rid of, and he hoped we shared the nation's joy on their tenth anniversary. No other African leader ever did or said anything as human and magnanimous as this gesture of Nyerere's, which all of us who had been invited appreciated enormously.

II

My arrival in Gaborone, the capital of Botswana, in July 1971 gave me many surprises. As I left the tiny airport, David Crowley who had met me, pointed to a large expanse of thorny scrub, and informed me that that was where the university would eventually be built. He went on to say that housing was in desperately short supply, and that a place for me to live had not yet been found. I learned very soon that we would be starting from scratch. After two days staying with a colleague who had arrived earlier and got one of the few quarters going, I was whisked off to Lesotho, where at Roma was the main, or indeed at that time, the only campus of the University of Botswana,

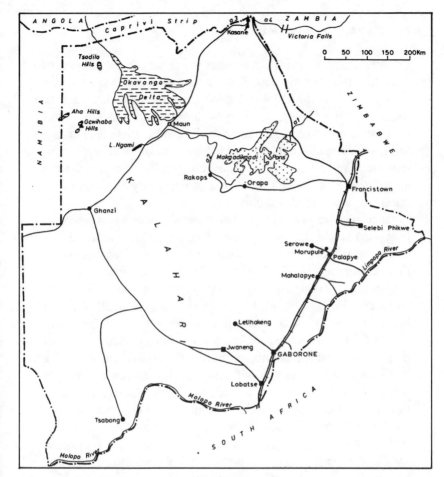

Fig. 3 Botswana

a Rivers

    1 Nata

    2 Boteti

    3 Chobe

    4 Zambezi

■ Towns
● Villages

—— Major roads
⌣ Other roads
+—+ Railways

▲ Gcwihaba Cave

Lesotho and Swaziland. There I met my departmental colleagues from Lesotho, and the new lecturer who, like me, was to start a new branch of the department of geography, in his case in Swaziland. Everybody was very welcoming and helpful. I was very impressed with the landscapes of Lesotho. It is a land of big broad-shouldered mountains girded by rank on rank of precipitous crags and cliffs, and the Roma campus lies in a magnificent amphitheatre of these. I wondered momentarily if I should request a transfer to this mountaineer's paradise.

Once back in Gaborone I was allotted a quarter in which to live. This was a tiny one-roomed flat. I was half-promised that when my wife arrived, we would probably be allocated something rather larger. With my few colleagues, one for each of the subjects to be taught initially, I prepared for the start of our first term, due on the 25th of July. Our base was a small block of offices for the pro-vice chancellor, the registrar, and the bursar and their tiny staffs. Nearby was a small library building, in fact a new church which had not yet been consecrated, and which we had rented. It was in this building that our university first got into motion. I remember the occasion well. We were, I think, fifty-five students and eleven academic staff who squeezed into the limited space available to be addressed by the then Minister of Education, Mr. Ben Thema, and by our pro-vice chancellor Dr. H. Vernon-Jackson, a Canadian. Suitable cliches, platitudes, and exhortations were breathed upon us. We had begun. Looking back, it really was a momentous occasion, though it did not appear so at the time.

The first two years were something of a struggle, but very absorbing. There were no teaching facilities of our own, and we had to use borrowed classrooms at the Botswana Training Centre close by, and laboratories at the Gaborone Secondary School a mile distant near the centre of town. Nor did we have much in the way of equipment and had to improvise. From 1973 things began to improve somewhat. With the sum of 1,000,000 rand (about £500,000) provided by Britain, the USA and Canada, the first buildings were erected on the campus site, ready for the start of our third academic year in mid-1973. Costs were pared to a minimum, and the quality of the buildings was poor. Inner walls of offices and lecture theatres were not plastered, but simply whitewashed over the rough brickwork. Air conditioning was omitted as a luxury, even initially in the small library building, and that in a climate where summer temperatures regularly reach 35° to 40° C in the shade, and where the windy air is laden with sand and dust. This parsimony was unavoidable, for in the early 1970s Botswana was still a desperately poor country. We did not complain as we were at last in our own buildings, and well set for the long struggle ahead. More staff began to flow in, and in my department I was joined by Robson Silitshena, a Zimbabwean, who has remained a stalwart colleague and friend right up to the present. Together we feel we have built something of value.

III

I must now say something about this remarkable country of Botswana to which we had committed ourselves. It is large in area, for those of precise mind about 220,000 square miles or 576,000 square kilometres, and thus a little larger than France, or a little smaller than the state of Texas. Eighty per cent of its area is covered by the geological formation known as the Kalahari sand. This area is commonly known as the Kalahari desert or locally simply as the sandveld. In fact the word desert is something of a misnomer. The Kalahari sand formation covers an enormous area of Africa, from the Zaire-Zambezi watershed in the north to the Orange river in the south, and from the west coast of Namibia in the west to the western parts of Zimbabwe in the east. This is the largest continuously sand covered surface in the world. Most of it, however, is not desert. Those parts which most nearly approximate to the popular conception of a desert with bare sand and shifting dunes lie in Nambibia and the northern Cape Province of South Africa. The Kalahari in Botswana, or Kgalagadi in its correct spelling, is covered by a mantle of vegetation which varies in type from woodland in the far north to sparse shrubs and tussocky grasses in the south. After good rains it has the superficial aspect of a lush savanna, but in drought it becomes sear, parched and blighted. This huge area is better called a thirstland, for there is no surface water, except in ephemeral pools after good rain has fallen. Nonetheless it supports large herds of migratory grazing animals, with attendant carnivores.

In the eastern and northern parts of Botswana are regions of very different character from the Kalahari of the centre, west, and south. In the north the environment is dominated by the very anomalous wetlands of the Okavango Delta and the Chobe riverine plains. Both derive their water from the Angolan highlands far to the north. The Chobe eventually joins the Zambezi in the far north-east corner of Botswana, but the Okavango empties its waters, an average of ten billion cubic metres annually, into a huge interior basin lying below an altitude of 3,000 feet or 1,000 metres, and occupying much of the northern half of the country. Shortly after crossing the border into Botswana, the Okavango river fans out into a very extensive inland delta. This is a complex maze of channels and open lagoons, papyrus-choked swamps, and islands. The upper half of this delta is permanently flooded, but the lower half is for only part of the year when the annual flood comes down from the north, fed by the heavy summer rainfall in the Angolan highlands. From this great wetland, most of the water evaporates or is transpired by the luxuriant vegetation, so that only a tiny fraction escapes, sometimes in years of high flood to the Chobe, and thus to the Zambezi and the ocean. More usually the remnant water flows southwards into the Lake Ngami basin, or via the Boteti river to be lost ultimately in the vast sink of the Makgadikgadi Pans (see figure 4). This whole area, comprising wetlands, open grasslands, riverine woodlands and arid bare salt pans teems with wildlife, variously adapted to the great range of available habitats. In fact, this region, linked to the dry Kalahari proper to the south, contains perhaps the most important remaining concentration of wildlife left in Africa. It is under serious threat as I will later explain.

Eastern Botswana comprises mainly the area not covered by the Kalahari sand. Here very ancient rocks of varied origin and character outcrop, and a wide range of soil types exists. Rainfall varies from 450 to 550 mm per annum and rivers flow for short spells after heavy rain. The landscape is more dissected by river courses which are part of the Limpopo river drainage system. Better rains, more easily available water supplies, and more varied and better soils than on the Kalahari sand have made this the most desirable part of Botswana for human settlement, and it is here that the bulk of the population is concentrated.

Botswana generally has a low potential for arable agriculture. The soils are usually poor in quality, but it is the climate which is the most critical environmental factor. Rainfall is poor in amount, varying in annual average amount from 250 mm in the south to 700 mm in the north. It is also very seasonal and very unreliable, varying greatly in amount from year to year. The rainy season lasts from October to April, but long rainless spells are far more common than actual rain occurrences. When it does rain, it is most usually in the form of short duration high intensity storms. Temperatures are normally high, reaching 40° C in the summer, so that rates of water loss through evaporation are very high. The dry winters can be cold especially at night when frost is not uncommon. Drought is endemic, and severe occurrences lasting several years have been experienced in a roughly eighteen to twenty-year cycle in this century. This is a harsh climate. With arable agriculture being such a risky and unprofitable venture, the dominant traditional economy has been based on the pasturing of livestock. The peoples of Botswana are essentially cattle-herding pastoralists, as indeed are the indigenous inhabitants of most of the semi-arid lands of the world.

The Batswana in their various sub-tribal groupings, are the most numerous of Botswana's peoples. They have occupied the country at least since the fifteenth century, being preceded by an earlier Bantu-speaking group known as the Bakgalagadi. The Bushmen, known locally as the Basarwa, or more correctly as the San, probably represent the truly original inhabitants. They are probably non-negroid or differentiated negroid by race, and certainly non-Bantu by language. They and related peoples, collectively known as the Khoi-san in linguistic terminology, must have occupied a much greater area of the sub-continent in the past, but over time they have been eliminated, driven out, or absorbed by Negroid (black) and later Caucasoid (white) invaders. Only small numbers remain, carrying on a hunter-gatherer existence in the Kalahari, a way of life which is fast disappearing. Other tribal groups in Botswana include the important Kalanga group in the north-east who speak a language akin to that of the Shona people of Zimbabwe.

In the nineteenth century Botswana, or Bechuanaland as it was then called, did not escape the effects of the enormous upheaval known as the *Difaqane*, the great flux of peoples in southern Africa driven by warfare and migrations which were initially triggered by the explosive expansion of the Nguni speaking tribes, whose most notable members were the Amazulu. Tswana speaking peoples were driven westwards out of their ancestral homes in what is now the Transvaal into Bechuanaland by the Nguni speaking group known as the Amandebele led by Mosilikatze. These ravaged the land and its peoples on their progress towards their final settlement as invading colonizers in what is now called Matabeleland in Zimbabwe, where they drove out or absorbed the indigenous Shona people. At the end of the century peace finally came to Bechuanaland. The country was taken over by Britain as a protectorate, thus saving it from almost certain incorporation into the Boer Republics or possible seizure by the Germans from South-West Africa. Thereafter, peace and the rule of law, accompanied by the slow introduction of new ideas and technologies, have led to steady progress and development, with a concomitant growth in population which is still accelerating.

With its harsh environment Bechuanaland seemed destined to remain a very poor country, with a limited economic base in its livestock. Meat products seemed to be the only possible export, apart from the traditional temporary migration of young men to South Africa to work in the mines there. Nonetheless the nation asked for and was granted its release from protectorate status, and in 1966 the country became the independent state of Botswana under the enlightened leadership of Sir Seretse Khama. It was at that time one of the poorest countries in the world, and the second most thinly populated, with only about half a million people to occupy its vast spaces.

During the past twenty years, for most of which time my wife and I have been working there, the situation in Botswana has changed radically. The population has doubled; the economy has grown and is still expanding with one of the fastest rates of growth in the world; the whole infrastructure of the state has been transformed; and from being one of the poorest states, Botswana is now one of the wealthiest developing countries, with foreign reserves of over two billion pula, enough to cover two years' imports. With all this, it has yet remained a peaceful, democratic society, with a multi-party system of government, and a relaxed attitude to race and colour. It is a veritable oasis in a region marked by struggle, revolution, racism, economic stagnation and decay, and government by dominant racial minorities, or corrupt and incompetent indigenous élites. Throughout this time of change, Botswana has remained a most stimulating and exciting place in which to live and work, and it has been a tremendous privilege to be part of and to play a part in its development.

This development has been founded on two major bases, with some contributing accessory ones. The most important has been the discovery of very rich mineral resources. These comprise diamonds, coal and copper-nickel, with the diamonds being far the most important. South African geologists of the de Beers company found two very rich kimberlite pipes at Orapa and Letalhakhane in the Kalahari in 1967. The Orapa pipe has proved to be the second largest in the world. By a tremendous joint effort by the de Beers company (part of the Anglo-American conglomerate) and the Botswana government, production of diamonds was started in 1971. At more or less the same time the copper-nickel ore deposit at Selebi-Phikwe in eastern Botswana was opened up, and nearby coal seams at Morupule also brought into production. New mining towns sprang up, and new roads and railway lines were constructed. The diamond mining industry has gone from strength to strength, and in the late 1970s another major pipe was discovered at Jwaneng in the southern Kalahari. This came into production in 1982, and the country now produces over twelve million carats of diamonds annually. The Morupule coalfield has also been developed further, and it now supplies a large new power station from which electrical energy is distributed via a power grid to the whole of eastern Botswana.

A second major factor in Botswana's rapid advance was the climate in the decade of the 1970s following independence. During this period the rains were very good, and in fact the period from 1972 to 1978 was the best on record. The land became green and pleasant, an amazing contrast to its aspect during drought years. With ample grazing and water, the cattle herd increased to over three million head from the mere one million left at the end of the 1960s drought. This favourable climatic episode created a sense of euphoria to supplement the growing optimism arising from the mineral developments.

However, in addition to these favourable factors, the government and people of Botswana deserve great credit for the progress of their country. This may be attributed firstly to their very sensible approach to joint endeavours with the mining companies who have the necessary skills and access to capital needed to turn dormant earth resources into real and usable wealth. Secondly and of equal importance has been the constructive and wise use of this wealth to further the development of the whole country and people. In many other countries such wealth would have disappeared into the private bank accounts of the governing clique, or would have been wasted and squandered on large-scale and useless prestige projects.

However, it has not all been plain sailing during this twenty-year period of progress. The 1980s have seen the return of severe drought conditions worse than those of the 1960s. A fall in the price of diamonds also served to exacerbate economic problems caused by the drought. The government kept its head, made its plans and dispositions with care and foresight, and has come through this trying time with the economy still in balance, and growth continuing. The drought has been handled far more effectively than in other similarly affected parts of Africa. No person has died of hunger in Botswana, and food aid from outside the country has been handled well on the whole. Now the drought has ended, rural reconstruction is taking place.

Botswana's peaceful progress and the maintenance of a functioning multi-party democracy is an unusual phenomenon in contemporary Africa. It owes much to the unexcitable and balanced character of the people, and their history up to independence. The country was poor and its population small and thinly distributed. Society was pastoral and patriarchal, with the *dikgosi* or chiefs wielding considerable traditional power. By and large they were respected and obeyed. There was no burgeoning class of disgruntled, ambitious and frustrated clerks, teachers and traders such as formed revolutionary cadres elsewhere. Little economic development had taken place, partly because of the lack of discovered resources, and partly because of uncertainty regarding the future. South Africa had for long expected to absorb the three territories of Bechuanaland, Basutoland and Swaziland, and the British government was very tardy in making up its mind to oppose any such development.

The drive to end the protectorate and achieve independent

status came from a remarkable man, Seretse Khama. I would rate him as perhaps the most distinguished of Africa's twentieth century leaders. He has remained comparatively little known or acknowledged compared with such as Banda, Nkrumah, Kenyatta, Kaunda, Nyerere etc because he was the leader of a small and until recently very poor country tucked away in southern Africa. He was also a political moderate and thus of no great interest to the world media which thrive on sensation and extremism. His outstanding virtues were undoubtedly sanity and a sense of proportion, bolstered by a delightful sense of humour, and the modesty of a confident aristocrat. His treatment at the hands of the British government, who exiled him for marrying a white woman, would have alienated and soured a lesser man. His character set the tone of post-independence Botswana, which is low profile, low key and dependable. He was chief of the largest Tswana sub-tribe, the Bamangwato, and every inch an aristocrat. He came from a family which had produced other fine men, like Khama the Great, his grandfather, and his uncle Tshekedi Khama who served as Regent during Seretse's minority and later banishment. Yet he retained a common touch and was eminently approachable, hating protocol in all its forms. His sense of humour was mischievous and has become legendary. One story told of him is that at independence he was asked what he thought might be a suitable name for the new official residence of the President. There had been some debate and various names such as State House and Presidential Palace had been suggested. He is reported to have said, with a wicked twinkle in his eye, "What about the Woodpile?" He could also prick pomposity with unerring accuracy. I remember once hearing him do this superbly. It was at a function organised by the university, of which he was chancellor, which was attended by a host of VIPs, including the whole diplomatic establishment. Two vice chancellors, ours and the one from Swaziland, had made long, elaborate and boring speeches. The President got up to make his speech and began "You know, I have degrees from several universities (he named them), but I just couldn't understand a word of what these learned gentlemen were saying". The concourse dissolved in laughter, and even the two VCs smiled rather ruefully. It was a terrible tragedy for his family and the nation when he died at the comparatively early age of sixty years. Fortunately his successors have striven hard to emulate and maintain the tone and pattern he set.

IV

Throughout this period of unprecedented progress in Botswana, the educational system has expanded rapidly, and the new university has been a part of this. Initially things went slowly. We began as I have indicated, as a branch of the tri-national University of Botswana, Lesotho and Swaziland. The main campus was at Roma in Lesotho where the university had been founded in 1964, and it was here that students from the other two countries went to complete their four-year degree programme after studying for two years in their own countries to Part I level. The courses we had to teach were as laid down by the departmental head in Lesotho, so that we had little latitude to develop our own ideas. Faculty meetings took place in rotation in the three countries, so that a lot of time was wasted in travelling. The three campuses lay at the apices of a triangle with sides 450 miles long, and which lay moreover within the Republic of South Africa, through which we had to travel. The arrangements whereby teaching in Botswana and Swaziland was confined to Part I level only, were regarded from the first as a temporary measure. As the campuses in Botswana and Swaziland developed, and the staff grew in confidence and experience, it was envisaged that they would expand their degree programmes up to final Part II level. How this was to be done became the subject of protracted and difficult debate. One thing which became transparently obvious was that Lesotho did not want to surrender any of its work to the other two campuses. The Lesotho government and the Roma campus people thought themselves very much *primus inter pares*, with a distinct emphasis on their primacy. The others however, saw the pattern of development as one of progressive devolution, leading to an eventual equal allocation of departments, staff and programmes within a fully-integrated regional university. Some progress was made, and in 1974 Part II teaching started in the Faculty of Humanities in Botswana and Swaziland. The Faculty of Science proved to be a very difficult stumbling block to further progress. In 1974 I was appointed to a six-man working group from the three countries, whose task it was to work out an equitable and acceptable three-fold division of the science departments. We produced a report in December 1974 which suggested two alternative schemes, both of great complexity, and looking back, I doubt if either would have worked satisfactorily. Subsequently a package of agreed developments was accepted by Council in June 1975. It was never to be put into effect. The Lesotho government was not prepared to see any real devolution from Roma, and following a bout of student unrest on the Roma campus, they unilaterally declared the creation of the National University of Lesotho, and nationalised all the assets on the Roma campus. This was done without any warning whatsoever on October 20th 1975.

This rash and selfish act placed the campuses in Botswana and Swaziland in a severe crisis situation. All the main university records, files and monies were in Lesotho and had been nationalised there. Our students who were studying at Part II level in Roma had to return to their own countries at once. We had to reorganise our administrative structures, and mount new courses and programmes forthwith. It was a traumatic time, but we succeeded. The governments helped as best they could, and in Botswana we were given emergency aid of R150,000 to purchase essential items of scientific equipment. The new University of Botswana and Swaziland rose from the ashes. It was regarded from the first however, as a necessary intermediate arrangement. Fully independent universities in Botswana and

Swaziland were to be the ultimate goal, and this was in fact finally reached in 1982. We were very proud of our achievement then.

It will be clear from the foregoing that our first few years in Botswana were both exciting and fulfilling. At the end of my six-year contract I was offered a further long contract and we accepted this with enthusiasm. A major attraction of the work arose from our pioneering situation. Administrative structures were simple and comprehensible, and easily manageable. All members of the teaching and administrative staff knew each other. Communication was easy and immediate. If there was a problem, one simply talked it over with colleagues, and quickly resolved it. One did not have to wait for endless committee meetings to filter it, discuss it at length, postpone a decision, appoint a sub-committee, or shelve it pending expected developments, or wait on any of the other time-wasting and decision-avoiding non-actions beloved of a well-entrenched bureaucracy. That was to come later. We were once flattered when the vice-chancellor from Roma, Dr. Cyril Rogers, a New Zealander, came to give us a pep-talk in the very early days before we had any facilities. He referred to us as the coalface workers. As the grandson of a coalminer I especially appreciated that.

It was a great moment when in 1973 we finally moved into our new buildings on our own campus site. At that time the man who had guided us through the very difficult early years, Dr. Hugh Vernon-Jackson, left us, his main task completed. He was succeeded by Dr. N.O.H. Setidisho, a Motswana with wide experience in education. He was to lead us very ably through the next eight formative years, and through the crisis of the break-up of UBLS in 1975 which I have described. Our numbers of staff and students slowly grew. As I have already mentioned, I was joined by Robson Silitshena in 1973. He had Bachelor's and Master's degrees from Sussex and London respectively, and was to obtain his doctorate from Sussex some years later. In 1975 we were granted a third lecturer post, and Dr. William Puzo came to

join us from California. By that time our first year intake in the
department had reached fifty-five students, and with the separation from Lesotho we began our own Part II courses up to full
degree level. Henceforward we would be teaching full four-year
degree programmes of our own design.

We were by no means out of the wood however, and still
faced many problems. Finance was a constant headache, and
getting funds for essential equipment was a continuous struggle.
I remember once being given a British grant which came with
strings attached. The equipment had to be of British manufacture, but what I wanted were the then new-fangled electronic
calculators. They were made by Hewlett-Packard and were
American. I won that battle after a six-month haggle, but there
were others. Some of the difficulties we faced, and indeed still
face, were avoidable and unnecessary. Financing development
has always been difficult. In the early years the country's poverty
was a good and sufficient reason for maximum economy in the
quality of our buildings and the level of equipment. However, as
the economy improved, and as Botswana's good name made it
increasingly attractive to foreign aid donors, parsimony still prevailed like a conditioned reflex. I remember once in the Local
Executive Committee of Council fighting for funds to build good
well-designed double-storeyed student hostels, and having to
contend with arid, unimaginative economic planners, expatriates
all, who tried to block this development. The same gentlemen
opposed the planting of trees and shrubs, and efforts to improve
generally the aesthetic aspect of our campus. I feel sure that in
the minds of many of these people there was an image of a
"bush" college, not a *real* university in embryo. Most unfortunately and regrettably this sort of attitude has also been demonstrated by a number of wealthy and influential Batswana, the
new élite. The public at large has shown more real interest, and
was given the means to show its support in practical terms by the
Botswana University Campus Appeal (BUCA), which in the
1970s raised 1,000,000 pula by public subscription throughout

the length and breadth of the country. This was a splendid example of self-help.

Our student body over the years has behaved commendably on the whole, especially when compared with other African universities. Of course they do not have much to complain about. They have government bursaries which cover all their expenses, have excellent accommodation and food, and are waited on hand and foot by an army of cleaners, bed makers etc. We have had minor strikes and boycotts, but these have been usually of a mildly political nature. The university has never been closed for long spells as has happened frequently in sister universities in Zambia, Lesotho, Swaziland, Tanzania and Kenya. Only on two occasions have the police over-reacted to student demonstrations with quite unnecessary violence, but this may have been due more to a letting-off of steam by bored young policemen than to anything more vicious or sinister. Part at least of the cause of this relative peace may lie in the Tswana character, which is calm and quiet and not given to histrionics. Foreign students from such places as Zimbabwe and South Africa have been prone to complain bitterly of what they choose to call a lack of political dynamism amongst the local students.

V

The academic staff of the university have a primary responsibility to develop the teaching function of the new institution, and to assist in all the administrative work as members of the manifold boards and committees which control its routine functioning. This latter work is enormously time-consuming but one must suppose it to be necessary. At the same time we have an obligation, specifically enjoined on us in our contracts, to carry out research in our several disciplines. Publication of research results in learned journals, and attendance at international conferences serves to establish the new seat of learning as worthy of note. In brief we have a duty to create a viable academic institution of great value to the nation, but also of good standing in the world at large.

My own particular interests lie in the fields of geomorphology (the study of landforms), climatology and environmental conservation, and Botswana offers ample scope for studies in all these fields. The landscapes of the country show a remarkable assemblage of landforms which must have evolved under very different climatic regimes over time. The great Kalahari sand sea is marked by very extensive systems of sand dunes, at the present day stabilized by a cover of grass and shrubs. These dunes must have been formed in a period or periods of great climatic aridity, such as today characterise parts of the Sahara or the central Australian deserts. Superimposed upon and across this sand sea however, are to be found river valleys, small lake basins, and the relics of what was once a huge lake in the area of the Makgadikgadi pans. These are all now fossil features, but they must have been active at times of wet climate in the past. A further small but highly significant landform feature lies in the Gcwihabe hills in the far north-west of the country. These hills are formed of a limestone outcrop and are surrounded by an enveloping sea of sand dune ridges. In the largest of the hills is to be found a large cave, complete with big cavernous chambers and connecting passages, and beautifully decorated with stalactites, stalagmites, and similar formations. Caves in limestone are the result of solution of the bed-rock by acidulated groundwater, and clearly can only be formed in a wet climate, in very marked contrast to the arid climate in which the dunes were formed.

Thus we have in the Botswana Kalahari a fascinating juxtaposition of humid and arid climate landforms. It is clear from this that the climate in the past has oscillated between wet and dry phases, each of which must have occupied large periods of time. An attempt to better understand these landforms, and to try to establish the time-sequence of the climatic phases which controlled their evolution seemed a worthwhile study. In recent years the scientific community, and through them historians, economists, and finally the public at large, have become increasingly aware of and concerned with the fact of climatic change, and with the considerable effects of this on human society in the past and present, and into the future. Also in a semi-arid country like Botswana, a better knowledge of how climate has varied in the past can lead to a better understanding of the present-day climate and its critically important vagaries, and so assist in the processes of long-term economic planning.

With my earlier work in Tanzania on the Tanga caves and their environs, I was naturally attracted first to the caves in the north-west, in that part of Botswana known as Ngamiland, and since 1972, with the assistance of Sylvia, colleagues and students, I have made a close study of these. Our first visit was made in the winter of 1972, and gave us some excitement. The Gcwihabe hills lie nearly 800 miles from Gaborone where we live, and in the 1970s the whole journey lay on unpaved roads and rough bush tracks, so finding our way there for the first time was an adventure in itself. There is no reliable water supply in the area, so that one's needs has to be carried in, together with all food supplies, fuel and vehicle spares, and of course field-work equipment.

Seven trips in all have been made to the Gcwihabe and the nearby Aha hills, where we also found caves. The whole of the work over this period has been most interesting and rewarding, but a number of incidents and events stand out in my memory. In the winter of 1972 we found two deep caves in the Aha hills with the aid of a local bushman named Bo, but we were frustrated in our attempts to get down them through lack of proper equipment, especially caving ladders. In the following summer, in October that is, we made a further attempt, but once more fate was not entirely on our side. We had ordered six twenty-five foot lengths of light-weight wire caving ladder from the UK, but this had not reached us by the time we left for the hills. This was a hurried trip with little time latitude. We hoped to succeed with fifty feet of ladder we already had, and two hundred feet of hemp rope. My optimism was bolstered by the fact that I had another experienced caver in the party, fellow Mancunian Alan Simpkins who was a government land surveyor. The others on this trip were Pete Lardner, an American colleague, and six of my students, all alas totally inexperienced. Once arrived in the hills we made quickly for the first of the deep holes. We fastened our fifty feet of ladder onto the rope and lowered it down. Alan and I went down to a boulder choke which partially blocked the shaft, pulled down the ladder, and lowered it down the next pitch, still tied onto the rope. I went down and was concerned to find that I was nowhere near the bottom. There was another pitch of unknown depth. Pulling down the ladder again did not seem advisable, as the rope ran over the boulder choke which looked and was extremely unstable. Exploring in remote areas is a sober business, and it is unwise to push the odds too far. As Kipling so wisely put it,

"Except ye owe the fates a jest,
Be slow to jest with them.''

We retreated, feeling very dejected. Next day however, our spirits soared. We were in radio contact with Gaborone and Maun, and got the news that our new ladders had arrived in Gaborone, and that Sylvia had persuaded some pilot flying to Maun to take them on there. Maun was however two days' journey distant and we only had three days left before having to start the journey back. Our only hope was the government surveyor in Maun, one Park Werner, a mature American Peace Corps volunteer. We asked him on the radio to get hold of a plane somehow, and then fly out to find us, and drop the ladders. This he did, no easy task in that wild and trackless country, and we were duly bombed by a large parcel of ladders. Unfortunately no snap-links had come with the ladders, and so we had to improvise by fastening them all together in one two-hundred foot length with fencing-wire. Thus armed we sallied forth again. We had just one day left in which to get down two as yet unplumbed vertical caves. We went to our second hole first. I went down to the point we had reached the previous May. Below me was a black pit. I threw down the mess of ladder and ventured over the edge. My headlamp was not too bright and I could not see very well, but feeling with my feet on the ladder I was brought up short by the inevitable tangle of wire. I had to spend the next five minutes hanging onto the ladder with one hand and swinging the rest of it with my free hand to try to disentangle it. I succeeded and pressed on down. The ladder just reached bottom. I unroped and gingerly explored around. I was in a large chamber from which I could find no exit, largely I think because masses of blown sand and collapsed rubble were blocking any continuation passages. I was at one and the same time elated to have plumbed the hole, but disappointed that there seemed no way on. I slowly climbed out, realising that I was not so young as I used to be. The effort in the great heat left me rather tired.

We moved quickly to the other hole, which was a few miles distant, and began the descent there. There was no cover, and we admired Pete's fortitude in sitting out, belayed to the front of the landrover, from which he controlled our safety line. The outside temperature was well in excess of 45°C. We slung down the ladder, and both Alan and I went down to our previous furthest point below the boulder choke. Alan ventured down the next pitch, but reported he could see no bottom, and that the end of the ladder appeared to be swinging in free space. Once more we considered our position. I was exhausted. The people on top, though reliable, were totally inexperienced. The cave was clearly a severe one, and in the event of any accident, rescue was unlikely in that remote spot. A small cascade of rock and dust from the unstable boulder choke above us lent speed to the decision-making process. We retreated again, but this was not the end of our troubles. As I was slowly ascending the ladder, I received a peremptory order from Pete to get a move on. Apparently a swarm of bees had descended on the scene of operations, and Pete, belayed to the vehicle, and handling my safety line, was quite unable to take any evasive action. African bees are notoriously vicious and when annoyed can be lethal. Fortunately these were not bent on mayhem, but simply greedy for the moisture which human sweat seems to supply. If you don't swat them they don't sting, but it is not too easy to remain cool with a mass of bees on your exposed anatomy. What was particularly bothering Pete was that they were beginning to crawl up the legs of his shorts, and he was powerless to stop them until he had my safety off his hands. My turn for trouble came when I reached a stance at the base of the upper funnel of the hole, and had to hold Alan as he strove to free the ladder from a snag lower down. A further crisis came when I noticed a large loose rock on the funnel slope was beginning to slide down towards the edge, whence it would fall and flatten my comrade. I shouted to Alan to get under cover if he could, which he did just in time. The rock went down with a thunderous crash, raising clouds of dust and dry bat dung. The language of my suffocating friend drifted up to me, but it is quite unrepeatable. We eventually got ourselves and the gear to the top, and beat a hasty retreat, still pursued by thirsty bees. We decided that in future we would stick to winter campaigning. Stifling heat, dirt, flies, bees, and to cap it all, warm beer, are a poor recipe for morale.

These Aha hill caves had given us a great deal of trouble, but we had derived little or nothing of scientific value from them. I must admit to having been driven by a most unscientific urge to make the first descents of these caves, but I had to be content with success in only one of them. Some years later, a party of competent and experienced cavers from the Cape branch of the South African Speleological Society succeeded in descending the cave which had given us so much trouble. They reported that the cave was nothing more than a deep shaft or sink-hole from which there were no continuation passages. I found some consolation in this discovery, for I had continued to wonder if I had been missing something of great scientific significance.

These relative failures in Aha were more than compensated for by very successful and productive scientific work in the

Gcwihabe hills. The large cave here had been shown to an Afrikaner trader named Martinus Drotsky, by bushmen in 1934, and it is now known as Drotsky's cave. It was later visited by the then director of the Bechuanaland Geological Survey, Dr. E.J. Wayland, and described by him in Volume 103 of the *Geographical Journal of the Royal Geographical Society*.

The Gcwihabe hills have already been briefly alluded to. They comprise four low hills which flank the fossil valley of the Gcwihabedum which here has the form of a narrow gorge with twenty-five foot walls of calcrete. In the largest of the hills lies the cave. Our work here involved a series of stages. We checked and extended a survey of the main passages carried out in 1969 by an expedition from Rhodesia, and in particular we levelled through the system to establish the precise height relationships between its different parts. This three-dimensional study was then related to the topography of the main hill and the adjacent valley, which we had also surveyed. We examined the geological structure of the area and produced a geological map, showing in particular the location of the faults in the rock, which control the position of both the valley and the cave. From a study of this data we were able to describe how the cave had evolved in a series of stages linked to the development of the Gcwihabedum valley. This in turn we were able to explain in terms of a pattern of oscillating climate, from humid to sub-humid, to semi-arid to arid, in a repeating cycle. Finally we were able to indicate actual dates in time for parts of this sequence. This was made possible by radiometric dating of carefully selected samples of sinter from stalagmites in the cave, and from calcretes in the valley outside. Sinter is precipitated in caves from percolating groundwater charged with carbonate dissolved from the bedrock, and this water movement can only occur when rainfall makes ample water available, initially at the surface from which it penetrates down into the rock via faults and joints. Periods of rapid stalagmite growth thus indicate times of good rainfall. Calcrete is also a form of re-precipitated carbonate, and it forms on the surface of the ground or in surface sediments, as carbonate charged groundwater is drawn to the surface by evaporative processes. It is thought to take place most rapidly at times of change from a wetter to a drier climate, and is common along dried up water courses and around pan edges. From this study we have been able to identify a number of periods when the climate was much wetter than at present, and very much wetter than during the equally significant times when the climate was completely arid, and the great sand dune systems were expanding. One major wet period for example, we can locate with some certainty in the period from 16,000 BP to 13,000 BP (BP = before present). Of considerable scientific interest is the fact that this period coincides with the time of the last major glacial advance in northern latitudes when much of northern Europe was covered with great ice sheets. Such facts help to make correlations possible between the northern and southern hemispheres, apart from their significance to an understanding of southern Africa's climates. The results of our work have been published in several scientific journals. By 1976 we had finished the major work at Gcwihabe, though further visits have been made in 1985 and 1987 to collect more material for dating.

A fairly natural extension of our geomorphological studies in the context of climatic change was to the Makgadikgadi Pans complex, also in northern Botswana.

Dick Grove of Cambridge University had drawn attention to the area as being of great palaeoclimatic significance in a paper published in the *Geographical Journal* in 1969. Some time later my friend David Grey, whilst prospecting for diamonds as a de Beers geologist, had noted the existence of fossil shoreline features along the southern edges of the pans. Sylvia and I worked with David in this area in 1976, and we became fascinated with the exciting possibilities for productive fieldwork there.

The Makgadikgadi Pans comprise a huge expanse covering

14,300 square miles (37,000 square kilometres), and they encompass what the geomorphologist calls pans, or salt lake flats between which are rolling grass-covered plains and scattered sand dunes, stabilized by coarse grasses which bind the surface particles. Here and there are small clumps of stunted low acacia thorn-trees, bent and battered by the wind. Large herds of zebra and wildebeest and attendant carnivores wander over these plains, their movements controlled by the seasonal availability of water in the pans, and the not too far distant Boteti river. This is to me a unique and surpassingly beautiful environment. It has an atmosphere of immense, mind-bending space. The horizon is elusive and dimensionless. Days are hot, even in winter when the wind drops, and in the shimmering light the slightest excrescence on the surface becomes magnified, so that one imagines seeing cities of towering buildings in the far distance. Pools of glittering water beckon, but they also are figments of the magical light, in fact perfect desert mirages. In winter, though the days may be warm, the nights can be cold. When a strong wind is blowing the cold can be bitter. Nights are brilliantly clear, and the quality of the light at full moon when the white pans reflect back the pale luminescence, or when the moon is down, the infinite multitudes of stars in the vast arc of the sky, beggar all description.

This fascinating area lies at the centre of a great basin of inland drainage below the 3,000 foot (1,000 metre) contour. It is the end-sink for waters escaping from the Okavango Delta via the Boteti river. This river carries water in good rain years as far as Ntwetwe pan, the largest of the pans, into which it disperses in a flat sandy delta. In runs of good rain years such as the major one from 1972 to 1978 parts of the pans flood to a shallow depth, though only the northern part of Sua pan floods regularly with water brought down by the Nata river from the uplands of Zimbabwe. Such floods attract immense flocks of water birds, including the colourful pink flamingo.

Since 1976 we have made many working trips to the Makgadikgadi. Winter is the best working season, when the tem-

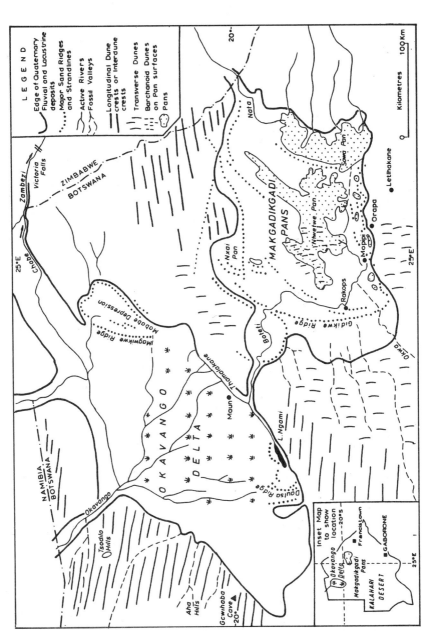

Fig. 4 Physical features of Northern Botswana

perature is ideal. Fortunately this is also the university long vacation, when ample time for fieldwork is available. Our task has been to attempt to prove the hypothesis that this whole area was a great lake on a number of occasions in the past, and then to try to work out the time sequences involved. Modern study of such vast expanses is greatly aided by the use of air photography and remote-sensed imagery such as that provided by the American LANDSAT satellites. From these it is possible to locate what appear to be particular landforms, in this case those typical of lake shorelines, such as gravel and sand spits, bars, beach ridges, and small deltas. With the bird's eye view thus made available one can see the spatial relationships of these different features. Once this preliminary interpretation has been made, the really arduous work starts. The features have to be located on the ground, and carefully studied. Survey and measurement have to be carried out, and height relationships especially established. This is no easy task in such flat terrain where basic survey data, such as bench marks, or trigonometrically heighted beacons are notably scarce, or simply absent. The characteristics of the sediment accumulations have also to be studied, and samples of material collected for later laboratory analysis. If material which is susceptible to radiometric assay for age determinations, such as calcretes, is present, this must be collected with care. This work has also been extended along the Boteti river towards the Okavango, and within the Lake Ngami and Mababe basins along the distal edge of the delta. (See figure 4.)

Travel and work in this great area is not without its excitements and hazards. The pans are surrounded and interpenetrated by sand spreads and low dunes, which make for very heavy going, even for four-wheel drive vehicles. Sometimes the sand ridges are the home of a variety of burrowing rodents which undermine the surface and leave large holes, hidden in the long grasses. One has to drive with the greatest circumspection to avoid these vehicle traps, into which it is most unwise to risk falling. The open pan surfaces themselves are also extremely treacherous. The surfaces dry out and form a hard thin crust, but this checks further evaporation of moisture from the damp clay underneath. To break through this crust with a heavily loaded vehicle spells disaster, and very careful driving is required. With experience one can learn to recognise the more dangerous patches, but the variety of surface texture and colour is very great, and one can never be sure of one's interpretations. I developed the technique of forward reconnaissance by bicycle, with Sylvia following behind in the landrover. On one or two occasions we had to throw caution to the winds to find routes to places we needed to reach. This entailed speeding flat out over open pan surface, trusting to speed and momentum to carry us over or through bad patches. This could be gloriously exhilarating and followed the precept of "nothing ventured, nothing done". Most of the time however, we had to remember that Dame Chance is a fickle and random arbiter, and is no respecter of persons. Only once did we really get bogged down badly, and on that occasion it took us four hours of heavy work to extricate ourselves. We always carried planks, rubber mats, and a heavy ratchet jack against such eventualities.

Animals can be a nuisance, especially the larger and more intimidating species such as elephant and lion. Elephants are common where water is not too far distant, and they once prevented us from carrying out some survey levelling in the Mababe depression. I'm afraid I lack the necessary sangfroid to carry on coolly with meticulous survey work with these large beasts looming in the near vicinity. Lions can be a bother, especially at night when they may come wandering into one's camp. This can be very trying, especially as in the dry winter months we like to sleep out under the stars. I remember on one occasion Sylvia and I were setting up camp near the edge of Nxai pan. The sun was just going down, and I was lighting our fire, when a grumbling growl eructed from the nearby bush just a few yards away. Leo was expressing displeasure at our presence. We quickly changed our minds about sleeping out, and had our tent pitched in double quick time, with the landrover parked by the rear entrance in case retreat to its steel-walled safety became necessary. Our dispositions made, we carried on with cooking and preparing for the night. When we eventually turned in Sylvia was less than happy, and asked what I proposed to do if our visitor decided in the night to make a closer inspection of our potential as food. As sleeping in the landrover would be cramped and uncomfortable, I said that if he did come closer I would bang on an empty petrol-can, and hope that the noise would frighten him away. The last resort was my shot-gun, but I didn't relish the idea of facing a lion at night with a single barrel twelve-bore loaded with bird-shot. Sure enough Sylvia woke me in the night in a state of some agitation, saying the lion was snuffling round the tent. I put my plan into action, but as I was half asleep, instead of banging a metal can, I was bashing a leather bag which made no noise at all. "You crazy fool," hissed Sylvia. "What on earth do you think you are doing?" Fortunately nothing further transpired, and we went back to sleep. Next morning we saw with interest the spoor of a large lion all round the tent. In the old days of course, and I think back to my Tanganyika days, one could carry a rifle when far from the haunts of man, though I never had to shoot an animal in self-defence.

Our work took us into many places where few people had ever been before, and sometimes we were first footing. Exploration is often a heady business, and very fulfilling. It is remarkably easy to over-emphasise one's own boldness, and one can quickly accept the satisfying illusion that one is no end of a fine fellow. It is therefore a useful and sobering experience to find evidence from time to time of earlier and much more intrepid explorers. These one can admire and envy. Just north of Ntwetwe pan for example there is a large old baobab tree, and under one of its massive lower limbs is carved the notice "Green's expedition" and the date "1858". Living today in Maun is an old man well into his nineties named Tommy Kays, and he will tell you of his adventures when in his teens, trekking with an ox-waggon from Windhoek in South West Africa to Maun, a journey of over 500 miles through rugged wilderness. The German geologist Passarge, who wrote the first major work on the Kalahari, likewise trekked with an ox-waggon, and was able to sense the subtle nuances of ground and landform in this featureless wilderness, without the aid of air photographs and all the modern paraphernalia with which we armed ourselves at the present day. Knowing of these early travellers, and aware of our own extensive if easier journeyings, it is amusing to read the considerable literature produced by some modern writers, who exaggerate and sensationalise their exploits in the Kalahari in slick and beguiling writing.

Our studies have proved beyond any doubt that the Makgadikgadi was indeed the site of a great lake in the past. At one stage it was linked to a neighbouring big lake in the basin now occupied by the Okavango Delta, to make a water expanse whose total area equalled that of present-day Lake Victoria. We have succeeded in mapping the former shorelines of this lake, and along them we have found all the typical features associated with lake or sea edges, such as gravel spits and off-shore sand bars, high beach ridges with masses of water-rounded boulders and pebbles, and old lagoon beds. Of particular significance have been one or two outcrops of old hard rocks thrown up by faulting, which stand out boldly from the predominantly flat landscape. On these we have found wave-cut notches and big pebble beaches. It is exciting to imagine these when the lake was at one of its high levels. They would have been isolated rocky islets far from land, pounded by the waves, and doubtless the nesting place of countless numbers of water birds.

We have called this great lake Palaeo-Makgadikgadi. However, it was never a permanent feature of the landscape here. We have been able to show that at some periods the whole area was a howling desert. Very extensive systems of sand dunes girdle the pans, while others are commonly found on the pan surfaces. Massive ridges of wind-blown sand are located along the western flanks of the pans, built up of sand deflated from the surfaces and driven westwards by the prevailing easterly winds during very dry climatic phases. Even today, in hot dry weather huge sand and dust storms are common. I was once caught out in one of these, which was an interesting experience. Another time our tent was ripped wide open by the howling wind. On yet another occasion Sylvia and I were encamped near the northern shore of Sua pan, in the month of October when it was horrendously hot and very windy, with the air like the breath from a brick-oven. We just could not move out, but lay in the tent all day, gazing out through the open door facing downwind. We were spell-bound by the pageant of nature that unfolded before our eyes. The wind was driving great clouds of dust and fine sand across the pan, and as they were driven, the clouds rolled and unrolled in huge vortices, with lines of towering, spiralling dust-devils cavorting and spinning in and out of the lumbering masses. This went on all day until near sundown, when the wind suddenly dropped, and an immense calm settled over the land. This seemed uncanny after the noise and tumult of the day.

Having established the existence in this northern Kalahari area of this remarkable juxtaposition of distinctive landform assem-blages associated with very differing climatically controlled proc-esses, we then had to try to answer the questions of how, why, and when. This is no place to go into detailed scientific explanations. Suffice it to say in summary that these landforms have resulted from two major sets of causes: earth movements and climatic change. Earth movements athwart the major drainage lines which run from north-west to south-east, namely the Zambezi, Okavango and the middle Limpopo, and their headstreams, have caused great changes in flow patterns. The Okavango-Boteti rivers in the past may have been the upper part of a great proto-Limpopo, with its headstreams in Angola. Arching and uplift of the earth's surface along an axis stretching from the central area of Zimbabwe and into eastern Botswana, blocked this river, and dammed back its headwaters to form a great lake. This was also fed by the upper Zambezi, which was then separate from the middle and lower present-day Zambezi. This huge lake then overflowed to the north-east over what is now known as the Victoria Falls escarpment. The upper, middle, and lower Zambezi became linked up to form the present river, and the Victoria Falls were born. A major inflow to the lake was thus cut off, and it shrank in area. Subsequently it waxed and waned in size as the climate varied from wetter to drier, both locally and in the Angolan highlands far to the north. The lake and its tributaries were active during the wetter phases, while in the drier times the great sand masses accumulated and shifted with the wind.

These mighty events probably occupied much of the past two million years or so, which is the geological period known as the Quaternary. By radiometric dating of calcretes, shells and rarer peats we have been able to gain some idea of the dates of some of these episodes, but only for the later phases back to about 50,000 years BP. In turn we have been able to correlate these dates with those we obtained in the Gcwihabe hills, and so get a better overall picture. This is far from complete, and much work remains to be done. But at least we now have a general outline of events, and their approximate sequence.

Homo sapiens has been around throughout at least the later part of these great environmental changes, which have continued up to recent times. Clearly his movements and ways of life based on what the environment had to offer in the way of resources, must have been profoundly affected by these changes. We know for certain that our Stone Age ancestors inhabited the Makgadikgadi region, for we find their stone tools very widely distributed. These tools were made from silcrete, a very hard rock commonly found in the area. It is hard and dense, and when fractured gives sharp edges and points, ideal for human purposes. One can try to imagine this environment when the lake was at one of its high levels. Fish would be abundant, and wild game, likewise attracted by the water, would abound. Woodland, a major source of raw materials, would be widespread in the wetter climate. In their old camp-sites, we find the stone tools Man hunted with, mixed with the bones of the animals he hunted and the fish he caught. An earthly paradise indeed. All good things are transitory however, and times came when the climate became drier, the lake retreated, and both humans and animals had to try to adapt to the changed conditions, and ultimately to succumb or migrate elsewhere. The desert advanced over the desiccating land, and blowing sand buried old settlement sites. Evaporating water left behind deposits of salts, and as carbonate-rich groundwater moved to the surface to evaporate, hard layers of calcrete were formed, often encasing and preserving the bone middens and stone tool assemblages. We thus have to envisage an alternation of good and bad times, with human groups continuously adapting and changing their life-styles and habits to optimise at all times their use of natural resources in the face of nature's imperatives. These matters lie within the field of study of the archaeologist, and we have had very fruitful co-operation with practitioners of this discipline in our Kalahari studies.

VI

Teaching and research were obviously our main pre-occupations as our new university developed. At the same time we were involved in the whole national development. As an environmental scientist I, and naturally my department at the university, were very concerned with the nature of Botswana's environment, and with human use of its natural resources. I have already described some of the major characteristics of these. Now I must add something about human interactions with the environment, and the results thereof.

The marginal nature of the environment, with poor soils, high temperatures and scanty unreliable rainfall not only makes all forms of land use risky in terms of an economic return from the effort applied, but also extremely dangerous. If land utilisation is ill-planned, badly managed and controlled, it is likely to lead to permanent degradation of soil, water and vegetation resources, and ultimately to the spread of desert-like conditions. This is not only a problem in Botswana. It is of very serious dimensions throughout sub-humid and semi-arid Africa, where desert encroachment is tending to spread and accelerate. Rapidly increasing human and livestock populations create a mounting and inexorable pressure on finite and fragile environmental resources. In Botswana since 1971 the population has doubled, and is now over one million. Similarly between the end of the 1960s drought and the mid-1980s the cattle population increased threefold to over three million head. The pressure of these animals on a finite amount of grazing already severely affected by drought, causes appalling damage to the vegetation cover, with related damage to the soil, soil moisture levels, and indirectly to the local climate. With the general paucity of surface water over most of the country except in the north-west, groundwater is a key national resource. It is a resource of unknown quantity however, and the rate of recharge of underground aquifers from present day rainfall and subterranean flow is largely unknown. Rapidly accelerating use of this resource for growing towns, mines, and to supply the livestock sector is in effect a mining operation on a finite resource. The main source of energy for rural people, for cooking and for warmth in winter, is firewood. Around major settlements woodlands are being depleted to sustain the supply and as the population continues to grow this problem will be aggravated. The great and valuable wildlife resources of the country are being threatened by the continual expansion of the livestock sector, as grazing spreads into the dry Kalahari, a movement made possible by the modern technique of deep borehole drilling for groundwater. Before these techniques were introduced, the Kalahari grazing could only be used on a seasonal basis, whilst ephemeral surface water was available after good rains.

A series of conflicts have arisen regarding the future use of large tracts of the country as the economy expands. For example, the central parts of the Kalahari sand veld have remained largely untouched until very recent times, utilised mainly by bushman hunter-gatherer groups. It is now a region of conflict between contending interests. The cattlemen want to extend their rights to grazing, but this is contrary to the status of much of the area as a vast game reserve where the herds of grazing animals and the bushmen can survive. At the same time the area has attractions for tourists, and the private tourist organisations are demanding access for what they argue convincingly would be a profitable and non-consumptive use of wilderness resources. The mining companies too are interested in the region, where prospecting for diamonds continues, and the search for oil will shortly begin. The mineral prospectors carve long cut-lines through the bush to facilitate their operations, and these remain to make access easier for poachers. The four-wheel drive vehicle and the modern rifle are quite lethal to wildlife once access to their previously largely inviolate habitats is opened up.

There is an enormous need for greater knowledge of Botswana's environment, and of its fragile nature, and with this a vital necessity to plan and manage its utilisation in such a way as to conserve it for future generations. The university has a key role in helping to meet these demands, and my department has a central position in this. As soon as we were free to plan our own department after the break with Lesotho, we changed our name to become the department of environmental science Although located in the faculty of science, we take students from all four faculties of science, humanities, social sciences, and education. We can thus spread our philosophy of rational utilisation and conservation of resources very widely. Our aim has been to give our students a firm grounding in the elements of the natural or physical environment — landforms, soils, climate, water and vegetation; and also on the nature of human societies and their activities in relation to the land and its resources. From these basics we go on to courses in human use of resources, human impact on the environment, the nature of natural hazards and how we can cope with them, and the elements of land management and planning. At all levels we emphasise practical work, such as air photograph and map interpretation, data collection and manipulation, the use and application of remote sensed earth imagery, and cartography. Relevance to Botswana's and Africa's problems is emphasised and stressed. Education in developing countries has to be geared to dealing with practical matters and urgent realities, and cannot allow much time for theoretical dilettantism. Our students have gone into a variety of careers — town, district and regional planning; land utilisation planning; soil survey; various branches of the civil service and private sector; and of course into the schools as teachers. They are many in number by now, and apart from their immediate work, much of it of direct environmental impact and significance, we hope and believe they are having a marked effect in raising the level of environmental awareness throughout the nation. A new development is the introduction of post-graduate programmes, the first of which is a MSc in Environmental Planning for professional land-use planners.

Sylvia and I have also been able to do something very positive about our concern for matters environmental through the agency of other local organisations. These are the Botswana Society, and the Kalahari Conservation Society both of them, following the modern taste for acronyms, being NGOs (non-governmental organisations). The Botswana Society was started after independence in 1969 by a group of locals and expatriates with a deep interest in the new nation's environment, culture and history. This society was following the long tradition of similar organisations which flourished in such countries as Tanzania, Kenya, Sudan and Uganda. Most of these societies published journals usually known as *Notes & Records*. The Botswana Society continues this tradition and its journal *Botswana Notes & Records* has been published regularly since the Society was founded, and in 1989 reached Volume 21. This constitutes an invaluable archive of a mass of varied scientific, cultural and historical information about the country. It is distributed worldwide to universities, research institutes and libraries, and has acquired an excellent reputation for sound scholarship. The Society also runs a series of monthly lectures on a very wide variety of topics about or relevant to Botswana. Perhaps its greatest impact on national affairs however, has been through a series of major symposia and seminars which it has organised on issues and matters of great importance to the nation. The series is worth listing: *Rural Development in Botswana* (1970); *Sustained Production from Semi-arid Lands* (1971); *The Okavango Delta and its Future Utilisation* (1976); *Drought in Botswana* (1978); *Settlement in Botswana and the Development of the Human Landscape* (1981); *Education for Development* (1983); *Managing Botswana's Environment* (1984); *Research for Development* (1985); *Developing Botswana's Environmental Strategy* (1987); *The Culture of Botswana* (also 1987); *Democracy in Botswana* (1988) and *Tourism in Botswana* (1990.) All these symposia have brought together local, and where appropriate, international scholars and specialists, together with civil servants and private sector representatives, in wide-ranging open debate completely free from any form of censorship or control by the government. Indeed the government has positively encouraged such openness. All proceedings have been published in book form, and these have been widely acclaimed internationally. Locally they have been acknowledged by government as being of very great value in the formulation of sound policies in both environmental and social fields.

Sylvia has been executive secretary of the Botswana Society since 1976, and has undoubtedly played a key role in the great success and beneficial influence of the society since then. Before that she worked with the Botswana Red Cross Society, and was its national secretary for some time. I managed to get involved in the 1971 symposium on *Sustained Production from Semi-arid Lands*, which was mounted just after my arrival in the country. Since then I have been involved in the planning of all subsequent symposia. The one in which I was most deeply involved was the

1978 Drought symposium. In 1976 I had been invited to a workshop at Clark University in Worcester, Massachusetts in the USA. Len Berry who had supervised my PhD work from 1964 to 1968 when he was professor of geography at Dar Es Salaam, was chairman of geography and dean of science at Clark. He had formed a group of scholars which was planning a major programme of research related to problems of development in several African countries, of which Botswana was one. This workshop was very fruitful in many ways, and it concentrated my mind on Botswana's semi-arid climate as the most fundamental limiting factor on development, with the drought hazard as a most severe constraint. On my return I suggested to the Botswana Society committee that we should organise a symposium on drought as soon as possible. The last serious drought occurrence had been in the decade of the 1960s, but since then the climate had been much more benign, and the 1970s had seen excellent rains year after year. Very worrying however, was research carried out by the Climate Research Unit at the University of the Witwatersrand in South Africa. This had found that in the summer rainfall region of southern Africa which includes Botswana, drought tends to recur at approximately ten-year intervals, alternating on an eighteen to twenty-year cycle with runs of better rain years. If the postulated model was correct, then the decade of the 1980s was likely to be drought threatened. We considered that a major symposium on this issue would serve to alert government and people to the threat looming ahead. The Society's committee endorsed my proposal, and planning began. A major problem with all these symposia has been the securing of adequate finance to pay for them, no easy task for a voluntary society. The drought one was easier than most in this regard. Clark University had agreed to co-operate in the symposium, and they had access to US government funding (through USAID). They agreed to try to tap this. Planning went ahead on this expectation. I sketched a programme, and suggested a list of participants both local and foreign who might be invited to attend and present papers, and this was accepted by the committee.

By this time I had completed over six years service with the university, and was therefore entitled to apply for sabbatical leave. This was granted for the first semester of the 1977/8 academic year, that is from September to December. Clark University very kindly offered to house me so off we went to America. I spent my time there writing a long background paper on the problem of drought in Botswana, which was to be used as the major background paper at the symposium.

Whilst at Clark, I was also able to go to Washington to tie up some loose ends regarding funding of the symposium. I was also able to go to the Annual Conference of the American African Studies Association which was held in Houston. Sylvia and I were able to tour extensively in New England, and were bewildered by the kaleidoscope of English place-names, all in the wrong relationship to each other. We enjoyed it all greatly and were very grateful to our American hosts.

The Drought Symposium was eventually mounted in June 1978, with strong local participation, and with specialists from Australia, France, Kenya, the Netherlands, Niger, the UK and the USA. It was a great success. The proceedings were published in a handsome volume by the Society in collaboration with Clark University Press, which was very well received everywhere. Without doubt this effort played a key role, as we had hoped it would, in alerting the government to the full nature of the drought hazard, and to the likelihood of an imminent new occurrence. In fact a severe drought did materialise in the 1980s as predicted, and lasted for seven years. Plans were made in good time to cope with the emergency, which in consequence has been handled very well. Nobody has starved to death through famine in Botswana, a notable achievement when compared with other drought stricken countries in Africa.

The Kalahari Conservation Society is a much later development than the Botswana Society, and clearly more specialised in its aims. It was founded on the initiative of Mr. Louis Nchindo, a Motswana, and managing director of Debswana, the joint Botswana government-de Beers company which runs the na-tions's diamond mines. It began its work in 1982, and has quickly become an influential lobby. Its principal aim is to create a greater awareness of, and to disseminate greater knowledge and understanding of the nation's wildlife heritage, and its habitats. I have been a member of its executive, technical and education committees since its inception.

One of the first acts of the Society was to organise a symposium, following the example of the well-established traditions and practice of the Botswana Society. The subject was "Which Way Botswana's Wildlife". This covered the whole spectrum of prob-lems associated with wildlife and its environment in Botswana, so that nobody, in government or outside, could be left in doubt any longer as to the nature of a rapidly approaching crisis situation.

I think few people would disagree with the claim that the continuous publicity and educational work of the Botswana Society, and more recently the Kalahari Conservation Society, together with the flow of environmentally aware graduates from the University into positions of authority and influence in government has been very significant. They have played a major role in helping to make Botswana at the present day a country which is widely recognized internationally as one where envi-ronmental concerns are well to the fore in the minds of politi-cians, policy makers and planners. Major international aid and funding agencies are fully alerted to the situation in Botswana, and to the possibility of assisting in very constructive work there. Botswana may in this regard be a model for the rest of Africa. Ample funds are flowing into the country, which is also able to make its own contribution to these. A National Conservation Strategy is in the course of formulation, and should be completed soon. Hopefully this will form the basic policy framework, the major context in which all development will be framed, to secure increasing utilisation of the country's natural resources while at the same time conserving them for the use of future generations.

In this development the university has a crucial role to play. A major, perhaps the biggest bottleneck in the execution of enlightened policies regarding the environment, as in all other fields, is an acute shortage of trained scientific and technological manpower. The university and the newer polytechnic must play the major role in producing directly the necessary professional personnel, and also in ensuring a flow of indigenous teachers into the secondary schools, to increase the supply of good candidates for training in all the professions and crafts. This is of necessity a slow task, which cannot be accelerated too rapidly. But we have made tremendous progress. The university we started in 1971 with fifty-five students, and no buildings of our own, is now a large handsome campus with over three thousand students, the bulk of them in residence. As I write we are building a completely new three-storey block of laboratories and classrooms with all ancillary facilities for environmental and earth science, as part of a new science complex costing 30 million pula (about £10 million).

My department will have by the 1990/91 academic year, nineteen academic and six technical staff, with over three hundred undergraduate students, an MSc programme in environmental planning, with an MSc in environmental education in the pipeline. The future will be exciting. There will be many problems to solve, but if the past is anything to judge by, we will succeed, and our university will play its full part in Botswana's continuing fruitful development.

EPILOGUE

Africa needs people who will never let themselves be discouraged.

Schweitzer

Having described my years of life and work in Africa, I can hardly just say *finis* and close my narrative. I suspect that the reader will expect some conclusion, some distillation if that is the right word, from the experiences described. I have tried, though to be sure not too successfully, to refrain from too much comment of a political nature. Now I must take off the restraints and speak my mind.

My attitude to what has been happening in Africa in the second half of the twentieth century is necessarily linked to my political stance, which is in turn based on my background, my experiences, and my reading of history. My basic premise is a very simple one. Society consists overwhelmingly of ordinary people, usually referred to in a semi-derogatory way as the masses. The major criteria by which the progress of society at large may be judged, should be concerned with whether the welfare and real freedom of such people are being enhanced and improved. I am totally disillusioned by all political -isms, especially those which preach revolution. Revolutionary political philosophies have usually been produced by intellectuals and theorists. Their dangerous ideas have been exploited subsequently by small, ruthless self-seeking groups who become the instigators, organisers, and ultimately the sole beneficiaries of revolution, which is, more often than not, violent and bloody. Seldom if ever have the common people benefited, for new parasitic ruling élites have simply replaced the old governing classes. One does not have to look very far back into history to find ample proof of this contention.

The historical events during roughly the decade of the 1960s when many African countries became independent, have often been referred to collectively as the Colonial Revolution. From it have emerged congeries of ostensibly independent states. Many of these are now run by corrupt and incompetent cliques who struggle amongst themselves for the fruits of power, and mercilessly exploit the common people whose standards of living have slowly deteriorated, while the stability and peace of their lives have been shattered. There are naturally some variations on this theme. In Malawi, for example, the dictator Banda has brought peace and a modicum of prosperity to the people, but at a very high cost in an almost total loss of political freedom. In most other countries there is neither freedom, nor peace, nor prosperity. Tanzania is a tragic case, where in spite of Nyerere's idealism and personal honesty, the country has been brought to the brink of collapse by slavish adherence to doctrinaire marxist policies, and colossal mismanagement by a ruling political élite which now calls itself the "Party of the Revolution" or *Chama cha Mapinduzi* in Swahili. Botswana is a special case and an exception. It is a country blessed with recently discovered mineral wealth, but whose rulers have so far tried to maintain a low profile and a true democracy, and to spread throughout the country the wealth that has fallen like manna from heaven in the form of diamonds. In the prevailing chaos Botswana stands out like a beacon of hope for the future.

One has to ask then whether this Colonial Revolution has benefited the common people in terms of the quality of their lives, and the opportunities made open to them for personal freedom, to be themselves according to their own wishes, within the protective envelope of a benevolent and effective system of law. It is difficult to give an affirmative answer, and indeed there is much evidence that the very opposite has occurred. Only small, usually urban minorities have really benefited from independence, and they jealously guard their new wealth and privileges. The principal role of these groups is to constitute the burgeoning bureaucracies and political oligarchies that have flourished and spread like weeds since independence. They bear down with crippling weight on the rural poor and enrich themselves from their substance. The peasantry and workers can only demonstrate the immemorial capacity of their kind to bend before the storm, to endure, and to survive. In Tanzania, and doubtless in other countries likewise, they have tended to turn in on their own resources, to produce for subsistence, and to organise their traditional lives as best they can. On a visit back to Tanga in 1974 an old friend expressed it well when he said "*Uhuru ndio neno tu, tena neno la bure*", which means "This freedom is only a word, and an empty word at that", and he went on to quote the Swahili proverb "*Ulimi hauna mfupa*" or literally "The tongue has no bone", which he proceeded to apply to all politicians.

The bureaucrats and politicians are aided and abetted in their tasks by a wide variety of advisers, analysts and commentators from elsewhere in the world. After independence Tanzania, for example, was invaded by a swarm of historians, economists and political scientists, who in the 1960s and 1970s produced a mass of books, pamphlets and learned papers, often of a decidedly Marxist slant. The country was a boon to leftist economists who advised the government. The international media joined in a chorus of adulation for Nyerere, who became a hero on the world stage. A lot of these people should be feeling very embarrassed by now. Some of these experts have re-appeared from time to time, and I recall with some amusement the remark of an American colleague concerning one of them — "She ought to wear a placard around her neck proclaiming, 'I have helped to ruin one country with my advice, now let me ruin yours'."

The peripatetic expert is in fact a notable phenomenon of the post-colonial Third World. The United Nations organisation actually uses this word to describe its officials and contractees who work in developing countries. There are two rather nice definitions of the species. The first — "an expert is an ordinary guy away from home". The second — "x (ex) is an unknown quantity, a spurt (spert) is a drip under pressure". These people are rarely paid by the host government, but by donor governments or agencies such as the UN or EEC. Large foreign universities and research institutes are another prolific source, of scholars who migrate through the Third World like nomads in search of fruitful grazing. The archetype is the consultant or adviser. Such people come to investigate problem areas, and then write reports on their findings, with recommendations regarding actions to be taken. They then normally go away, additional items chalked up on their curricula vitae, and fat — usually $US — cheques under their belts. The local personnel then have to assess and evaluate as best they can the advice given, and try to take some action. Quite often what is recommended is irrelevant to a poor developing country, or is beyond the locals' comprehension, or is quite unrealistic of execution or attainment, and if carried out with insufficient trained manpower and funds, is doomed to failure. The locals are then blamed, or sneeringly castigated for incompetence. Countless millions have been spent on irrelevant aid in support of ill-judged schemes, much of it totally unproductive of anything useful or of value. In fairness I must add that there are some persons who fall into this category of experts who are dedicated scholars and specialists who are deeply and genuinely interested in African problems; I count several amongst my friends.

A related species to the expert, but of a rather different complexion, is what for want of a better word may be called "the philanthropist". First there are the legions of mainly young, inexperienced people sent out for short periods, usually of two years, by the various volunteer organisations. These include the US Peace Corps, the British Volunteer Service Organisation and similar bodies from Germany, the Netherlands and the Scandinavian countries. Our daughter Philippa worked in Nigeria for three years under VSO auspices. Then there are the people employed by the charitable institutions such as Oxfam and a multitude of similar bodies. In assessing the significance of these organisations one has to be careful. Undoubtedly they do offer opportunities for young, idealistic and adventurous persons to work, often at grass-roots level in developing countries, and for only meagre material rewards. They gain real experience of what the problems of under-development really are, and not how they are portrayed in school and university courses, or by the media. One must note, however, that some of the big relief agencies have become large bureaucracies, whose administrative processes consume a lot of their funds. They sometimes behave like all such organisations do, in attempting to secure monopoly spheres of influence, in competing for funds, and in quarrelling amongst themselves. Their patterns of behaviour in these regards are rather similar to those of the old-style missionaries that I have commented on elsewhere in my narrative. On the whole, however, their contributions must be regarded as very positive, certainly more so than those of the monstrous army of bureaucrats and experts.

Yet Africa needs aid desperately. The colonial powers undoubtedly pulled out prematurely. This is an opinion that I have heard expressed directly or indirectly by a number of thinking Africans, and is not simply my idea. It is unpalatable, however, to many of Africa's present élite, to many commentators on the African scene, and to radical historians. For such people the fable of the emperor's new clothes should be compulsory reading. Lesser mortals are more realistic. I remember as early as 1971 when I was in Dar Es Salaam for the Tenth Anniversary of Independence celebrations, sitting and drinking with an elderly retired TANU official. He had had more than enough to drink, and became very confidential. Leaning over he whispered to me, "You know, we would like you to come back, not to rule us of course, but to help run things. These young men are very irresponsible, and don't do their work properly."

Colonies by the mid-century had become burdens. They were a worry and a financial drain, and an embarrassment in the brave new post-war world, especially in the face of ignorant and hypocritical American pressure. So Britain, France, Belgium and Portugal pulled out, sometimes as in the case of the Belgian Congo, with catastrophic abruptness. Where vociferous white settler communities were present, they succeeded in slowing down the process of abdication, but could not stop it. The results of these irresponsible acts are today very obvious and need no emphasis from me.

It is perhaps appropriate at this point to sketch briefly the positive aspects of the colonial episode in Africa's history. To do this is to swim against a very strong tide of routine condemnation that has become a conditioned reflex. There is a marked unwillingness on the part of most commentators to admit and evaluate the enormous positive contribution of the European to Africa. To attempt to do this is not to ignore or deny the negative aspects, but sooner or later a balance must be struck.

Positive aspects worthy of note include the creation of new states — the exact opposite of balkanisation; the establishment of the basic infrastructures of modern states such as a communication system, an education system, the rule of established law, the introduction of crops and agricultural techniques suited to tropical conditions, often after long and heart-breaking experimentation and frequent failure, the founding of towns and cities where before (parts of West Africa excepted) there was only the village. I have no space to develop this theme in depth, but can only examine some aspects of the points listed above.

Regarding the creation of new states, the common criticism is that these were created with artificial boundaries resulting from foreign imperial rivalries, and were enforced on unwilling populations. Surely however, all political frontiers, being human artefacts, are by nature artificial and frequently the cause of chronic or intermittent conflict; witness the Franco-German border, or frontiers in eastern Europe which have been fought over for centuries. The idea that somehow all political frontiers should coincide with ethnic boundaries is so superficial as to be ludicrous. Let us suppose the European powers had not gone into say, East Africa in the last century. The Turkish empire from the north (Egypt) and the renascent Arabs from Zanzibar in the east were establishing their hegemony over vast areas in the interior, from what is now Zimbabwe in the south to the southern Sudan in the north, and from the coast westward to the great lakes of the interior and beyond. They were using the petty quarrels and internecine strife of a multitude of small states to their own ends, which were in no way constructive. Out of this mighty flux there might have emerged in due course more powerful entities, by vying with each other and with the intruders for control of larger areas. The larger would have swallowed the smaller, creating uneasy and unwilling minorities, and peaceful stability would not have been attained for a very long time indeed. The emergence of strong centrally organised states in western Europe for example, took centuries, and there is no reason whatever to suppose that the process could have happened more quickly in Africa. Colonialism did at least impose peace and stability for a few decades, and this allowed new states to be formed as a basis for civilised progress. At the very least colonialism was a catalyst of constructive change, or a short-circuiting of the alternative process.

The demise of colonial control has led to a situation which could have been completely averted by a longer period of time for consolidation. In East Africa for example, the regionalisation of common services such as communication, finance and currency, banking, postal and telecommunications, and scientific research was well advanced by 1960 in the East African Common Services Organisation. Leaders who pay so much lip-service in endless windy rhetoric to African unity have broken up this organisation in their own petty and selfish interests. Britain's policy had been the exact opposite of the precept of divide and rule. Her successors have balkanised East Africa.

The basic infrastructures of modern states had to be constructed from scratch, *ab initio*, in most parts of Africa once new frontiers had been defined, a point which is seldom appreciated. I have dealt with the problems of educational development in Chapter 7, and the same considerations apply in other fields. The indigenous system of communication was a network of foot trails, and even the wheel was unknown over large areas. Roads, railways, ports and harbours had to be created from a zero base. Again the common criticism, repeated *ad nauseam* is that the new communication served only the imperial interests. A little thought will clarify this point. Roads and railways are very expensive and have to serve perceived needs at the operative time. Who would have paid for railways to be pushed into remote areas to stimulate some imagined and vague future development where nothing was known of the geology, the existence of mineral wealth, the soils, or the climate; or between colonies to serve some hypothetical future linkup? Yet in spite of these powerful drawbacks, railways were built, at great toil and expense in East Africa to foster economic development. Where would Uganda have been without the railway from the coast at Mombasa? Also in East Africa the Tanganyika railway system built by the Germans was linked to the Kenya-Uganda system, in the east by the line from Taveta to Voi, and in the west via the new ports and steamer services on Lake Victoria. This was an integrated inter-state system serving a very large and productive area. Since independence it has been broken up into its parts, each under a separate control.

Agriculture was enormously advanced through the work of key research institutes, and the creation of extension systems into the rural areas, as I have described in Chapter 4. Cotton, coffee, tea, sisal, cashew were all introduced as valuable cash crops, and better strains of the basic food crops such as banana, maize, sorghum and cassava developed, and the techniques of cultivation improved in the face of natural conservative reluctance. In Tanganyika success in agriculture was being achieved, and production expanding under the colonial regime. After independence the momentum thus created carried on for some time, into the 1970s, in fact. This however, has petered out, wrecked by foolish doctrinaire policies, and finally by the utterly disastrous forced villagisation policy (*vijiji vya ujamaa*). The result is the present sad situation with a disillusioned peasantry, and totally inadequate food production.

The rule of law was established over vast areas by systems of courts applying both introduced European concepts and local traditional law, and by the creation of efficient, incorrupt police forces. The ordinary man could find ready redress for his grievances in his local area, and could travel safely and without fear throughout the length and breadth of his country. This benevolent and beneficial system has deteriorated or even disappeared in many areas since the 1960s, and the rule of law can hardly be said to exist there. In many parts of the continent there is regression to a much earlier state of disorganisation and even chaos, in which economic development becomes difficult or impossible.

My thesis is that in the long perspectives of history, much of the blame for this regression will devolve upon the colonial powers, not as is the current dogma, for neglect during their period of control, but for a cynical abandonment of major responsibility. They did this for purely selfish motives, because as I have said, colonies were a profitless burden. Moreover, once these states had become politically independent it quickly became obvious that they could fill the classic supposed role of colonies as enunciated by the Marxists — as sources of cheap raw materials, as markets for manufactures, and as the successor states began to fight within and amongst themselves, as very lucrative markets for expensive armaments. Much of this selling moreover, could be made to appear righteous by being labelled as aid — but aid with hidden strings. These countries could be exploited without any of the costs and problems of government and real development. The new governing élites, in spite of their passionate empty rhetoric at endless grandiose and ruinously expensive conferences about the evils of colonialism and neocolonialism, have co-operated closely in all this. For them too it has been extremely profitable, and they have fought viciously amongst themselves for the lucrative spoils of office that flow like milk and honey in Canaan.

Out of the present chaos new structures, new states and new societies might in time emerge. The historian assures us that this is what has always happened in the past. Historians tend to be short-sighted, however, and they fail to see that one major and crucial factor has changed. The time-dimension in which they work has collapsed into itself like a black hole in space. There is no time. If chaos and misery on a stupendous scale are to be avoided, the slow evolutionary processes of the past will have to be short-circuited again. So, I repeat, Africa needs aid now on a large scale. But what form should this aid take?

This is a daunting question to try to answer. It is easiest to say what might have been done when we gave independence to the colonies, and which still might be accomplished at this late stage. The new states were inevitably short of administrative, technical and managerial manpower. They still are in spite of the swarms of expatriate aid workers in Africa. These latter are unfortunately an amorphous mass of individuals and groups recruited by governments and agencies of great variety. Many of the persons concerned are taking steps in careers which lie elsewhere; others are young inexperienced volunteers on short working stints; yet others are simply in search of fat international salaries or lucrative consultancies; some are dedicated to working in Africa for as long as they can be helpful. These modern aid workers usually stay for a short spell, and then go elsewhere. They are essentially birds of passage, and cannot build up a commitment to one country and one service. If individuals make errors, or are generally useless, it is of little consequence to them. When the results of error or irresponsibility become evident, they have gone. Their careers do not suffer in most cases. Quite often such expatriates are resented by locals, and localization is the cry everywhere. The complaint is frequently made that an expatriate, hopeful of a further contract, may connive to block the promotion of a local. In any case, short-term contract workers have little time to train locals as they are often too busy trying to learn themselves.

The old Colonial Service officers were a totally different breed. They were professionals, dedicated to working for their entire careers in one colony. They were certainly not in search of high salaries and perks, and quick wealth. In the old days there were no such things as expatriate allowance, school fees assistance, and all the other perquisites taken for granted by the modern expatriate aid worker. They were adjudged by the quality of their work, and error or idleness could blight their careers. In short they were fully answerable for their actions. Serving for long periods in one country they could, indeed usually had to, learn a local language, and could become familiar with the customs and traditions of the local people.

What we should have done when we pulled out from control of the colonies, was to have offered them a continuing professional service, entirely paid for by the former colonial power, and on a pure, explicitly defined partnership basis. The personnel involved would have been part of a long term career service, ideally in a Commonwealth context so far as the English speaking countries were concerned. The people involved would have been placed with the host country at the latter's request, and would have been under local control regarding location, responsibilities, etc. The newly independent states would surely have welcomed such a cheap, reliable service, and the officers themselves would have had a secure career without the constant worry about being localized, or where the next contract might be found. In turn the local officers would have had no fear of being blocked by an insecure expatriate. Such a scheme would have offered a true partnership for progress on a long term and secure basis. The British toyed with this idea but failed to grasp it boldly. They created instead a parody — the Overseas Civil Service, which was in no way a full professional career service, and which could not offer any security to dedicated experienced people often with years of service in Africa. Individuals had to secure their own contracts, and the British government might, or might not, then offer to supplement the local salary. Some people took the risk and stayed on. I am one who did, but we are a disappearing breed. To create such a service at this late date might still be possible, but it would require a bold effort of political will on the part of the contributors to such a partnership. It would certainly be cheaper and far more effective than continuing to pour millions into aid programmes that often fail in execution for lack of experienced personnel. It is competent, experienced and highly motivated people who generate progress and development, not money and external advice. Locals have no real chance of acquiring the really meaningful experience which they would obtain by working in close tandem with older, long service, thoroughly experienced professionals with a real interest in the country and their work there. Incompetence based not on incapacity, but on inexperience and lack of guidance creates a dangerous sense of inferiority. This tends to be self-perpetuating, and creates vicious circles of decline and breakdown, which in turn lead to disillusion and stagnation.

For what I have suggested I am well aware that I will be attacked and criticised on a variety of grounds. Some will say that I am naive, and that I over-simplify; others that I am arrogant and paternalistic; yet others that I am an ageing pessimist; and finally that I am advocating a Trojan Horse as a means to re-impose close control of states that were once colonies.

So be it. It is difficult to feel much optimism for Africa well into the next century. The exploding population, the spawning of millions of people for whom in the prevailing chaos there is no work nor any hope of any; the despoliation of basic irreplaceable resources of soil, vegetation and water; and the spread like a diseased rash of desert-like conditions over huge areas of the continent, with the concomitant decline in food production, spell imminent catastrophe. The political oligarchs and their incompetent bureaucracies seem to be incapable of tackling these problems in any consistent and effective way. At the same time, the crystallisation from the common mass of a wealthy, urban-based minority class, increasingly jealous of its position and fearful of losing it, marooned in a fluid morass of restless urban jobless and rural poor, whose standards of living remain static or are declining, can only lead to sullen discontent and frustration.

This may seem a nightmare vision, and I desperately hope that I am being too pessimistic and am utterly wrong. But as things are at present I grieve for Africa. The African has been the outcast of history; scorned, scourged, derided and exploited by others for centuries, and the present shows no improvement. Aid is given with increasing reluctance or doled out by the arid, uncomprehending mandarins of the IMF and World Bank. Much of the aid which does flow tends to be given in the context of big power rivalries. Africa is bled of its resources of crops and minerals for which poor prices are paid. We have even reached the stage where there is a net outflow of wealth from the continent as poor states struggle to service and repay the huge debts contracted as totally useless and unproductive "aid". Expensive armaments are fed in to stoke the fires of internecine African struggle and warfare, and we make the incredibly immoral excuse that we need this loathsome and abhorrent trade to keep our own people in employment. It is the present and not the colonial episode recently past that constitutes the most cynical, exploitative and destructive phase of Africa's long association with Europe and the rest of the world.

Strangely enough, and many people will perhaps find this difficult to believe, there is one major area of real hope in Africa, and this is the Republic of South Africa. A dynamic economy with the full infrastructure of a modern state has been created there, though unfortunately the main beneficiaries of this to date have been a minority of the population, the white elements. They have attempted to ensure their own continued dominance through the enforcement of the misbegotten system known as *apartheid*. Apart from purely moral considerations, this system can be described as at best woefully in error, or at worst utterly and blindly stupid. But things are now changing, through the sheer force of economic and social logic, reinforced by the pressure of local and international opinion. The black elements of the population must attain their rightful place, which springs from their enormous numerical dominance in the total population. One must fervently hope and pray that this will be achieved by peaceful means. White technical and organisational abilities and skills must be transferred and diffused throughout the black population, which has a tremendous and pent-up vitality, and is ready and greedy for this. The combined talents of every population group, in all spheres from the scientific to the artistic, harnessed in combination will assuredly develop the great human and material resources of their country. South Africa may thus become the power-house from which the whole of sub-Saharan Africa can be helped forward to develop fruitfully its enormous potential. Africa might thus pull itself up by its own efforts, rather than through the suspect philanthropy of others. It is thus possible to see South Africa as perhaps one of the most exciting places in the contemporary world, where a great experiment in racial harmonizing is about to take off. Should this fail however, through the intransigence and short-sightedness of white and black extremists, or lack of constructive encouragement from the rest of the world, then South Africa might well go the way of much of the rest of Africa. The future then would be bleak indeed.

ACKNOWLEDGMENTS

The author thanks Neil Parsons and Philippa Cooke for critically reading early drafts.

The author and publishers thank the following for permission to quote brief extracts from their books:

1. Sir Arthur Grimble; John Murray Ltd, London; *A Pattern of Islands*
2. The Estate of Karen Blixen; The Bodley Head for Putnam & Co, London; *Out of Africa*
3. Paul Johnson; Weidenfeld and Nicolson, London; *The Offshore Islanders*
4. Professor A. H. Rweyemamu; Africa Institute of South Africa; *South African Journal of Contemporary African Studies Volume 3*